Human Resou Management Applications

7th Edition

Stella M. Nkomo
University of Pretoria

Myron D. Fottler
University of Central Florida

R. Bruce McAfee
Old Dominion University

CENGAGE Learning®

Andover • Melbourne • Mexico City • Stamford, CT • Toronto • Hong Kong • New Delhi • Seoul • Singapore • Tokyo

Human Resource Management Application, 7e
Stella M. Nkomo, Myron D. Fottler, and R. Bruce McAfee

ISBN-13: 978-81-315-2096-3
ISBN-10: 81-315-2096-X

Cengage Learning India Private Limited
418, F.I.E., Patparganj
Delhi 110092
India

Tel: 91-11-43641111
Fax: 91-11-43641100
Email: asia.infoindia@cengage.com

Cengage Learning is a leading provider of customized learning solutions with office locations around the globe, including Andover, Melbourne, Mexico City, Stamford (CT), Toronto, Hong Kong, New Delhi, Seoul, Singapore, and Tokyo. Locate your local office at: www.cengage.com/global

Cengage Learning Products are represented in Canada by Nelson Education, Ltd.

For product information, visit our website at **www.cengage.co.in**

Printed in India
Fourth Indian Reprint 2015

Preface

The purpose of this book is to provide a single source of cases, exercises, incidents, and skill builders to supplement the basic text in human resource management. These materials offer a fresh approach to students based on dynamic, real-life organizational events, confronting both human resource managers and line managers who often implement human resource programs and policies. This book's contents are uniquely designed to increase analytical problem-solving skills and may be used in basic courses at the undergraduate and graduate levels. Topics range from traditional applications of human resource management theory to the more controversial issues of cultural awareness, telecommuting and Web 2.0 technologies, the financial impact of human resources, phased retirement, alcohol and drug abuse on the job, new federal legislation on discrimination issues, employment-at-will, work and family, and the human resource aspects of merger activities. The settings cover a wide variety of organizations with an emphasis on the growing service sector.

This book offers opportunities for learning experiences in its six major sections: (1) Human Resource Management in Perspective: Environment and Legal Issues; (2) Meeting Human Resource Requirements: Job Analysis/Design, Planning, Recruitment, and Selection; (3) Developing Effectiveness in Human Resources: Training, Career Development, and Performance Appraisal; (4) Implementing Compensation and Security: Compensation, Incentives, Benefits, and Safety and Health; (5) Enhancing Employee Relations: Discipline, Motivation, and Labor Relations; (6) International HR and Term Project. Each of these sections, except Part 6, contains cases, exercises, incidents, and skill builders.

Most cases are based on actual events occurring in private- and public-sector organizations. All names have been changed. The first two cases in the introductory section are designed to act as pre- and post-measures of the students' knowledge of human resource management. That is, the two cases in Part 1 can be used at the beginning of the course to pique interest in the material or at the end to test how much students have learned. The student becomes the decision maker in these classroom-tested cases. Questions are provided at the end of each case and incident to guide discussion, and/or the instructor may ask students to use the case analysis model suggested by the authors on the book's Web site.

The exercises include opportunities for students to simulate the human resource work environment through role playing, identifying and solving human resource problems, completing in-baskets, and applying human resource management theories. The role plays and in-basket exercises require students to act just as they might in a real management situation. Virtually all of the exercises can be completed within 45 minutes and all contain a set of detailed procedures to follow.

The incidents are mini-cases composed of critical human resource management events and are designed to help students develop problem-solving skills. They are intended to raise questions around issues that do not have definitive answers and may be used to stimulate class discussions or to introduce students to human resource management topics.

Skill builders are short, individual assignments that can be completed by students outside of class. The skill builders develop the specific technical skills needed by human resource professionals and line managers to effectively manage human resources.

The final item in this book—the Term Project—provides instructions for a group project and/or term assignment to enhance the learning of human resource management. This project is designed to be challenging and comprehensive by requiring students to draw upon material learned throughout the course.

The instructor's manual includes an analysis of the cases and incidents, solutions to the exercises and skill builders, and alternative approaches for using and presenting the materials in the book.

New to This Edition

Responding to the requests and recommendations of instructors, students, and HR professionals, the authors have included a number of new items in this edition:

- Exercise 3: Developing Environmentally Friendly HR Policies at City University
- Incident 7: Human Resource Information Systems Data Breach
- Case 11: Investigating a Sexual Harassment Case
- Case 39: The Use of Social Media in Employee Recruitment and Selection
- Exercise 44: Selecting from Imperfect Applicants
- Exercise 68: Executive Bonuses and Incentives
- Exercise 78: Domestic Partner Benefits
- Case 89: Violence at Work
- Exercise 91: Developing an Employee Dress Code
- Incident 92: Facebook Posting: I Hate My Stupid Boss
- Case 104: Outsourcing Jobs to India
- Case 106: A Clash of Cultures in the Workplace: German Managers in South Africa

In addition to numerous updates and revisions, the authors have significantly updated the data, scenarios, and information presented in the following:

- Exercise 5: Scanning the Contemporary Work Environment: Shifting Demographics
- Incident 10: The Cultural Diversity Training Program
- Exercise 16: The Older Worker Questionnaire
- Exercise 17: Is This Unlawful Discrimination?
- Exercise 18: What Is Sexual Harassment?
- Exercise 20: Group Debate Project
- Exercise 31: Work and Family Issues
- Skill Builder 33: Phased Retirement Options
- Exercise 40: Evaluating the Recruiting Function
- Exercise 55: Design and Evaluation of Training Programs
- Exercise 61: EvalSim—A Performance Evaluation Exercise
- Case 65: The Overpaid Bank Tellers
- Exercise 70: WageSim—A Compensation Administration Exercise
- Skill Builder 74: You Be the Judge: Is This Job Exempt?
- Case 77: Controlling Employee Benefit Costs

- Incident 84: The Medical Leave Problem (FMLA)
- Term Project 107: Human Resource System or Subsystem Evaluation

Acknowledgments

Many people have assisted in making this book possible. We are grateful to the following case contributors: Myron Glassman, J. Stewart Black, Gerald Calvasina, Susan Corriher, Diana Deadrick, Yvonne du Plessis, J. Kline Harrison, Sam Holliday, Hank Hummel, Ronald Karren, Margaret Foegen Karsten, Arno F. Knapper, Steve Maurer, M. Susan Taylor, and James Wimbush. Special thanks to Juanita Craig, Ralph Pederson, Jim Bavis, David Abernethy, Diane Marie Eckland, Rusty Rainey, and other friends who shared with us their professional knowledge and experiences in human resource management for developing materials for the book.

The authors wish to acknowledge the contribution of the reviewers of the previous edition of this book. They are:

- Dr. Tina C. Elacqua, LeTourneau University
- Cheryl Crozier Garcia, Ph.D., SPHR, GPHR, Hawaii Pacific University
- Karen Jacobs, LeTourneau University
- Dr. Kimberlee Keef, University of Memphis
- Joe Mosca, Monmouth University
- Elizabeth E. Regimbal, Cardinal Stritch University
- Stacy Rogers, SPHR, CPRW, Sullivan University
- Romila Singh, Ph.D, University of Wisconsin–Milwaukee
- Thomas Tudor, University of Arkansas at Little Rock

Stella Nkomo would like to thank the Faculty of Economic and Management Sciences at the University of Pretoria for its support in the revision of this edition. She also wants to thank her research assistant Anna-Marie Nieuwoudt for her assistance. She also appreciates the steadfast support of her husband, Mokubung, and her son, Sebenza.

Myron Fottler would like to thank his wife, Carol, for her assistance and input into the current and all previous editions of this book. Her contributions were particularly important in the development of several cases and incidents based on her own experiences and those of friends and relatives. He is also extremely grateful to Megan McLendon, Whitney Windham, and Sarah Cox, who have done a tremendous job preparing new materials and editing old materials for this seventh edition of our book.

Bruce McAfee would like to thank the College of Business and Public Administration at Old Dominion University for their support. He also appreciates the support of his wife, Chris, and his son, Ethan.

This book would have been impossible without the outstanding work of the people at South-Western/Cengage Learning.

Finally, we would like to thank our students for their invaluable suggestions for revising and clarifying the materials in this book.

Stella M. Nkomo

Myron D. Fottler

R. Bruce McAfee

CORRELATION TABLE

TOPIC	CASES	EXERCISES	INCIDENTS	SKILL BUILDERS
Adverse Impact	12,38			
Affirmative Action	12	20		24
Application Blanks		43		48
Arbitration		101		
Benefits	76,77	31,78,79,80	81,82,83,84,97	
Career Development	51,53			
Collective Bargaining	99	100		
Compensation	1,65,66,67,99	68,69,70,71,72,78	73	74,75
Cultural Awareness		106		
Disabilities		19	21,45	
Discipline	1,20,88,89,90	91,101	47,92,93,94,95	
Disaster Preparation			85	
Discrimination	8,12,38,60	16,17,18,19	9,10,21,22,23, 45,93	24
Diversity Issues	8	20	9,10	
Dress Policy		91	93	
Ethics	1,13	64,71,72	45,81	
Employment at will	15			
Executive Perks		68,80		
Exit Interviews			46	
FLSA				74
FMLA			84	
Family Issues		31	84	
Health/Safety	52,77,85	86	81,84,87	
HR Challenges		4		
HR Data Breach			7	
HR Environment/Policies		3,5		
HR Forecasting				32
HR Functions	2	6,29		
HR Strategy	1,2,26	4,40		
HR Structure	2			
HR Trends		5		
Incentives	66,67,76	68,69,80	73	
Immigrants	14	20		
International HR	8,103,104,105	20,106	9	
Interviewing		41,42,43,49	46	50
Internet Blog			92	
Job Analysis	38	30		49,58
Job Descriptions		30		49,58

Labor Relations	98,99	100,101		102
Layoffs/Downsizing	25	28,29	96	
Management Development	51,53	54		
Mentoring	53			
Mergers		4	97	
Motivation	66		96,97	
NLRA		100		102
Nepotism			47	
Orientation	52		57	
Outsourcing	104	29		
Pay Inversion		72		
Performance Appraisal	25,59,60	61,62,63,64		
Privacy Issues	14,39,88,90		92	
Promotion	1,12,51			
Recruiting	34,35,36	40		49
References		43		
Retirement			81	33
Safety/Health	52,77,85	86	81,84,87	
Selection	14,34,35,36,37,38,39,103,105	41,42,43,44	9,22,45,47	48,49,50
Self Appraisal	59		84	
Seniority			21	
Sexual Harassment	11	18		
Sexual Orientation		78	23	
Social Networking	39	92		
Substance Abuse	88		94	
Surveys of Employees	8			
Telecommuting		20		49
Termination	88	20,28,100,101		
Testing	37,38,88	43	94	50
Training	52,53,105	55,56,106	10,57	58
Turnover/Retention	66	6	46	
Unfair Labor Practices	98,99			
Union Organizing	98			102
Utilization Analysis				24
Violence At Work	89			
Wage Structures				75
Wage Surveys	65			
Whistle Blowing	13			
Work Schedules	27			

Contents

PART 1 Human Resource Management in Perspective: Environment and Legal Issues — 1

THE HRM FUNCTION/ENVIRONMENT

1. **CASE** The New Director of Human Resources 3
2. **CASE** The Human Resource Function of Harrison Brothers Corporation 9
3. **EXERCISE** Developing Environmentally Friendly HR Policies at City University 14
4. **EXERCISE** Human Resource Challenges during Mergers 17
5. **EXERCISE** Scanning the Contemporary Work Environment: Shifting Demographics 20
6. **EXERCISE** Evaluating the Financial Impact of Human Resource Management Activities: Reducing the Cost of Turnover 21
7. **INCIDENT** Human Resource Information Systems Data Breach 26

DIVERSITY ISSUES

8. **CASE** Managing Diversity: Johnson Chemical International 27
9. **INCIDENT** Too Much Diversity? 35
10. **INCIDENT** The Cultural Diversity Training Program 36

THE LEGAL AND REGULATORY ENVIRONMENT

11. **CASE** Investigating a Sexual Harassment Case 38
12. **CASE** Analyzing Promotion Data: Applying the 80% Rule 41
13. **CASE** Blowing the Whistle: Accounting Practices at Glenfair Electronics 45
14. **CASE** LGA Industries: Employing Undocumented Immigrants 46
15. **CASE** The Broken Employment Contract? 50
16. **EXERCISE** The Older Worker Questionnaire 54
17. **EXERCISE** Is This Unlawful Discrimination? 56
18. **EXERCISE** What Is Sexual Harassment? 60
19. **EXERCISE** Understanding the Americans with Disabilities Act 62
20. **EXERCISE** Group Debate Project 64
21. **INCIDENT** Giving Up Seniority to Accommodate a Disabled Colleague 68
22. **INCIDENT** "Beautyism" in the Workplace 69
23. **INCIDENT** Sexual Orientation Incidents: Bootstrapping Discrimination 71
24. **SKILL BUILDER** Data Analysis for Affirmative Action Plans 73

PART 2 Meeting Human Resource Requirements: Job Analysis/Design, Planning, Recruitment, and Selection — 81

ANALYSIS/PLANNING/OUTSOURCING/MERGERS/LAYOFFS

25. **CASE** Employee Layoffs at St. Mary's Hospital 83
26. **CASE** Strategic Human Resource Management 86
27. **CASE** The Alternative Work Schedule 89

28. EXERCISE Which Employee Should Be Terminated? 91
29. EXERCISE Outsourcing the Human Resource Management Functions 93
30. EXERCISE Job Analysis: Writing Job Descriptions 97
31. EXERCISE Work and Family Issues 100
32. SKILL BUILDER Human Resource Forecasting Assignment 103
33. SKILL BUILDER Phased Retirement Options 106

RECRUITMENT AND SELECTION

34. CASE Recruiting Recreational Vehicle Surveyors 109
35. CASE Recruiting and Selecting High-Level Managers through the Internet 112
36. CASE Recruiting and Selecting Low-Level Workers among Seniors 114
37. CASE Selecting Patient Escorts 115
38. CASE A Solution for Adverse Impact 118
39. CASE The Use of Social Media for Employee Recruitment and Selection 122
40. EXERCISE Evaluating the Recruiting Function 123
41. EXERCISE Selection Decisions 127
42. EXERCISE Selection Interview Role Play 135
43. EXERCISE Which Selection Procedure Is Most Effective? 139
44. EXERCISE Selecting from Imperfect Applicants 140
45. INCIDENT The Ethical Selection Dilemma at Integrity Motors 143
46. INCIDENT The Exit Interviews and Employee Retention 145
47. INCIDENT Nepotism 146
48. SKILL BUILDER Evaluating Job Application Forms 147
49. SKILL BUILDER Staffing for a Telecommuting Job 150
50. SKILL BUILDER Test/Interview Validation 152

PART 3 Developing Effectiveness in Human Resources: Training, Career Development, and Performance Appraisal — 155

ORIENTATION/TRAINING/CAREER DEVELOPMENT

51. CASE Career Development at Electronic Applications 157
52. CASE The Safety Training Program 159
53. CASE The Mentoring Problem at Walnut Insurance 161
54. CASE Management Development: The I-MBA Request 164
55. EXERCISE Design and Evaluation of Training Programs 166
56. EXERCISE On-the-Job Training 170
57. INCIDENT The Orientation Problem 172
58. SKILL BUILDER Identifying Training Needs through Task Analysis 174

PERFORMANCE APPRAISAL

59. CASE The Self-Appraisal Problem 176
60. CASE Mills Paper Company: Performance Management or Age Discrimination? 180
61. EXERCISE EvalSim—A Performance Evaluation Exercise 183
62. EXERCISE Performance Appraisal Interview Role Play 187
63. EXERCISE Which Performance Appraisal Format Is Most Effective? 191
64. EXERCISE Ethical Performance Appraisal Issues 192

PART 4 Implementing Compensation and Security: Compensation, Incentives, Benefits, and Safety and Health — 195

COMPENSATION

65. **CASE** The Overpaid Bank Tellers 197
66. **CASE** Rewarding Volunteers 199
67. **CASE** Evaluating Nontraditional Incentive Systems: Howe 2 Ski Stores 202
68. **EXERCISE** Executive Bonuses and Incentives 205
69. **EXERCISE** Allocating Merit Raises 211
70. **EXERCISE** WageSim—A Compensation Administration Exercise 213
71. **EXERCISE** Ethical and Practical Compensation Dilemmas 218
72. **EXERCISE** Pay Inversion: Is It Practical and Ethical? 221
73. **INCIDENT** Merit Increases 223
74. **SKILL BUILDER** You Be the Judge: Is This Job Exempt? 225
75. **SKILL BUILDER** Developing a Wage Structure 229
76. **CASE** Managing Nonmonetary Compensation 231

BENEFITS

77. **CASE** Controlling Employee Benefit Costs 234
78. **CASE** Domestic Partner Benefits 237
79. **EXERCISE** Flexible Benefit Plan Choices 239
80. **EXERCISE** Executive Perks 242
81. **INCIDENT** Retiree Health and Pension Benefits 244
82. **INCIDENT** The Educational Leave Problem 245
83. **INCIDENT** The Lost Vacation Days 247
84. **INCIDENT** The Medical Leave Problem (FMLA) 249

SAFETY ISSUES

85. **CASE** Disaster Preparedness 251
86. **EXERCISE** Safety and Health Programs 253
87. **INCIDENT** The Safety Problem 254

PART 5 Enhancing Employee Relations: Discipline, Motivation, and Labor Relations — 257

DISCIPLINE

88. **CASE** The Drug Testing Problem at Standard Chemical 259
89. **CASE** Violence at Work 263
90. **CASE** Surfing the Internet on Company Time 265
91. **EXERCISE** Developing an Employee Dress Code 266
92. **INCIDENT** Facebook Posting: I Hate My Stupid Boss 268
93. **INCIDENT** Can He Wear an Earring at Work? 269
94. **INCIDENT** Spiked Milk 270
95. **INCIDENT** Caught in the Act: Immoral Behavior at Work 272

Motivation

96. Incident Motivating and Maintaining Morale during Downsizing 273
97. Incident Motivating Employees during a Buyout 274

Labor Relations

98. Case Union Organizing at SGA Industries 276
99. Case The Give Back: A Case of Union Busting 280
100. Exercise Applying the NLRA 281
101. Exercise Labor Arbitration 283
102. Skill Builder Employee Communications during Union Campaigns 286

Part 6 International HR and Term Project 287

International HR Issues

103. Case Selecting a Manager for a Nigerian Facility 289
104. Case Outsourcing Jobs to India 291
105. Case Fred Bailey: An Innocent Abroad 293
106. Case A Clash of Cultures in the Workplace: German Managers in South Africa 297

Term Project

107. Term Project Human Resource System or Subsystem Evaluation 302

PART

1

Human Resource Management in Perspective: Environment and Legal Issues

The HRM Function/Environment

1 CASE

The New Director of Human Resources

Mount Ridge Engineering Systems designs, builds, and operates standardized, coal-fired utility plants in Kentucky. These small generating plants (35 megawatts and 55 megawatts) are built adjacent to an industrial plant that utilizes steam in its operations. Mount Ridge sells the steam to the industrial plant and electricity to the local utility. Under federal regulations, utilities are required to purchase this independently produced power if it is cost competitive. When Garrett Levinson founded the company, he firmly believed that the future of electric generation in the United States would depend upon coal as the primary fuel and standardization as a method of cost control and efficiency. This new technology, known as "cogeneration," is rapidly coming of age as many companies turn to these systems as a way to cut energy costs. Mount Ridge's very efficient plants have allowed it to pursue a cost leadership business strategy.

When the firm was formed four years ago, Joyce Newcombe was hired as director of human resources. Newcombe had recently graduated with an MBA from a large university in the Southeast. At the time of its establishment, the company had four employees in addition to Newcombe: the president and founder, a senior vice president of operations, a vice president for administration, and a vice president of cost and estimation. From the start, Mount Ridge had both the financing and plans to build seven plants over the next five- to eight-year period. Joyce Newcombe was hired to develop all of the necessary human resource programs, plans, and policies needed to staff the plants once they became operational. She explained, "When I was hired, all we had was a dream and a plan. I had an office with a desk, chair, and telephone. I literally had to develop an entire human resource system." During the first year, Newcombe developed benefit packages for both corporate and plant personnel, an employee handbook, job descriptions, a salary program, a supervisor's manual, and other basic personnel policies. In less than three years, the company built five plants. The size of the workforce grew from 5 to 39 people at corporate headquarters and from 0 to 183 employees in the plants (see Exhibit 1.1 for the company's organizational structure).

The company became remarkably successful in a short period of time. Newcombe was promoted to vice president. In addition to having two plants currently under construction in the state, Mount Ridge plans to build an additional two to three plants in the Northeast. The demand for cogeneration plants is strong in New Jersey, Connecticut, Maine, and Massachusetts, where state energy regulators are concerned about high electricity prices. Forecasts indicate that the company will grow to a total of nine plants and approximately 650 corporate and plant employees over the next two to three years.

The company faced a dilemma with regard to determining benefits and salaries for its employees. These had to be competitive, but not so high as to attract workers from Mount Ridge's "customers"—its industrial hosts and the local utility. In addition, since profits were to be reinvested into the business to finance future plant expansion, a profit-sharing plan was not feasible. Another important goal of the company was to remain nonunion by offering

EXHIBIT 1.1 *Organization Structure*

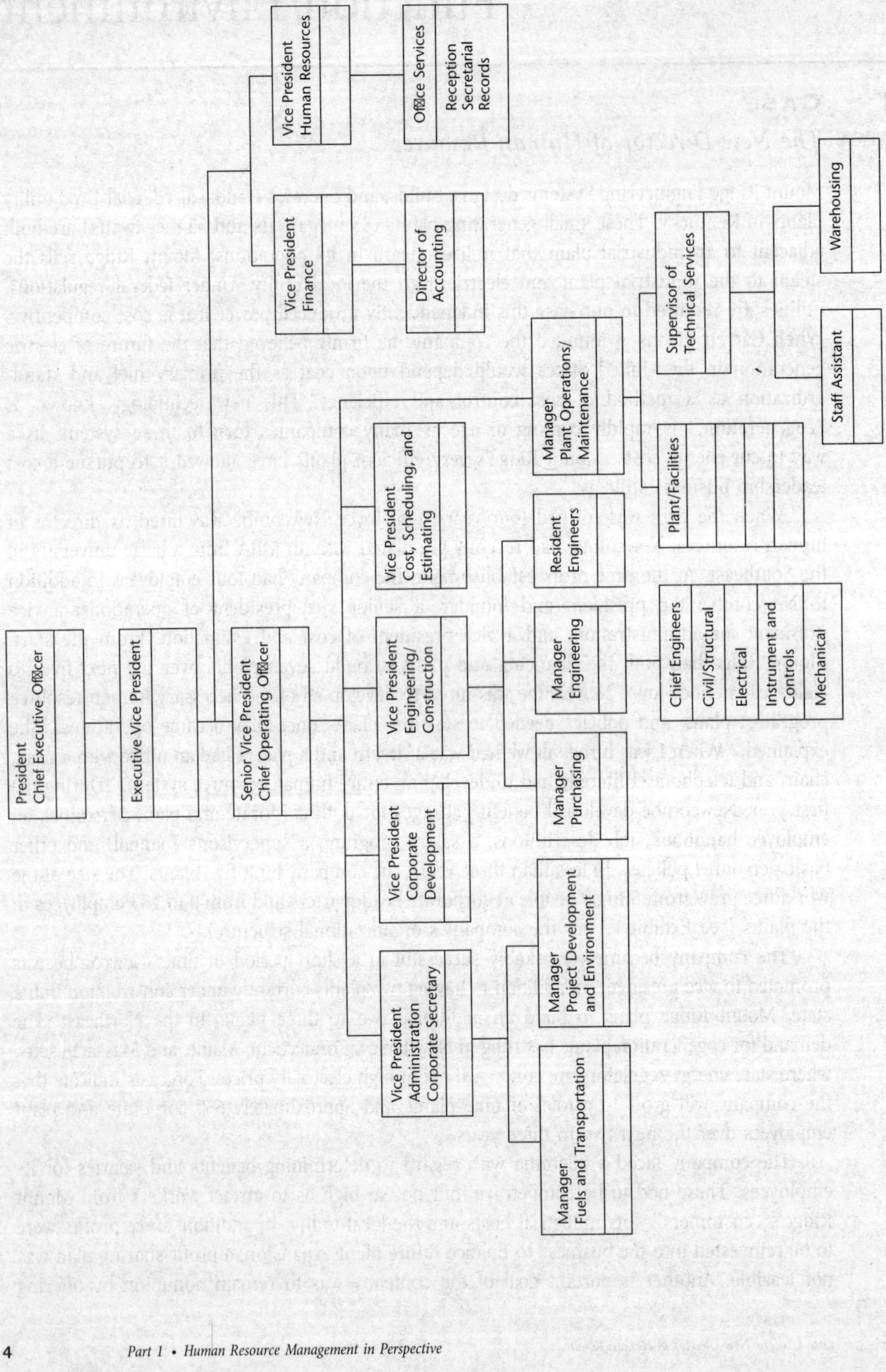

employees a good quality of work life and attractive benefits. Balancing these two goals was often difficult. Low-cost production was critical to Mount Ridge's competitive position. The importance of these goals is reflected in the words of President Levinson: "Mount Ridge places great value on its relationship with our industrial and utility clients. Our internal employee relationship has an equally important role in order to maintain an enjoyable and productive workforce for the future. Management believes that companies that are good to their employees reap the benefits in terms of increased productivity and loyalty." As part of an effort to build this philosophy into its human resource programs, employee appreciation dinners are held annually at each of the five plants. The president and other corporate officers attend each of the dinners given throughout the state. These dinners have been well-received by employees.

Plant Operations

Most of Mount Ridge's plants are scattered throughout the state. Each plant employs approximately 45 workers. The typical plant structure is shown in Exhibit 1.2. Each plant is run by a plant superintendent who reports directly to the manager of plant operations and maintenance. While personnel operations are generally centralized at corporate headquarters, the plant superintendent and shift supervisor of each plant are largely responsible for the day-to-day administration of personnel policies. Newcombe admits, "One of our biggest problems has been getting management—especially plant management—to understand the legal and governmental regulations affecting human resource procedures." Although Newcombe developed a detailed employee handbook and supervisor's manual, over the years there have been situations where supervisors have not followed company policy. Newcombe recounted one such incident that occurred in one of the older plants during her third year with the company.

The Termination

One of the first plants built was the Edison plant. It is located in a medium-sized rural community in the eastern region of Kentucky and employs 45 workers. Bud Johnson, who started at the plant as a laborer, worked his way into a position as an auxiliary operator. An auxiliary operator is responsible for assisting the control room operator and the equipment operator in the basic operations and maintenance of the plant's generating system. In the two years that Johnson was in this position, he learned quickly and knew a good deal about the equipment operator's job. On many occasions, Johnson was asked to fill in when the equipment operator was absent or when there was a problem that no one else could handle. One day Johnson approached the plant superintendent, Larry Braxton, about a promotion to equipment operator:

Johnson: Larry, you know I can handle the equipment operator position, and I'd like to be considered for a promotion.

Braxton: That's not the point. We all know you are capable, but we just don't have any openings right now. Besides, the job qualifications require that you spend sufficient time as an auxiliary operator before moving up to an equipment operator. Just sit tight.

Johnson: Well, I hope some openings will come up soon. I really would like to make more money, and I know that I am qualified. You know I can learn quickly. Look at how fast I moved up from being a laborer.

After this conversation, Johnson was again called on several times to help out with the equipment operator's job and to explain the readings and gauges to Wilma Barker, one of the

EXHIBIT 1.2 *Typical Plant Structure*

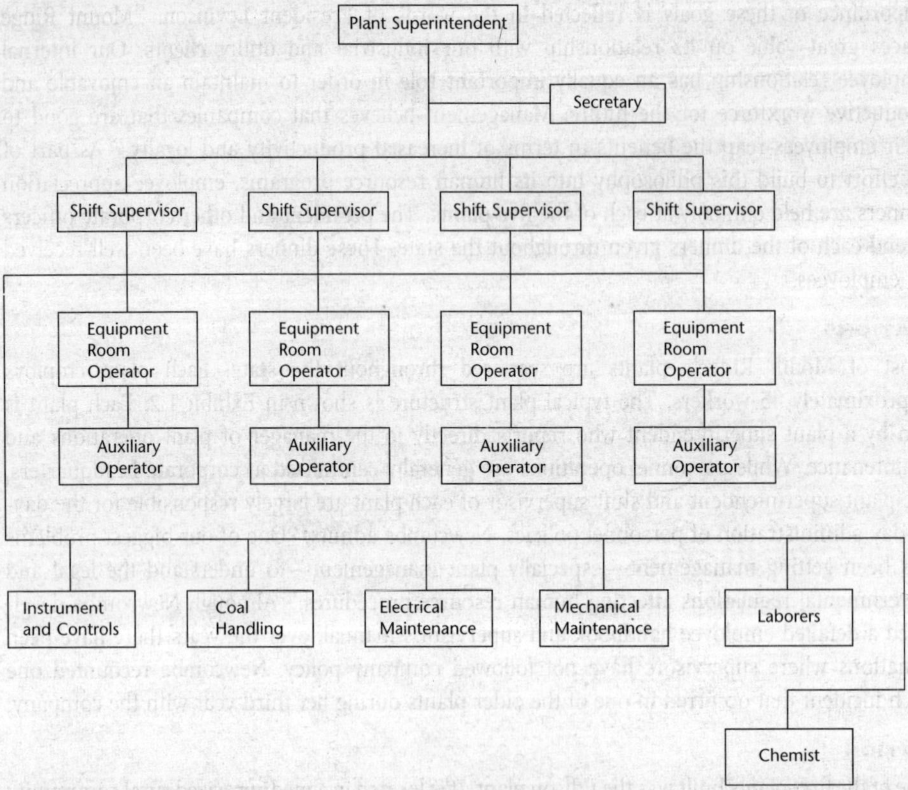

1 Plant Superintendent
1 Secretary
1 Chemist
1 Instrument and Controls
4 Shift Supervisors
8 Equipment Room Operators
16 Auxiliary Operators
2 Electrical Maintenance
2 Mechanical Maintenance
3 Coal Handlers
6 Laborers
- 1 Assigned to Electrical Maintenance
- 1 Assigned to Mechanical Maintenance
- 2 Assigned to Coal Handling
- 2 Assigned to Plant Clean Up

45 Total Plant Staff

equipment room operators. When Johnson did not receive a pay increase or promotion after his annual evaluation, he met with Braxton and told him that he was dissatisfied with his pay and felt that because he often performed the equipment operator's job, he ought to be paid at that rate instead of his present rate as an auxiliary operator. Braxton told him he would have to remain at the pay of an auxiliary operator and that he should be satisfied with that for the time being. Johnson became quite upset and stormed out of Braxton's office. The next day, Johnson did not report to work and did not call in to report his absence.

Company policy stated that when an employee is absent and fails to notify his or her supervisor, the employee may be terminated. When Johnson returned to work the following day, he told Braxton that he had decided to quit his job because he was very dissatisfied with his pay. Johnson was asked to sign a termination notice form required by company policy and was told by Braxton that he would receive a copy of the form in the mail.

A week later, Newcombe received a phone call from Johnson. Johnson told her that the reason given on the copy of the termination form he had just received in the mail was incorrect (see Exhibit 1.3). He had not left to take another job but had left because he was dissatisfied with his pay and lack of promotion at the plant. He explained that he had spoken with the plant superintendent about this several times. Johnson told Newcombe that he wanted his personnel records to be corrected and that he had been asked by Braxton to sign a blank form. He alleged that Braxton had added the incorrect reason after he had signed the form. Johnson also stated that he thought the Department of Labor would have something to say about this whole incident.

Questions

1. Discuss the relationship between corporate human resources structure and operations at the plant level. What impact, if any, did that relationship have on the situation described by Newcombe?
2. How should Newcombe have handled this situation?
3. What, if any, disciplinary action should have been taken against the plant superintendent (Braxton) at the time of the incident?
4. If Johnson's allegations were true, what are the legal ramifications of Braxton's behavior?
5. Describe Mount Ridge's business strategy. What is the relationship between its business strategy and its human resource practices?
6. What strategic human resource issues will Newcombe likely face as the company expands to the Northeast? How might this expansion affect the structure of the organization and its human resource department?

EXHIBIT 1.3 *Termination Form for Bud Johnson*

NOTICE OF TERMINATION

This form MUST BE completed for EVERY termination

DEPARTMENT USE ONLY

1. SOCIAL SECURITY NUMBER
1 2 3 – 0 9 – 7 6 2 5

Johnson Bud O.
2. NAME Last First Middle

348 Bismark Street
3. MAILING ADDRESS Number Street

Mount Ridge, Kentucky
City State Zip

587-6089
4. HOME PHONE

Auxiliary Operator
5. JOB TITLE

6. Termination date: 11/1/06 — Last day worked: 10/31/06

7. Recommended for other employment Yes ☐ No ☒
8. Replacement Required Yes ☒ No ☐

9. Immediate Supervisor: Larry Braxton — Phone

10. Plant Location: Edison

11. Sex M ☒ F ☐

12. Ethnic Background

REASON FOR TERMINATION

13. LAY-OFF — No replacement required ☐
14. DISCHARGE
☐ Absenteeism (give dates)
☐ Not qualified (explain)
☐ Other (explain)
15. VOLUNTARY QUIT
☐ Leave of absence granted (ending ....)
☐ Dissatisfied pay (overtime, rate, etc.)
☐ Dissatisfied distance to work (miles..................)
XX To take another job (employer, rate)
☐ Leaving town
☐ Dissatisfied working conditions (explain)
☐ Other (explain)

16. EXPLANATION (Use additional sheet if necessary)

PAYROLL DEPARTMENT

17. EMPLOYEE number
18. HIRE DATE
19. RATE
20. HOURLY ☐ SALARIED ☐

	Days	$
Regular pay thru		
Vacation		
Severance		
Pay in lieu of notice		
Deductions:		
W/H (Federal & State)		( )
FICA		( )
Other, i.e., Insurance		( )
TOTAL		$

EMPLOYMENT OFFICE

Larry Braxton — 23. Plant supervisor

Bud Johnson — 24. Employee signature

______, SIGNATURE ACKNOWLEDGES RECEIPT OF THIS NOTICE
Date

SUPERVISOR'S REPORT OF TERMINATION

WERE WRITTEN WARNING NOTICES OR PERFORMANCE EVALUATION GIVEN?
☐ YES (ATTACH COPIES) ☐ NO

WHAT WAS EMPLOYEE'S REACTION TO COUNSEL, WARNING NOTICES, OR PERFORMANCE EVALUATION?

REASON FOR TERMINATION. (UNEMPLOYMENT INSURANCE CLAIMS ARE A MAJOR COST TO THE COMPANY. WHEN FACTUAL INFORMATION IS LACKING, THE STATE EMPLOYMENT DEVELOPMENT DEPARTMENT GENERALLY FAVORS THE EMPLOYEE'S CLAIM—EVEN THOUGH IT MAY NOT BE MERITED. THEREFORE, THE EXACT REASONS FOR TERMINATION ARE EXTREMELY IMPORTANT. IN ADDITION, THIS INFORMATION CAN BE ESSENTIAL FOR THE RESOLUTION OF UNFAIR LABOR PRACTICE AND EQUAL EMPLOYMENT CASES.)

2 CASE

The Human Resource Function of Harrison Brothers Corporation

COMPANY HISTORY

Harrison Brothers Corporation was founded in upstate New York on September 15, 1898, by Aubrey and William Harrison. Harrison Brothers is a multi-line traditional department store that carries mainly men's, women's, and children's clothing. In recent years, the store has expanded to include household furnishings and other items for the home. The long-term goal of the company is to become the leading chain of department stores in the Northeast, selling moderate- to higher-priced merchandise to middle-class, fashion-conscious customers. Harrison Brothers is one of the largest privately owned retail stores in the United States. A majority of its twenty stores are located in the Northeast. Its largest store is located in a major urban center and has 950 employees. The company is highly decentralized and maintains a very small corporate office.

INDUSTRY CHALLENGES

Traditional department stores like Harrison Brothers are beginning to experience the effects of a number of changes in the retail industry. Not long ago, major department stores succeeded by being all things to all customers. However, today's customer is looking for both value and specialization. Superstores and giant discounters are also popping up. At the same time, the industry faces the challenge of keeping a well-trained, highly motivated sales staff and management team. James Harrison, CEO of Harrison Brothers, describes the company's strategic challenges for the next five years: "We can no longer continue to do the same old things that gave us a reputation for fair value. We must reposition ourselves—floor to floor—offering exciting brand names, excellent sales help, and frequent sales. We need a sales staff that knows the merchandise and understands customer preferences. Buying expertise is also critical because fashions and consumer tastes never stay the same. We have five strategic goals:

1. Convert non-selling space into revenue-generating selling space.
2. Build up underdeveloped merchandise categories.
3. Invest aggressively in private brands like Polo, Nautica, and Tommy Hilfiger.
4. Reduce costs through the use of advanced computer systems to project sales and manage inventory.
5. Improve productivity of sales associates, buyers, and department heads."

James Harrison took over the business after earning an MBA at a prestigious business school in the Northeast. Unlike previous family members, he wanted to take a much more deliberate approach to charting the future of Harrison Brothers. To do this, he hired a consultant to assist in assessing the company's strengths and weaknesses. Harrison felt the employee quality and performance would be one of the keys to the future. As part of his analysis, the consultant sought to learn more about the human resource function within Harrison Brothers. He decided to interview a few of the human resource and other key managers at the store level. Both groups were also asked to complete a questionnaire of their perceptions of the responsibilities of the human resource function (see Exhibit 1.4).

EXHIBIT 1.4 *Results of Questionnaire Completed by HR Managers and Non-HR Managers*[a]

HR Responsibilities	HR Managers	Store Managers
Staffing	4.5	4.5
Training and Development	3.5	4.5
Performance Management	4.5	4.0
Compensation	3.0	3.5
Safety	2.5	2.5
Knowledge of Business	2.0	4.5
Managing Change	2.0	4.5

[a]Respondents were given a list of human resource responsibilities and asked to rate their importance to store performance using a scale of 1 (not very important) to 5 (very important). The responses were aggregated for all stores. The numbers in the table represent the mean ratings for each item. The questionnaire was completed by all the human resource managers and store managers at each store.

THE WESTPARK STORE*

Brenda McCain has been the human resource manager at the Westpark store for the past four years. Prior to her employment at Harrison Brothers, Brenda had several years of experience in retail stores and came to Harrison Brothers after being a buyer at one of its major competitors. McCain has a degree in fashion merchandising from a college in New Jersey. Currently, there are 950 employees at the Westpark store. The staff includes salespeople, sales support employees (dock, marking room, clerical, and accounting), maintenance, security, and management. The human resource department consists of five people (see Exhibit 1.5). During the peak holiday season, a number of people are hired as floating sales staff. These temporary workers may number close to 100.

THE HUMAN RESOURCE MANAGER'S JOB

McCain talked about the human resource department's areas of responsibility: "Our business has really grown in the last two years. We are carrying more specialty and designer clothing lines and have added items we hope will appeal to moderate- to high-income customers. When I came here four years ago, I found too many of the human resource operations being performed by the operations manager, Pat Hartlake, and one of the department heads, Rich Jenkins. Since that time, I have attempted to set up procedures and policies to assure proper staffing of the store. I spend most of my time just managing the human resource department. I think it is important to keep abreast of the performance of workers, and I like to observe their work habits regularly. I also spend a good deal of time on selecting applicants for the sales and support jobs. There is heavy turnover on the sales floor in our business, and the average salesperson at Harrison Brothers is either part-time, an older employee, or one who is 'in-between jobs'—if a better job came along, they would snap it up immediately. For example, of the 119 part-time people hired in the last four months, 65 have left."

McCain went on to explain their selection procedures: "The main sources of our applicants are newspaper ads and word-of-mouth by present or past employees. We select people based on how well they do in the interview. Right now, I conduct about 25 to 30 interviews a week and perhaps more during the holiday rush. I have enough experience in

**The interview at the Westpark store reflects what the consultant heard throughout the company.*

EXHIBIT 1.5 *Harrison Brothers Organization Chart*

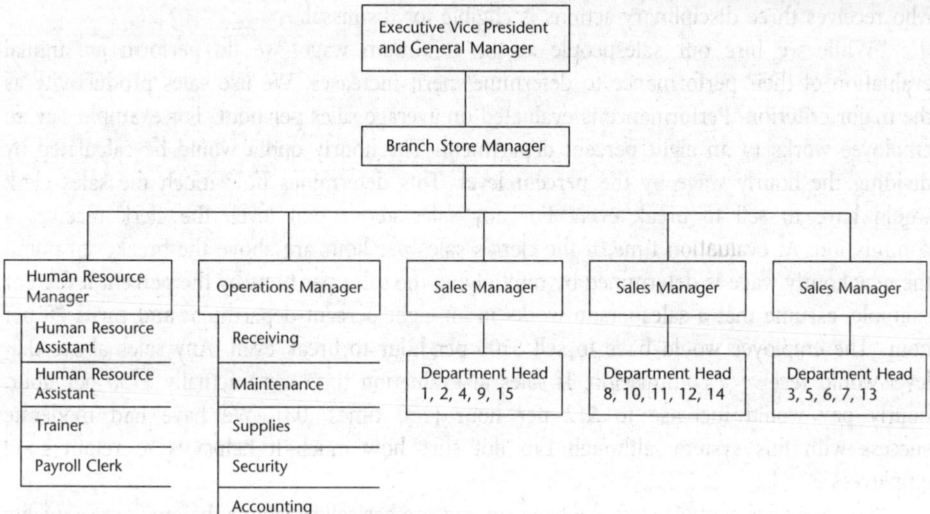

Department Identification

1. Children's (boys, girls, infants)	9. Cosmetics
2. Shoes	10. Domestics
3. Dresses	11. China/etc.
4. Men's	12. Housewares
5. Women's coats	13. Fine jewelry
6. Fashion accessories	14. Sporting goods
7. Intimate apparel	15. Toys
8. Furniture/Carpet/Bedding	

(Each department head supervises several sales clerks.)

retail to know what it takes to be a good salesperson. We place a lot of weight on their motivation, personality, and drive. Little or no useful information is gained from high school or college records or references. I do check their application forms for an indication of job stability, though.

"The training of new salespeople occurs every two weeks and every week during the holiday season. Now and then we get some employees who cannot effectively complete the cash register training. Our trainer, Joanne Flynn, tries to expose them to selling techniques and how to properly interact with customers. Although we have a trainer, I do spend a good deal of time with her and will help out if the training classes are too large.

"When I came here, discipline was a continual bone of contention between the employees and supervisors. Employees felt the present procedures were inconsistently enforced and applied. Each supervisor was administering punishment depending on his or her own interpretation of the problem. Now, I am totally responsible for all disciplinary actions. I discuss the alleged wrongful act with the employee's supervisor to assess the magnitude of the act. I then talk with the employee before deciding upon the appropriate consequences. In this way, we have better consistency in the application of disciplinary rules. Any employee who receives three disciplinary actions is eligible for dismissal.

"While we hire our salespeople at the minimum wage, we do perform an annual evaluation of their performance to determine merit increases. We use sales productivity as the major criterion. Performance is evaluated on average sales per hour. For example, say an employee works in an eight percent department. The hourly quota would be calculated by dividing the hourly wage by the percent level. This determines how much the sales clerk would have to sell to break even. For any sales above that level, the clerk receives a commission. At evaluation time, if the clerk's sales per hour are above the breakeven point, the new hourly wage is determined by multiplying the sales per hour by the percent level. For example, assume that a salesperson works in an eight percent department and earns $8 per hour. The employee would have to sell $100 per hour to break even. Any sales above that level would receive a commission. If sales at evaluation time were actually $150 per hour, hourly pay would increase to $12 per hour (150 times .08). We have had moderate success with this system, although I'm not sure how much it helps us to retain good employees.

"For our sales support staff, we have supervisors basically evaluate the employee's quality and quantity of work. Last year, though, we incorporated a form of employee development into the evaluation process. Supervisors are required to discuss the employees' career opportunities and professional development with them. I initiated this as a form of career planning and hopefully as a way to keep good employees. Unfortunately, supervisors have been slack in doing the assessment. They seem to be more anxious to get the performance evaluation completed. Several employees came to me to say they had not received a 'professional assessment' since the program was instituted.

"There is a lot more we need to do here in human resources, but we are somewhat constrained by cost considerations and the realities of the retail industry. The turnover in the sales areas gives me little free time to develop new programs and ideas."

Interview with the Store Manager

Jennifer Daft recently joined Harrison Brothers after being recruited from a major specialty retailer. Jennifer had a number of years of experience in management and retail. During the interview, she talked about her perceptions of the human resource department in her store. "I think they are too internally focused most of the time. Brenda and the rest of her staff seem to be struggling to keep up with the day-to-day activities. I don't know if they are understaffed or not. Our store has experienced very high turnover. With the new strategic direction of our company, however, I need human resources to be more of a key player. It's not hard to get the merchandise we want to sell, but we need people who know how to merchandise it and how to sell it to customers. There are a lot of changes going on in the company. It's not going to be a smooth ride for a while. We're all going to have to learn how to do things differently and better to stay competitive. Our human resource people are no exception."

Interview with the Operations Manager

Pat Hartlake, the operations manager, talked about interactions with the human resource department: "I have a good working relationship with the human resource department, but it took some time to develop that relationship. McCain has a good understanding of the retail business, and I am impressed with her knowledge of store operations. They have been somewhat slow in filling the vacant sales positions, and they don't always respond as quickly as they should. They seem terribly understaffed and overworked most of the time.

"Let me give you an example of what I mean. A few weeks ago, I was faced with an employee situation that was evolving to the point where I felt termination was necessary. I went to the Human Resource Department to discuss the case to be sure I had covered all bases. With all of the laws today, one needs to be careful in making decisions. They never seem to be able to produce answers to questions without hedging. I had to wait almost two weeks before I got any help from them. In the meantime, the situation with the employee continued to deteriorate. I can understand their reluctance to terminate sales staff because of the difficulty in recruiting new people. In a way, however, the old system seemed to be a lot less complicated. Department managers knew how to handle situations that came up in their departments. Don't get me wrong! I know that as we continue to grow we're probably going to need an even larger human resource department."

QUESTIONS

1. How does McCain view her role as human resource manager?
2. What is Harrison Brothers' business strategy?
3. What is the structure and staffing of the human resources department?
4. Analyze the data in Exhibit 1.4. What are its implications?
5. Given the organization's size and strategic goals, evaluate the development of the human resource function at Harrison Brothers. What problems do you see? How could its major human resource functions be improved?

3 EXERCISE

Developing Environmentally Friendly HR Policies at City University

I. OBJECTIVES

A. To understand the critical role HR can play in an organization's green initiatives to ensure and support sustainability goals.

B. To identify environmentally friendly HR policies and initiatives within the key HR functions.

II. OUT-OF-CLASS PREPARATION TIME: 1 hour

III. IN-CLASS TIME SUGGESTED: 45 minutes

IV. PROCEDURES

A. Read the entire exercise before class. Students may want to conduct some research before class on environmental responsibility and sustainability. They can also visit the following Web sites:
www.carbonfootprint.com
www.greenatwork.com

B. The class should be divided into groups of four. The groups should be given 20 minutes to brainstorm ideas for green initiatives that fall within HR's responsibility. Each group should complete Form 1.1.

C. The instructor should then ask each group to present their list to the rest of the class. After the first group shares its list, the rest of the groups should only add things that are new or different.

D. If time permits, the entire class should discuss the following questions: 1) What is HR's role in building a greener organization? 2) What are the potential benefits in terms of attracting and retaining talent? 3) How should Andrea proceed in order to develop an overall strategy for "greening" the HR function at the university?

BACKGROUND

Alice Vanderbilt has been the Director of Human Resources at City University for the past five years. The sprawling state university is located about 15 miles north of the city center in a bustling suburb known for its rolling hills and plentiful trees. The campus itself is quite beautiful with lots of green areas and ponds. Two major thoroughfares are within close proximity. The student enrollment was 17,000 six years ago but has grown to 20,000 students. The University has many degree programs but has gained a reputation for excellent engineering programs. Recently the university built a research complex that houses a number of research projects focusing on innovation in environmental engineering.

A majority of its 20,000 students commute from the various towns and communities daily to attend day and evening classes. Only about 30 percent of the students live on campus. International students represent less than 5 percent of the student population. There are 1,300 faculty and staff. During the week, the campus is a hub of activity. Most of the in-state residential students drive home for the weekend and return on Monday morning or late Sunday evening. Despite the growth of the city over the years, there is no public transport system except for a light rail trolley system that mainly services the city center with a few routes to key suburbs south of the city. There is no line running to the university. Thus, most of the City University's staff members drive to work in their own cars. Most students also have their own cars since many students work part-time. Parking demands continue to outstrip available space. Last year, the campus paved over one of the green areas to make space for an additionally 1,500 cars. A new 4-story parking deck is also under construction.

Three months ago, Dr. Jeanette Marshall was installed as the 20th president of the University. Dr. Marshall has already embarked on a number of initiatives since taking office. At a management planning session two weeks ago, she announced a new initiative, Green Leadership for a Sustainable Campus. At the session, she shared her vision for greening the campus: I want City University to become "the most green-friendly university in the country."

At the session the following objectives were developed:

- To create an environmental culture where everyone is committed to protecting the environment.
- To leverage the University's knowledge and expertise to "green" the campus.
- To encourage positive environmental behavior in staff.
- To implement and encourage green practices for the entire campus.
- To reward best practice in "greening" the campus.
- To partner with the local community on green projects of mutual interest.

Each manager was given the assignment to identify green initiatives and policies for their area of responsibility. All managers were expected to have a draft proposal completed within the next two months for review and discussion by the larger group. Since the planning session, Alice had been giving a lot of thought to what she could propose. Alice also believed she needed to first come up with some basic ideas for green initiatives and would then work toward an overall HR strategy for greening the workplace. She admitted to herself that she had really not thought about HR implications of environmental sustainability. Yes, recycling was obvious but what else can be achieved through the HR function?

FORM 1.1 *HR Green Initiatives*

HR Functional Area	Possible Green Initiatives and Policies	Potential Benefit(s)
Recruitment and Staffing		
Orientation		
Compensation and Benefits		
Work Practices and Policies		
Performance Management		
Reward Systems		
Employee Cafeteria		
Employee Communications		

4 EXERCISE

Human Resource Challenges during Mergers

I. OBJECTIVES

A. To sensitize you to the actual and potential human resource challenges facing organizations contemplating or implementing a merger.

B. To familiarize you with various human resource strategies and tactics for managing a successful merger process.

II. OUT-OF-CLASS PREPARATION TIME: 30 minutes

III. IN-CLASS TIME SUGGESTED: 50 minutes

IV. INSTRUCTIONS

A. In groups of three to five students, read the "Situation," below as well as the merger challenges listed on Form 1.2.

B. Each group will be assigned one or more of the merger challenges listed in Form 1.2. Search the Web sites outlined in the Internet Skill Builder in Part 1, the Internet sites listed below, or other sites to identify one or more human resource strategies and tactics to address each of your assigned merger challenges.

C. One person from each group will present the strategies and tactics developed to address their assigned merger challenges together with the group's assessment of the highest priorities. Each group should also identify which of the challenges and strategies/tactics for addressing each will be most crucial for implementing a successful merger.

Useful Web sites for this research include the following:

http://www.workforceonline.com/

http://www.hrmgt.com/

http://www.hrworld.com

http://www.pohly.com/admin7.shtml

SITUATION

Katherine Montgomery is the Director of Human Resources for a faith-based hospital in the Southwest. In addition to a BS in Nursing, she also has an MA in Human Resources Management and has been active in her local Society for Human Resources Management. Recently, Katherine has heard rumors that her hospital may be in merger discussions with the academic medical center in the same city. The academic medical center is larger in terms of beds (804 versus 658 beds), total revenue, staff, and external research grants. In addition, the medical center is state-associated and many employees are either union members or have civil service job protection. Katherine's hospital is private, not-for-profit, and has no labor union representation. Based on a private communication with her human resources counterpart in the academic medical center, she is aware that neither of them has been involved in merger negotiations or planning.

Today, the city newspaper reported that the two institutions were taking part in merger talks and the expectation was that a final merger agreement would be signed within three months. Katherine is upset because she knows that most mergers fail primarily due to poor communications and incompatible corporate cultures. She is also saddened that her department was not included in the initial merger negotiations since she is well aware of the literature on merger challenges and has detailed knowledge of one healthcare merger failure in another city. She also strongly believes that the greater the degree to which the human resources department is involved in the merger process, the greater the likelihood of merger success.

As she contemplates her course of action, she lists the human resource challenges both organizations would face before, during, and after the merger. These appear in Form 1.2.

Until now, she has not had to consider which human resource strategies and tactics would be most appropriate for addressing each of the challenges she has identified in Form 1.2. She has called Professor Martin Smith in the Department of Management at the local university and asked if he or some of his graduate students could assist her in completing Form 1.2. With that input, she then intends to schedule an appointment to speak with her CEO in order to indicate how her department could assist in the merger process. Specifically, she plans to present him with a human resource plan for successfully integrating the two hospitals based on Form 1.2.

FORM 1.2 *Potential Human Resources Challenges Facing the Merged Organization*

Potential Challenge/Problem	Appropriate Strategies/Tactics
1. Rumors, misinformation, and inadequate information	
2. Conflicting corporate cultures	
3. Existing state government civil services rules and union contracts	
4. Neither organization fully aware of the skills, knowledge, and abilities of the other's management or staff	
5. Likely staff reconfiguration, reassignments, and layoffs	
6. Determination of which human resources practices to retain	
7. Management of staff morale and stress levels	
8. Turnover of valued employees	
9. Unclear job assignments and reporting relationships	
10. Lack of understanding of new policies and procedures	
11. Overall strategy to market her department's role and potential value to the CEO.	

Indicate Highest Priority Concerns: ______________________________

5 EXERCISE

Scanning the Contemporary Work Environment: Shifting Demographics

I. OBJECTIVES

The purpose of this exercise is to help you understand the potential influence of trends and changes in the external environment on the design and implementation of human resource management practices.

II. OUT-OF-CLASS PREPARATION TIME: None

III. IN-CLASS TIME SUGGESTED: 20–30 minutes

IV. PROCEDURES

A. This exercise should be done in groups of four to five students.

B. After completion of the exercise, each group will present its ideas to the rest of the class.

C. Listed below are some of the major predictions about changes or trends in the labor/employment environment that will take place. Read each trend and list some ideas about the impact of these trends on the major human resource management functions: staffing and placement, training and development, salary administration, performance evaluation, job design, promotions, and career planning. That is, what human resource issues will organizations face because of these changes?

Trend	Impact on HRM
1. Increasing government regulation of health care	
2. Aging of the workforce	
3. Increase in outsourcing, offshoring, and employee leasing	
4. Increasing diversity of the American labor force (e.g., women and minorities in the labor force)	
5. Multigenerational workforce	
6. Increasing use of social networks	
7. Increasing number of foreign-born employees	
8. Global warming and growing environmental awareness	
9. Labor shortages at all skill levels	
10. Threat of stagnant economic growth in United States and globally	

Suggested Internet Resources

U.S. Department of Labor	http://www.dol.gov
EEOC	http://www.eeoc.gov
Society for Human Resource Management	http://www.shrm.org
Conference Board	http://www.conference-board.org
OSHA	http://www.osha.gov
U.S. Census Bureau	http://www.census.gov
United Nations	http://www.un.org
International Labor Office	http://www.ilo.org

6 EXERCISE

Evaluating the Financial Impact of Human Resource Management Activities: Reducing the Cost of Turnover

I. OBJECTIVES

A. To provide you with practice in analyzing data and drawing conclusions regarding managerial implications.

B. To make you aware of the potential costs of controllable, dysfunctional turnover and its impact on net income or profit.

C. To make you aware of the potential benefits of human resource management activities to an organization's "bottom line."

II. OUT-OF-CLASS PREPARATION TIME: 2 hours

III. IN-CLASS TIME SUGGESTED: 45 minutes

IV. PROCEDURES

Read the entire exercise, including the "Background" on the Charlotte Health System and the three exhibits. Using the data in the exhibits, do the calculations (on your own, prior to class) requested on Form 1.3. Then, assemble groups of three to five students during the class period and discuss each of the questions. At the end of the class period, have a spokesperson for each group discuss the group's answers and rationale with the entire class.

BACKGROUND

The healthcare industry has undergone dramatic change and restructuring during the decade of the 1990s and early 2000s. Mergers, consolidations, and downsizing have become the norm as organizations struggled to provide more cost-effective, high-quality services demanded by managed-care organizations and corporate employers. A major response to these pressures has been the development of "integrated delivery systems," which typically combine multiple units of hospitals, physician practices, outpatient facilities, long-term care facilities, and insurance.

The goal of these systems is to provide "seamless" care through internal referrals, a common electronic medical record, common policies and procedures, etc. However, the reality has been somewhat less than a total success. Among the problems identified have been differences in values and incentives between the organizational units, lack of top management knowledge of some of the units acquired, and inability to "integrate" the different units clinically and managerially.

The Charlotte (North Carolina) Health System was developed from a base of a public hospital to which various delivery sites were added after Harry Majors became CEO 15 years ago. Since his arrival, Majors and his executive team have created the dominant health system in North Carolina. Despite this success, the system continues to be under pressure from employers and managed-care organizations to further reduce its costs and document both clinical quality and cost-effectiveness.

Almost four years ago, Majors and the board of directors decided that the time had come to "professionalize" the human resource function since the organizations they had purchased or aligned with exhibited varying degrees of sophistication and vastly different policies and procedures. Betty Williams was recruited from another health system as the new VP for Human Resources. Williams came to her job after completion of an MA degree in Human Resources Management from the University of Alabama and 16 years of experience in the

EXHIBIT 1.6 *Human Resource Management Department Budget for Years One through Four*

	Department Budget per Year			
Budget Cost	**One**	**Two**	**Three**	**Four**
Salaries and Benefits	$110,000	$233,000	$288,000	$324,000
Equipment and Supplies	24,000	39,000	48,000	57,000
Communications	41,000	62,000	73,000	81,000
Totals	$175,000	$334,000	$409,000	$462,000

field. During the three years she has been at Charlotte Health System, she has hired three new HRM staffpersons in recruitment, employee benefits, and compensation.

H.R. Cost Justification

As the Board has considered how to reduce the cost of service delivery in the system, the corporate office in general, and the Human Resources Department in particular, have come under increased scrutiny. Williams has been told she needed to justify the additional budget allocation to her department over the past three years. Exhibit 1.6 shows her department's budget for year one (the year prior to her arrival) as well as the three years since her arrival. The board has calculated the "extra" costs of the Human Resources Department over the past three years (using year one as the base) to be $680,000. The largest percentage cost increases were in "salaries and benefits" and in "equipment and supplies." Most of the latter increases were the result of upgrades in computer hardware and software.

The Board has scheduled a meeting for next Monday. One of the agenda items is to examine the costs of the Human Resource Management Department with the possibility of a budget cut for next year. Williams has been asked to make a presentation to justify her budget and how expansion of her department has contributed to the system's "bottom line." She has considered a number of changes she made which she believes have improved overall system performance. Among these were the development of system career ladders to increase employee retention, in-house management training programs to improve management competence, development of "model" staffing ratios to reduce employee stress and burnout, quarterly performance reviews to increase employee feedback, absenteeism incentive programs, and initiation of an annual employee survey to identify problem areas.

After some discussion with her staff, Williams decided that it would be easier to "document" the benefits of increased employee retention. Exhibit 1.7 shows the employee

EXHIBIT 1.7 *Annual Turnover Rate by Category for Years One through Four*

	Percent Turnover per Year			
Personnel Categories	**One**	**Two**	**Three**	**Four**
Executive (n = 127)+	12.8	11.5	9.2	8.3
Physician (n = 367)	18.1	17.6	17.9	15.6
Other Professional (n = 615)	22.6	22.1	18.3	15.6
Nonprofessional (n = 804)	29.0	26.3	27.1	24.3
Totals++ (n = 19.3)	23.8	22.3	21.3	18.8

+*n is the average number of employees in each category over the four-year period.*
++*This is the weighted average turnover rate for all four categories for each of the four years.*

EXHIBIT 1.8 *Average Costs of Turnover per Individual Over the Four-Year Period by Personnel Category*

Turnover Costs	All Categories+	Personnel Category Executive	Physician	Other Professional	Nonprofessional
	(n = 1913)	(n = 127)	(n = 367)	(n = 615)	(n = 804)
Separation Costs:					
Exit Interviews	50.73	62.50	73.00	51.00	38.50
Administrative Costs	119.27	127.00	132.50	116.00	114.50
Separation Pay	348.01	2,254.00	1,034.00	—	—
	518.01	2,443.50	1,239.50	167.00	153.00
Replacement Costs:					
Job Advertisements	1,346.49	1,805.00	2,416.50	1,127.50	953.00
Pre-Employment Administration	353.28	405.00	416.50	386.50	291.00
Entrance Interviews	324.86	486.00	724.50	284.00	148.00
Assessment Testing	271.69	382.50	695.00	214.50	105.00
Staff Time	249.00	417.50	522.00	212.00	126.00
Travel/Moving Expenses	293.68	1,215.50	1,110.50	—	—
Processing New Employees	87.50	87.50	87.50	87.50	87.50
Medical Examinations	175.00	175.00	175.00	175.00	175.00
	3,101.50	4,974.00	6,147.50	2,487.00	1,855.50
Training Costs					
Informational Literature	80.00	80.00	80.00	80.00	80.00
Formal Training	147.53	340.00	516.50	35.00	35.00
On-the-Job Training	68.15	—	—	212.00	159.50
	295.68	420.00	596.50	327.00	274.50
Reduced Productivity during Learning Period	3,133.37	4,000.00	6,500.00	3,452.00	1,215.50
Total	$7,048.56	$11,837.50	$14,483.50	$6,433.00	$3,528.50

+*weighted average*

turnover by category for year one (the year before Williams's arrival) as well as for each of the following three years since her arrival. These data show a decline in turnover for all four personal categories over the four-year period.

Williams and her staff have calculated the average cost of turnover per employee by personnel category and these calculations are shown in Exhibit 1.8. Most of these calculations can be documented from personnel records. The exception is the "reduced productivity during the learning period." For these calculations, the staff calculated the average monthly productivity for a small sub-sample of the individuals who left and compared it to the average monthly productivity of those who replaced them during their first three months. They then calculated the dollar cost of this lost productivity for a one-year period.

Their assumption is that the lower productivity continues at the same level for a 12-month period and then disappears. More realistically, the lower productivity probably declines over time but continues for longer than a 12-month period. However, they feel their method of calculation is a good approximation of reality since their overestimation of the productivity loss is offset by the shorter time period of their calculations.

Exhibit 1.8 shows that the total cost for each individual who leaves the Charlotte Health System averages $7,049 but this varies from a high of $14,484 for physicians to a low of $3,644 for nonprofessional employees. These costs are divided into separation costs, replacement costs, training costs, and costs of reduced productivity (for the new employee) during the (assumed) one-year learning period.

QUESTIONS

1. Are the calculated benefits of reduced turnover sufficient to justify the $680,000 in increased costs associated with the expansion of the Human Resource Management Department? Would your answer be the same if "reduced productivity during the learning period" was excluded from the analysis?
2. In addition to improved employee retention, what are some other areas of potential economic benefit to the organization from having a Human Resource Department? What calculations would you do to prove such benefits?

FORM 1.3 *Calculation of Benefits of Higher Employee Retention Using a Base of Year One*

Personnel Category	Savings in Year: Two	Savings in Year: Three	Savings in Year: Four	Total Savings
Executive				
Physician				
Other Professional				
Nonprofessional				
All Categories	______	______	______	______

Calculation of Savings or Loss:

1. Total Incremental Savings from Higher Employee Retention for all Personnel Categories for Years 2, 3, and 4.

2. Total Incremental Costs of the Human Resource Management Department Budget for Years 2, 3, and 4. –$680,000

Net Savings or Loss ______

Benefit/Cost Ratio (1) ÷ (2) ______

7 Incident

Human Resource Information Systems Data Breach

Sweets, Inc., a candy manufacturer, is finalizing the implementation of a comprehensive human resource information data system covering its 400-plus employees. It has been working on the system for two years and hopes to finish it within the next few months. This system will eliminate virtually all of the paper forms used by the Human Resource Department. The firm has been transferring all of the information contained on these forms to its computer. When the process is complete, the firm will be able to store, analyze, retrieve, and distribute most of its HR information.

Shortly, the company will be able to post job openings on the Internet and retrieve incoming job applications. It will know what skills and abilities all of its employees possess and what training each has received. It will be able to access performance appraisal information on all employees to determine job performance levels and necessary training. The firm will be able to examine pay and benefit information to determine individual and aggregate compensation levels. It will also be able to easily prepare various documents such as Form EEO–1. All of this information will be available with just a few key strokes.

Until yesterday everything had gone smoothly. Then, a major problem developed that turned everything upside down. A laptop computer containing sensitive data went missing from one of the HR offices. Was it stolen? Did someone borrow it to work on at home? Was it just moved to another office? No one knew for sure and a frantic search began, but it was without success.

The human resource director decided he had better call the company president and the head of computer operations to explain what had happened. The president wanted to know immediately what information was stored on the computer and how this information could be retrieved by others, assuming it was stolen. The HR director stated that he was not sure if the laptop had been stolen, but that employee compensation information was probably on the computer, including each person's name, address, telephone number, and social security number. The confidential information was password protected, so the average citizen could not retrieve it, but an experienced hacker might be able to do so. All three executives were aware of recent incidents in which sensitive computer data had been compromised at many large corporations and that these corporations had issued warnings to those affected. The question that needed to be addressed was what action Sweets, Inc. should take given its present situation.

Questions

1. What action do you recommend that Sweets, Inc. take now? Explain your reasoning.
2. What steps can the firm take to prevent this problem from occurring in the future?
3. What additional information needs to be gathered before any decisions are made or action taken?

Diversity Issues

8 CASE

Managing Diversity: Johnson Chemical International

Jeff Rice, vice president of corporate human resources at Johnson Chemical International, was very anxious about the meeting he was about to have with John Henderson (CEO), Gary Polaski (secretary and general counsel), Steven Hong (vice president of operations, Haverford plant), and Matt Beale (vice president of public affairs and communications). The last two days had been quite tense in the company ever since an e-mail (see Exhibit 1.9) was sent throughout the company's Haverford plant.

Johnson Chemical International is one of the world's leading manufacturers of specialty chemical products. The company was founded in 1902 by Herman Johnson, who was an MIT-trained chemist. Over the years, Johnson Chemical has built a reputation for producing high-quality products developed through cutting-edge technology and research. As a privately held corporation, Johnson Chemical does not report sales or earning figures. It has plants and operations in 30 countries and manufacturing facilities in 10 countries (Argentina, Canada, Kenya, Indonesia, Greece, United Kingdom, Japan, Taiwan, Malaysia, and Brazil). Johnson Chemical employs more than 14,500 people worldwide with its headquarters located in Chicago. Employment in the United States is about one-half of its total workforce worldwide, with a majority of those employees in the Chicago area. Because of its need for highly trained scientists and technicians, the company recruits a substantial number of employees with training in the science and engineering fields.

The U.S. manufacturing operations are conducted at the Haverford plant, about 15 miles outside of Chicago. The state-of-the-art plant is about three million square feet and is one of the most modern chemical manufacturing facilities in the world. The facility also has state-of-the-art laboratories and houses the company's research division. In addition to its hourly employees, the company employs a large number of R&D employees consisting of scientists, technicians, and engineers. Because of its need for highly trained technical employees, the company conducts extensive recruiting at the major colleges and universities with outstanding science and engineering programs. A majority of Johnson Chemical's top management has come from the technical ranks of the company. Its current CEO, John Henderson, is a chemical engineer and the former president of international operations.

THE MEETING

John Henderson: Come on in, Jeff. Good morning, folks. I want to thank you for meeting with me this morning. We have a major problem on our hands. A crude e-mail has sent a tidal wave through the company. It's already hit the press. We've had several calls from the media asking for us to comment on what has happened. Matt, how are we handling the calls?

Matt Beale: John, I have issued a press release that basically states that Johnson Chemical does not tolerate any form of racist or sexist jokes and the individual responsible will be dealt

EXHIBIT 1.9 *The E-Mail Message*

The e-mail message

Morning Puzzle: Do you recognize these acronyms?

UFO
IBB
NAACP

Answer: UFO = Ugly ------- Orientals; IBB = Itty bitty breasts; and NAACP = -------, apes, alligators, coons and possums

with appropriately. Our information systems folks are trying to determine the origins of the e-mail.

Gary Polaski: John, don't worry. We are on firm legal grounds if we fire the individual or individuals responsible for using the company e-mail to send racist and sexist jokes. I think we should take very strong action when we find out who is responsible.

Steven Hong: Well, we better do something fast because it is certainly affecting plant operations. People aren't working but are busy talking about the e-mail. I'm afraid that it really has taken people off track for the time. It also seems to be unleashing some grievances that our women and minority employees have about their treatment in the company. The men and white employees seem to be worried that they're going to all be blamed for the e-mail or, even worse, that they agree with the sentiments in that e-mail. John, I'm worried about the impact of this on employee morale.

Jeff Rice: John, since the e-mail I have had several women and minority employees, especially the African-American employees, come to my office to talk about problems and other incidents in the company. To be honest, it has caught me off guard. We have an excellent equal opportunity/affirmative action program in place and have made some strides in hiring women and minorities in the last five years (see Exhibit 1.10). I am wondering if we've really done enough.

John Henderson: I'm not sure what you mean, Jeff. Our company has enjoyed a good reputation as a leader in the industry when it comes to equal employment opportunity. How could this happen?

Jeff Rice: Well, I was thinking about this last night. You know, John, in the last few years we have begun to have a more diverse group of employees after years of being a company with

EXHIBIT 1.10 *Employment Trends*

There has been a 10 percent increase in employee growth at the Haverford Plant.

The percent of women employees has increased from 10 to 15 percent.

The percent of African-American employees has remained at 6 percent.

The percent of Asian employees has increased from 5 to 10 percent.

Plant turnover averages 2 percent, but is ten times higher for women and African Americans.

The percent of women in management/supervisory positions increased from 2 to 2.7 percent.

The percent of African Americans in management/supervisory positions increased from 1.5 to 2.0 percent.

The percent of Asians in management/supervisory positions increased from 2 to 3.5 percent.

There has been an 8 percent increase in minority scientists (most of that represents Asians).

The percentage of women scientists has grown by 2 percent.

The highest ranking woman in the company is Meredith Jensen, vice president and deputy counsel.

The highest ranking African-American manager is vice president for equal opportunity and employee relations.

The highest ranking Asian manager is vice president, plant operations.

primarily white male employees. Perhaps, it was only a matter of time before these tensions emerged.

John Henderson: Well, we're going to have to get a handle on the issues. Jeff, I want you and your staff to find out what the issues are and give me a report on your findings in 60 days. After we review your report, we'll have to determine what we need to do. Get whatever help you need from consultants. I expect a negative media backlash on this thing, and we're going to have to show that we are a company prepared to deal with tough issues. I have prepared a companywide message that will be sent to all employees this afternoon (see Exhibit 1.11).

Rice's Report

Two months after the meeting, Jeffrey Rice sent John Henderson and the rest of the executive staff a 20-page confidential report of his findings. Excerpts from his report are contained in Exhibits 1.12–1.18. With the assistance of a consulting firm, Rice organized focus groups with African-American employees, women employees, Asian employees, and white male

EXHIBIT 1.11 *Letter to Employees from John Henderson, CEO*

Dear Johnson Employees:

By now, you have heard about the e-mail that was sent through the company's computer system that contained offensive comments. I want to be very clear: We will not tolerate behavior that makes our work environment uncomfortable and hostile for others. The telling of racist, sexist, or offensive comments is not appropriate behavior at Johnson Chemical. It is disrespectful of fellow employees. Using company e-mail to perpetuate offensive views of others violates company policy. Rest assured that we will see that those responsible for sending the e-mail are duly disciplined.

I am counting on you to respect your fellow employees and to commit to ensuring a working climate that is tolerant of our diversity.

John Henderson

John Henderson

employees. Focus groups were recruited on a volunteer basis and were facilitated by the consultants to assure confidentiality and candidness (see Exhibit 1.12). The topics covered in the focus groups are shown in Exhibit 1.13. The views expressed by each group are summarized in Exhibits 1.14–1.17. In addition to the focus groups, an employee attitude survey was also administered to all plant employees. The results of the survey are shown in Exhibit 1.18.

QUESTIONS

1. Evaluate Johnson Chemical's actions in dealing with the e-mail.
2. Examine the data contained in Exhibits 1.10 and 1.12–1.17. What seem to be the most significant diversity issues at Johnson Chemical?
3. What is the cost of these problems to the organization? What will happen if they are not addressed?
4. Where and how do these issues need to be dealt with?
5. What support, skills, and training do managers need to deal with these issues?
6. What human resource management systems or policies need to be examined and possibly modified?

EXHIBIT 1.12 *Letter of Invitation to Participate in Focus Group Discussions*

As you know, we continue to be committed to having an equal opportunity work climate at Johnson Chemical. In an effort to achieve this goal, we invite you to participate in a focus group to help us collect data around issues of diversity. The focus groups will be organized so that we bring together different categories of employee groups over the next two months.

To assure confidentiality and anonymity, the actual discussion sessions will be facilitated by an outside consultant group we have contracted to assist us in our efforts. Discussion will focus on your experiences and thoughts on topics related to our human resource policies and systems, and equal opportunity work climate.

I hope you will be willing to participate in one of the focus groups. Thank you in advance for your help. If you have any questions, please call my office. I'll be happy to provide additional information.

Sincerely,

Jeffrey Rice

Jeffrey Rice, Vice President
Corporate Human Resources

EXHIBIT 1.13 *Focus Group Discussion Areas*

1. Comment on your experience and view of the following areas of the company:

   A. Recruitment and hiring: sources of recruits; selection criteria; orientation of new employees

   B. Promotion: fairness of rating system; adequacy of opportunity

   C. Training and career development: access to training; selection of trainees; adequacy of and availability of career development counseling

   D. Performance management: pros and cons of the performance appraisal process; supervisor feedback

   E. Benefits: adequacy; administration of benefits

   F. Affirmative action program: effectiveness of target of opportunity efforts; attitudes toward

   G. Treatment: personal experiences of bias or barriers because of one's race, ethnicity or gender, or other areas

EXHIBIT 1.14 *Statements Made by Participants in African-American Employee Focus Group*

Recruitment of African-Americans scientists and engineers is inadequate.

African-Americans have to be "more qualified" than other groups to get a job in the company.

African-American students from historically black schools participate in summer intern programs but are rarely hired as full-time employees.

African-Americans employees do not have access to the same training and development opportunities as white employees. Selection for training and development rests with supervisors. This allows supervisors with negative views of the potential of African-Americans to control who gets access to training.

The promotion system is driven by potential ratings given by supervisors, and African-Americans are disproportionately given low potential ratings for promotability.

White supervisors are not comfortable working with African-American employees, and many do not know how to give helpful performance feedback.

Most of the African-American employees are pigeonholed into staff positions in management.

African-Americans can't break into the "informal network," and are excluded from many social activities.

Because there were so few African-Americans in higher level positions, there are no mentors and role models.

African-Americans are stereotyped as being non-technical, lazy, and not suitable for management.

Racial slurs and jokes are often heard on the plant floor.

There is the "rule of three"—no three African-American employees should be seen together in the cafeteria or other places. If so, majority group employees assume something is going on or ask, "Why are the African-American employees all eating together?"

EXHIBIT 1.15 *Statements Made by Participants in Women Employee Focus Groups*

Women are not treated as individuals but subjected to sex role stereotypes. They are viewed as emotional, non-technical, and subordinate. Women who display different behaviors (assertive, good technical skills) are characterized as "pushy or macho."

A myth persists that many of the women in the company don't need to work.

Many male supervisors don't know how to work with women as peers and, therefore, treat female subordinates in condescending ways.

Women are often made to feel that their ideas are inconsequential. They are cut off in meetings, especially when a woman is the only female in a group meeting.

There are too few women in management and supervisory positions.

None of the top women in the company are in line positions.

There are no women in senior management.

Women receive lower potential ratings than men in the company.

Women are excluded from the "old boys" network.

Women are always being tested with offensive sexual jokes or comments.

Affirmative action stigmatizes women and makes them look like victims rather than leaders.

Company benefits do not have programs to help women balance work and family.

EXHIBIT 1.16 *Statements Made by Participants in Asian Employee Focus Groups*

Asian employees are stereotyped as having excellent technical skills but not having suitable skills for management.

Asian employees are not promoted because supervisors tend to give them low ratings on communication skills.

Asian employees are stigmatized by affirmative action and shouldn't be lumped with other minority groups in the company.

There are a very small number of Asian managers in the company relative to their numbers in the company.

Most employees are ignorant of the diversity among Asian employees (e.g., Chinese, Korean, Japanese, etc.).

EXHIBIT 1.17 *Statements Made by Participants in White Male Employee Focus Groups*

White men are stereotyped as racist and sexist.

The company's affirmative action plan has lowered opportunities for white employees.

White supervisors have to be careful when managing minority employees.

African-American employees are hostile toward white supervisors.

The company's focus on equal employment opportunity doesn't include white men.

Women employees are overly sensitive; plant environments are tough.

EXHIBIT 1.18 *Results of Employee Survey: Percentage of Employees with Favorable Responses*

Question	All Employees	African-Americans	Asian	Women
My department is effectively managed.	75	57	74	60
People in my department have the skills and abilities to be an effective team.	85	79	82	78
I feel proud to work at Johnson Chemical.	75	60	70	61
I am satisfied with my opportunity to get a better job.	79	39	65	44
I like the work I do.	85	75	84	74
My manager gives me feedback that helps improve my performance.	52	38	51	35
My department has a climate that respects employee diversity.	65	49	60	48
My manager is sensitive to the relationship between my work life and my personal life.	61	58	59	49
My supervisor applies company policies and rules regardless of race, gender, etc.	77	54	65	55

9 INCIDENT

Too Much Diversity?

Bill Baldwin, president and founder of Baldwin Scientific Instruments, had just finished meeting with Tran, a Baldwin assembler of Vietnamese descent. Tran was very upset about the treatment that he and his Vietnamese co-workers had been receiving from their first-line Latino supervisors, a brother and sister who were originally from Peru. Tran had reported that the two supervisors did not respect any of the 10 Vietnamese assemblers, that they were intentionally mean and rude to them, and that they spoke negatively about them in Spanish behind their back. He pointed out that the assemblers are the key to the firm's success, and asked the president to take immediate action to restore the respect they deserved.

Baldwin was aware that distrust and friction existed between the Latinos and Vietnamese. Fortunately, there had never been any fights or even loud arguments. However, he noticed that during lunch both groups sat apart and spoke in their native languages. At the annual company summer picnic and Christmas party, both groups also sat separately, and, while cordial, were never very friendly toward one another. Baldwin realized that part of the problem might be that the Latinos were often in supervisory positions whereas the Vietnamese were mostly assemblers. This structure reflected the fact that the Latino supervisors had far more experience and length of service than the new Vietnamese employees did. Bill also realized that another part of the problem might be that the head of the assembly department, a non-immigrant Californian who supervised the brother and sister, was not an effective leader because he refused to address employee relations problems. He knew a lot about assembling instruments, but allowed problems to fester among the diverse workforce rather than solve them.

As Baldwin was pondering what should be done, the sales manager walked into the office and gleefully announced that another large order had just come in. Baldwin knew this would necessitate the hiring of five more skilled assemblers, and that advertisements in the southern California area newspapers would result in mostly Latino and Vietnamese applicants. He wondered what the firm's hiring policy should be, given that he did not want to create more problems.

QUESTIONS

1. If you were Bill Baldwin, what actions would you take in response to Tran's request?
2. What hiring policy should the firm follow?
3. Does the firm have too diverse a workforce?

10 INCIDENT

The Cultural Diversity Training Program

Dr. Jennifer Barnes is an Assistant Professor of Organization Behavior and Human Resource Management of a major state university in the Southeast. Her university is located in a large city which is 61 percent black. In recent years, the university has aggressively recruited black faculty and graduate students. Specifically, the university has funded new faculty positions and graduate fellowships for minorities.

Recently Dr. Barnes read about a new university-sponsored cultural diversity training program that was required for all academic administrators/supervisors and offered to faculty and staff. Since Dr. Barnes teaches two human resource management courses, she decided to enroll in the one-day seminar in anticipation of utilizing the material in her own courses. She expected the program would cover the full range of workforce diversity including age, race, gender, ethnicity, physical abilities, and sexual orientation. She also thought there might be some discussion of the impact of parental status, religious beliefs, and dual-career couples. Finally, she expected to experience a high level of involvement in the process through the use of case studies, sensitivity training, incidents, and role playing.

When Dr. Barnes attended the program, she was quite disappointed. There was a series of lectures by seven different speakers, including one external consultant on cultural diversity and several university administrators. While the seminar coordinator told the participants she wanted their input and involvement, the speakers were scheduled for one-hour blocks and used most or all of their allotted time with their formal presentations. Throughout the day only seven comments or questions were asked by participants. In addition, the only concept of diversity discussed by the presenters was racial diversity.

Other types of workforce diversity were mentioned in passing by one presenter but were otherwise ignored. The emphasis for most of the presentations was on the changing workforce demographics and the consequent necessity for the university to be more open, accommodative, and responsive to black students, employees, or potential employees. One of the speakers noted that while blacks constitute 60 percent of the city's population and 30 percent of the area's population, only 15 percent of the students and 4 percent of the faculty are black. Moreover, only three percent of the academic administrators at the university are black. The unspoken assumption was that the participants (most of whom were white) harbored racial animosity toward blacks. Therefore, they needed to modify their attitudes and behavior in order to better recruit, retain, and relate to black employees or students.

Dr. Barnes felt that both the content and process of the seminar left much to be desired. After the seminar, she discussed her experience with her department chair. The chair agreed to discuss it with the Dean of the School of Business. After doing so, he reported that it had been decided at the highest levels of the university that "in our environment, diversity means black." She interpreted that comment to mean that the political "powers that be" in the university were only interested in the racial aspect of diversity. Consequently, she did not expect to see future changes in the diversity training program.

QUESTIONS

1. What is cultural diversity?
2. Why is cultural diversity an important issue for all organizations? What are the potential disadvantages of ignoring it as an issue? What steps should a proactive organization take to respond to this challenge?
3. Evaluate the content and training method used by the university in this training program. Do you have any suggestions for improvement? How might such changes be implemented?

The Legal and Regulatory Environment

11 CASE

Investigating a Sexual Harassment Case

I. OBJECTIVE

The purpose of this exercise is to help you understand the procedures for investigating an allegation of sexual harassment in the workplace.

II. OUT-OF-CLASS PREPARATION TIME: Read the material on sexual harassment in your textbook as well as the background below before class.

III. IN-CLASS TIME SUGGESTED: 20–30 minutes

IV. PROCEDURES

D. This exercise should be done in groups of four to five students.

E. Each group should read the scenario and the sexual harassment policy.

F. Each group must develop a sexual harassment investigation plan that details how they will go about determining if wrongdoing has occurred. After completion of the group discussion, each group will present its investigation plan to the rest of the class.

SCENARIO

James Tilden is the Human Resource Manager at SenGlas, Inc., which manufactures specialized glass for industrial use. The company has 300 employees and a management staff of seven including Tilden's position. SenGlas has been in business for over 50 years and has a well-established human resource department.

On Friday morning, the company's shipping coordinator, Mary Booth, came into Tilden's office quite agitated and said she was fed up. She wanted to file a formal complaint against one of her co-workers, Bob Simonsky, a fork-lift driver, for his harassing behavior toward her. Simonsky had been working with SenGlas for twenty years. Booth joined the company five years ago and had held administrative positions before getting promoted to her present position in the warehouse. Both of them worked on the second shift in the plant. She told Tilden that Simonsky was continuing to treat her in a very nasty manner because he didn't want to work with a woman. Booth said she had tried for a long time to ignore his actions toward her. However, she said his behavior toward her was getting out of hand and that she no longer looked forward to coming to work and was suffering from headaches every day. She claimed Simonsky's behavior created a hostile work environment for her and she could no longer bear it.

In her written complaint, Booth specifically alleged the following:

- That Simonsky had made false accusations about her behavior toward another employee, Ginny Miller. Simonsky had told Miller that Booth was threatening to hurt her physically;
- That Simonsky on more than one occasion had revved his fork-lift engine and drove straight toward her while laughing when she tried to give him orders about a delivery;
- That he had slammed the metal forks of his fork-lift on the ground in an intimidating manner;

- That he continuously refused to take any directions from her about which shipping trucks to load or unload;
- That twice he had thrown a cigarette butt at her;
- That he would regularly tear up instructional notes she left for him;
- That Simonsky had told another worker, Henry Mueller, that "Booth had f- - - - - with the wrong person and that when he got through with her not even Jesus Christ himself would be able to save her."
- That two other fork lift drivers, John Griffin and Henry Jackson, had overheard Simonsky say that women did not belong in the warehouse area and that he preferred working with men.
- That when she first started in the position as shipping coordinator that Simonsky had told her, "I hate that maggot. I should have killed her when I had the chance," referring to Sally Jenkins who held the shipping coordinator position before her.

Although Tilden had only joined the company six months ago, he had heard about Simonsky's bad temperament from many people in the company. On one occasion Simonsky had even been rude to him. Tilden asked Booth if she had reported the incidents to her supervisor. She indicated she had and her supervisor had told her he would speak to Simonsky. Tilden decided he had better review SenGlas' sexual harassment policy (see Exhibit 1.19) before investigating Booth's allegations.

EXHIBIT 1.19 *Excerpt from SenGlas's Sexual Harassment Policy*

SenGlas prohibits sexual harassment of its employees and applicants for employment by any employee or non-employee. Such conduct may result in disciplinary action up to and including discharge. This policy covers all SenGlas employees regardless of position held. The Company will not tolerate, condone, or allow sexual harassment, whether engaged in by fellow employees, supervisors, associates, clients, or other non-employees who conduct business with the Company. All SenGlas employees are entitled to work in an environment free from sexual harassment and a hostile or offensive working environment. We recognize sexual harassment as unlawful discrimination, similarly to conduct that belittles or demeans any individual on the basis of race, religion, national origin, sexual preference, age, disability, or other similar characteristics or circumstances.

According to federal law, sexual harassment is any behavior that includes unwelcome sexual advances, requests for sexual favors, making sexual or romantic advances toward an employee, and persisting despite the employee's rejection of the advances or other verbal or physical conduct of a sexual nature when:

- submission to, or rejection of, such conduct is used as the basis for promotions or other employment decisions;
- the conduct unreasonably interferes with an individual's job performance or creates an intimidating, hostile, or offensive work environment.

No manager or supervisor shall threaten or imply that an employee's refusal to submit to sexual advances will adversely affect that person's employment, compensation, advancement, assigned duties, or any other term or condition of employment or career development. Sexual joking, lewd pictures, and any conduct that tends to make employees of one gender "sex objects" are prohibited.

If an employee believes that he/she has been subject to sexual harassment or any unwanted sexual attention, he/she should:

- make their unease and/or disapproval directly and immediately known to the harasser;
- make a written record of the date, time, and nature of the incident(s) and the names of any witnesses; and
- report such complaints to their supervisor immediately. If the supervisor is the cause of the offending conduct, the employee may report this matter directly to the Human Resource Manager. All complaints will be promptly and thoroughly investigated. Such investigations will be completed within two weeks of the complaint. Confidentiality of reports and investigations of sexual harassment will be maintained to the greatest extent possible. Any manager, supervisor, or employee who, after appropriate investigation, is found to have engaged in sexual harassment of another employee will be subject to disciplinary action, up to and including termination of employment. The disciplinary process outlined in the SenGlas Disciplinary Policy (HR Handbook, page 15) will be applied.

If any party directly involved in a sexual harassment investigation is dissatisfied with the outcome or resolution, that individual has the right to appeal the decision. The dissatisfied party should submit his or her written comments to the Vice President of Operations at SenGlas who will review the matter.

SenGlas will not in any way retaliate against any individual who makes a report of sexual harassment nor permit any employee to do so. Retaliation is a serious violation of this sexual harassment policy as well as federal laws. All such violations should be reported immediately. Any person found to have retaliated against another individual for reporting sexual harassment will be subject to appropriate disciplinary action, up to and including termination.

Note: Sexual Harassment Complaint Forms are available on the Intranet.

12 CASE

Analyzing Promotion Data: Applying the 80% Rule

Thomas L. Rutherford, human resource director of Food Chain Supermarkets, Inc., was jolted by the conversation he just had with Walter Jackson, an employee in the company's distribution warehouse. Jackson had complained that black employees were being passed over for promotions in favor of white employees who had less experience and seniority. Jackson had gone on to explain that he had resigned his position in the meat department of the warehouse because, despite his experience and job performance, he felt he would not get promoted. He explained that he had been passed over for promotion three times since he started work with Food Chain Supermarkets.

After Jackson left his office, Rutherford immediately began to investigate his claims. He called in Mark Walters, his personnel assistant, and explained to him the conversation he'd just had with Jackson. "The last thing I want on my hands is a discrimination suit," Rutherford told Mark. "I want you to get some data on promotions that have occurred in the last couple of years in our warehouse operations. Also, while you're at it, get the same information for our stores. Also, here are the names of three black employees given to me by Jackson. Pull their files and try to get any facts on what happened with their promotion requests."

Mark replied, "I don't think it will be too difficult to pull together the information, Tom, now that we have finally gotten our personnel records centralized. But I'll probably have to talk with some of the department managers and supervisors also." Rutherford suggested that he also interview the three black employees. As Mark left his office, Rutherford began to think about the company's human resource practices and Jackson's allegations.

BACKGROUND

Food Chain Supermarkets, Inc. is a regional chain of supermarkets located in the Midwest. Additionally, the company operates a central warehouse, bakery, and its own transportation system. Its main office, distribution center (warehouse), and a dozen stores are located in Reed County. Presently, the company employs over 1,600 people in the county. According to recent census data, Reed County's labor force is about 22 percent black. The company has plans to refurbish its stores and to open four additional stores over the next two years. Rutherford was hired in anticipation of this growth to help better manage the company's personnel needs.

The distribution center has five departments: grocery, meat, frozen food, produce, and transportation. Each department has two shifts. The starting times of various employees on the same shifts are staggered. Both receiving and shipping functions are carried out at the warehouse. Order puller, order selector, order picker, and picker are synonymous terms for the same position. A warehouse crew leader is a working supervisor who not only assigns duties but also performs the same duties as subordinates. Management positions in the stores consist of assistant produce manager, produce manager, grocery manager trainee, relief grocery manager, deli manager, relief assistant manager, assistant manager, head cashier, and assistant head cashier.

Background information on some of the key people in this situation include:

Clifford Gemson: Clifford Gemson was hired as a produce clerk in June 2007. He had originally applied for a management position. He had three years of grocery store management experience including six months in produce management with another company. Gemson worked in two stores between June 2007 and April 2008. On several occasions,

Gemson asked his district manager (J. Perkins) and his store manager (C. Fagen) about promotion to vacant produce manager positions. The first vacancy was filled on October 8, 2007, by Bob Watkins, a white employee. Watkins, a produce clerk, had eighteen months of experience with us. Watkins, who had no management experience, was replaced by another white employee, Sheila Wilson, on November 8, 2007. Wilson was selected on the basis of her Food Chain Supermarket experience as a produce clerk and an assistant produce manager for six months. Gemson was not considered for either vacancy.

Roy Thompson: Roy Thompson was hired by Food Chain Supermarket at our warehouse on September 18, 2004 as a maintenance (sanitation) employee. His duties included forklift driving, sorting damaged food, and rebuilding pallets. His prior work experience included supervisory duties and self-employment. Thompson trained a white employee of Food Chain (Neal Marcy, hired May 12, 2007) who was promoted to crew leader of the maintenance (sanitation) department on June 16, 2007. Before Marcy was hired, Thompson asked his supervisor (E. Jones) for the crew leader job to which Marcy was promoted. Jones told Thompson that he would never be a crew leader as long as he was supervisor. Jones denies saying this. According to Thompson, his supervisors had repeatedly told him that he had both excellent attendance and performance. On August 15, 2008, a junior white employee, Earl Hanes (with less company experience than Thompson), was promoted to a sanitation crew leader for the same shift and in the same department that Thompson worked. According to Jones, Hanes was better qualified because of his previous work experience.

Leslie LeBlanc: Leslie LeBlanc was hired by Food Chain Supermarket on July 8, 2005 as a frozen food picker. Her next position was frozen food loader. LeBlanc was trained to act as a "fill-in" crew leader, and in fact did fill in as a crew leader until Ricky Anderson, a white employee, was hired. LeBlanc trained Anderson in the duties of a "fill-in" crew leader who then assumed LeBlanc's place as "fill-in" crew leader. Anderson was offered a full-time crew leader's position, which he refused. LeBlanc was never offered this job. LeBlanc had previously informed Food Chain Supermarket management of her prior experience as a shift leader at a textile mill.

Walter Jackson: Walter Jackson was employed by Food Chain Supermarket on April 14, 2004 at the warehouse in the meat department. (Milk, dairy products, and meat are in the same department.) Jackson's job duties prior to April 2008 included milk picking, unloading, and forklift driving. In the spring of 2008, a crew leader told Jackson that he was up for promotion to crew leader in the department. Terry Gibson, a white employee, received the job on June 7, 2008. Gibson was initially hired on January 11, 2004, resigned February 5, 2004, and was rehired November 3, 2004. Jackson had more company and departmental experience than Gibson. However, he was never considered for the position. Gibson's prior duties were solely picking meat and Jackson had supervised Gibson when Jackson served as "fill-in" crew leader prior to Gibson's promotion. The supervisor asserted that Gibson had broader departmental experience than Jackson. Since that time, two other employees in the meat department with less seniority and experience have been promoted over Jackson.

Human Resource Practices

When Rutherford was hired four months ago, the president had explained that because of the physical dispersion of the stores, human resource policies were decentralized with a great deal of responsibility placed on the district managers. Promotion recommendations and decisions were made by supervisors of the different departments in the warehouse. In order to be promoted to a warehouse crew leader, an employee had to be on the same shift and in the same department as the opening. The factors utilized in promotion decisions at the warehouse were character, integrity, good sound morals, correct attitude, and initiative. The company felt that the supervisor was in the best position to judge whether or not an employee was promotable. There was no system for employees to apply for promotions. Written performance evaluations were limited to office employees, merchandisers, and store managers. At the retail stores, store supervisors made promotion recommendations to the district manager. Promotions were limited to persons recommended by the store managers. The district managers agreed with the store managers 90 to 95 percent of the time. The district manager decided who would be promoted, transferred, demoted, hired, or terminated for all positions up to the department head. Job vacancies were not routinely posted. Employees could be transferred from store to store as needed.

Rutherford recalled a conversation he recently had with one of the district managers, Joe Perkins: "We really don't need to post jobs since each district manager is usually aware of openings in his or her district and which employees are ready for promotion. Further, an employee doesn't have to ask in order to be considered for a promotion. Although we don't have a written evaluation system, the job performance of an employee is conveyed by word of mouth from one level of supervision to another."

Two Weeks Later

Rutherford received the reports and data prepared by Mark on promotions within the warehouse and stores for the past two years (see Exhibit 1.20). Mark also prepared summaries of what had happened to Jackson and the other three black employees mentioned by Jackson. As Rutherford began reading through the report, he wondered what changes would be needed at Food Chain Supermarket in order to create equal opportunities for all employees. He never wanted to have another conversation like the one he had with Jackson two weeks earlier.

Questions

1. Analyze the table in Exhibit 1.20. What conclusions do you reach? Is there evidence of discrimination in promotion decisions?
2. Do you believe that Gemson, Thompson, LeBlanc, and Jackson were discriminated against?
3. What are some of the potential disadvantages of a "word of mouth" promotion system?
4. What should Rutherford do now?
5. What kinds of policies can the company design to better integrate minorities into management positions?

EXHIBIT 1.20 *Report on Promotion Rates*

TO: T. L. Rutherford, Director of Human Resources
FROM: Mark Walters, Human Resource Assistant
RE: Promotions

I have collected the data you requested on promotion rates at our warehouse and stores for the last two years (see table). I have also summarized what I learned about the Jackson situation and the other three promotion cases he mentioned.

Promotion Rates

		Total Employees		Total Promotions		Promotion Rates	
Unit	**Year**	**White**	**Black**	**White**	**Black**	**White Rate**	**Black Rate**
Warehouse/Stores	2008	1,603	284	171	21	10.66%	7.39%
Warehouse/Stores	2007	1,414	291	122	27	8.62	9.27
Warehouse	2008	411	173	42	13	10.21	7.50
Warehouse	2007	223	192	18	21	8.07	10.90
Stores	2008	1,192	111	129	8	10.80	7.20
Stores	2007	1,191	99	104	6	8.73	6.10

Note: In 2008, blacks represented 5.8 percent of 137 store promotions and 9 percent of the work force. In 2007, 94.6 percent of the managers were white and in 2006, 94.7 percent were white.

13 CASE

Blowing the Whistle: Accounting Practices at Glenfair Electronics

Bob Schein, vice president of human resources at Glenfair Electronics, sat at his desk thinking about the meeting he had just had with Anwar Patel, an accountant. He had listened intently to Patel describe what had transpired in the finance department during the last few weeks. Patel joined Glenfair after completing his degree in accounting five years ago. For the past three years, he had been preparing Glenfair's sales revenue reports. As a listed company, Glenfair was required by the Securities and Exchange Commission to issue public sales and profit forecasts. Glenfair Electronics had over 10,000 employees and a reputation for producing high-quality electronic components used in a number of manufacturing applications. The company had begun to experience a slowdown in product demand, and their share price had declined as well in the last year and a half.

Patel had told Schein that he had been instructed to use a different and more aggressive accounting method for forecasting and calculating projected sales revenue for the coming year. He believed that such an approach could mislead shareholders about Glenfair's likely future sales performance. The previous chief financial officer (CFO) had taken a rather conservative approach and did not stretch the boundaries of acceptable practices. Since the beginning of the year, however, Patel was working under a new CFO, John Beatty. Beatty had joined Glenfair earlier in the year after not obtaining a promotion to CFO at his previous company. Everyone perceived him to be smart and ambitious and it was clear that he was determined to make his mark at Glenfair. When Patel pointed out that the proposed accounting methods were very different from Glenfair's traditional practices for reporting sales revenue, he told Schein that Beatty had said, "Well, I am the new CFO, and I have a different view and approach." However, it was his next remark that disturbed Patel the most. According to Patel, Beatty went on to say, "Sales should turn around next quarter, and we are justified in reporting higher expected sales revenue in the coming months. Besides, Anwar, don't you want your Glenfair stock to do well?" Projected higher sales revenue could indeed burnish Glenfair's earnings outlook and probably help its stock price.

When Patel persisted in questioning the accounting methods, Beatty allegedly told him to do his job as instructed. Since that conversation, Patel felt that Beatty had become hostile toward him, and they no longer had a friendly relationship. Despite his fears, Patel felt he had to come to Schein for advice. Schein could see that Patel was worried about Beatty finding out about their meeting.

Schein was disturbed by what he had heard from Patel and sat at his desk thinking about what he should do as vice president of human resources.

QUESTIONS

1. If you were Schein, what would you do, if anything? Explain.
2. What should Schein do about Patel's claim that Beatty has become hostile toward him?
3. What rights and protections do whistle-blowers have in the workplace today?

14 CASE

LGA Industries: Employing Undocumented Immigrants

David Martin was excited to start his new position as the manager of staffing, training, and development for LGA Industries, a carpet and rug manufacturer located in a mid-sized Texas town. LGA Industries had been producing well-known and high-quality carpets and rugs for the past 100 years. Over the years, its workforce had grown to just under 2,000 employees. Martin had just completed a master's degree in Human Resource Management from the University of Texas at El Paso. In the last few years, LGA Industries had found it increasingly difficult to locate and hire employees to meet the growing demand for its products. Their traditional sources of labor were drying up as many high school graduates left the small town to seek employment in places like Dallas and Houston. The pay for unskilled jobs was $8.50 per hour. Martin learned that 45 percent of hires in the last four years consisted of immigrants from Mexico and other Latin American countries. The Latino population of the town, which had been less than 5 percent in 1990, was now about 25 percent.

Martin's predecessor, who retired last month, had been with LGA Industries for 15 years. Martin was anxious to introduce some of the new and up-to-date HR practices he had been taught at the university. Within his first two months on the job, he was to fill five new plant positions. The company had received a large order that needed to be completed within the next six months. Given the increasing difficulty that LGA had finding employees for new positions, the company had begun using an employment agency. When Martin contacted the agency, they assured him they would have no problem sending him prospective applicants. When five candidates showed up at his office about a week later, Martin was quite impressed with how quickly the agency had responded. When he interviewed the candidates, he found it odd that they were not able to tell him much about their previous employment experience. Three of the candidates appeared to know only a few words of English. Martin decided to talk with the HR manager at LGA Industries about the candidates. He was surprised when the manager told him not too worry—the agency was quite reliable and had sent them good candidates in the past.

Martin was curious and decided to look at the files and records of previous hires. He was not able to locate the I-9 Forms for any of the newly hired Latino employees, nor could he find them on the HR database. Martin knew from his academic training and previous work experience that employers were required to complete an I-9 Form for all employees to verify eligibility for employment in the United States. When he asked the HR manager about the missing forms, Martin was told that the employment agency took care of them whenever they sourced candidates, and the forms were probably on file in their offices. About a week after the new employees were on board, Martin received an anonymous note in his inbox that read, "LGA Industries hires illegal immigrants." He showed the note to the HR manager who told him that he should not believe everything he reads and that LGA had little choice but to get labor wherever it could.

Martin was quite upset when he went home that evening. He suspected his new employer was hiring undocumented immigrant workers. The next morning he called the employment agency and asked for a copy of the I-9 Forms of the five employees they had just hired at LGA Industries. He was told that the forms were not ready and were usually kept at the agency.

Martin knew the Immigration Reform and Control Act (see Exhibit 1.21) required that if an employee does not have the proper documentation within three business days of his/her start date, the employer must terminate the employee. The next day his manager bluntly told him there was no need for him to worry or follow up with these new employees.

QUESTIONS

1. What factors appear to be affecting LGA Industries' staffing practices?
2. Who is responsible for meeting the requirements of the Immigration and Reform and Control Act with respect to the completion of I-9 forms?
3. If you were Martin, what would you do now?

EXHIBIT 1.21 *Excerpts for I-9 Form Completion under the Requirements of the Immigration Reform and Control Act (IRCA)*

Form I-9

The Immigration Reform and Control Act of 1986 (IRCA) made the knowing employment of unauthorized aliens illegal. Under IRCA, employers may hire only persons who may legally work in the U.S., i.e., citizens and nationals of the U.S. and aliens authorized to work in the U.S.

With the enactment of IRCA, the legal obligations of employers, hiring new employees have been greatly increased. Employers are required to verify the identity and eligibility for employment of all persons they hire after November 6, 1986. It is also unlawful for employers to knowingly hire a person who is not authorized to work in the U.S., or continue to employ such a person. Thus, IRCA requires employers to complete a Form I-9 for each new employee.

Employers may be held liable for an employee's failure to complete Section 1. The employee has three business days from the date of her or his hiring to provide the employer with the documentation of identity and work authorization needed to complete Section 2 of the I-9 Form ("three business days" requires an employer to count weekends and holidays as business days if the employer is open for business on those days). The employee must present original documents (not photocopies) that establish identity and employment eligibility. If an employee does not have the proper documentation within three business days of his or her start date, the employer must terminate the employee. However, if, within that time, the employee produces a receipt showing that he or she has applied for a work authorization or identification document, the employee must be given 90 days to produce the required documentation. The employer must complete Section 2 of the I-9 Form within three business days of the date an employee is hired. Employees must not be required to produce specific documents. The employer must accept the documents enumerated in the Form I-9 "Lists of Acceptable Documents" in any of the combinations indicated on the form.

On the other hand, demanding excessive documentation can also result in substantial fines. IRCA's anti-discrimination provisions prohibit employers of four or more employees from discriminating against certain protected individuals (including permanent residents, temporary residents, special agricultural workers, refugees, and asylees) with respect to hiring, discharging, recruiting, or referring for a fee.

I-9s must be retained for the duration of an employee's employment, plus one year, or for a minimum of three years from the date of hire, whichever is longer. Employers must keep a record of employees whose work authorizations will expire and re-verify the authorization to work of such employees prior to expiration.

Employer Obligations for Document Retention

Employers must retain the I-9 Form for every employee for the full duration of that individual's employment, with the exception of the individuals previously classified as exempt from the I-9 requirement. Additionally, every employer must keep each employee's I-9 form on file for either three years after the date of hire or for one year after employment is terminated, whichever is greater. Employers should accurately organize and maintain all I-9 records. The Department of Homeland Security and/or the Department of Labor may ask to review I-9 documentation. I-9 documents must be provided to these federal agencies upon request.

Offenses

Failure to properly complete an I-9.

Knowingly hiring, continuing to employ, or contacting to obtain the services of an unauthorized alien.

Providing or knowingly accepting false social security cards.

Pattern and practice of I-9 compliance failure.

Monetary Sanctions

Paperwork violations may result in fines from $100 and $1,100 for every individual for which a mistake is made.

Substantive violations may result in fines from $200 to $11,000 per unauthorized employee depending on whether it is the first offense or a repeat offense.

In 1996, Executive Order 12989 was passed, which imposes a one-year ban on federal contractors who knowingly hire unauthorized non-immigrant workers.

Criminal penalties including fines and imprisonment may also be imposed if there appears to be a deliberate pattern or practice of violations of these requirements or where a company knowingly hires ten or more non-immigrant workers who are illegally in the USA.

Source: Lurie, D. (March 2005). "The I-9 Form: Everything HR Professionals Need to Know About the I-9 Employment Verification Process." Society for Human Resource Management White Paper (www.shrm.org).
www.dol.gov/compliance accessed February 6, 2010.

15 CASE

The Broken Employment Contract?

Arthur Wayne was shocked as he walked out of Sara Bell's office. It was hard for him to understand what had just transpired. Bell, treasurer of EcoCare, a large health insurance company located in Michigan, had just told Wayne of the decision to terminate his employment and had requested his immediate resignation in return for a severance pay arrangement whereby he would continue to receive his salary for six months or until he found other employment. As he looked at the date on his watch calendar, May 7, Wayne realized that he had been hired exactly five years ago by Bell. Bell had told Wayne that EcoCare was not satisfied with his administration of the company car program and that, given the number of complaints about the program from other employees, it was in the best interest of the company to ask for his immediate resignation. Wayne, assistant to the treasurer, had been in charge of the program for the past year. During a meeting the day before with both Bell and the vice president of operations, George Findlay, he had been unable to explain why there were so many complaints about the program. One such complaint had involved the claim that someone had set back the odometers on several company cars while the vehicles were under Wayne's control.

After his termination, Wayne requested that the decision to ask for his resignation be reviewed by the company president and the chairperson of the board of trustees of EcoCare. Wayne felt that he had been wrongfully discharged and had been under the impression that he had a contract for continued employment as long as his performance was satisfactory. He further maintained that his supervisor had not properly followed the termination policies and procedures of EcoCare.

In preparation for the review, the president asked the director of human resources, Chris Miller, to investigate the facts of the situation and the events leading up to Wayne's termination.

HUMAN RESOURCE DEPARTMENT'S INVESTIGATION

In order to prepare its report for the president, the human resource department decided not only to review Wayne's personnel file but also to interview Wayne, Bell, and others involved in the case. Two weeks later, Miller prepared the following summary of what had been learned.

> *After seven years with a local bank in Michigan, Arthur Wayne sought the assistance of an employment agency to obtain a job that would give him more opportunities for advancement. Wayne had graduated with a degree in Business Administration and had completed 15 hours toward his MBA in Finance. The employment agency referred him to our company. After several pre-employment interviews and a psychological test, Wayne was hired as an assistant to the company treasurer, Sara Bell. His duties primarily consisted of analyzing and preparing certain financial reports under the direction of Bell. Wayne came to us with excellent work experience and admirable references from his previous employers.*

According to Wayne, he felt at the time of his employment that he had a contract with EcoCare that was partly oral (Bell's statements during the job interview) and partly written. Wayne told us that during his pre-employment interview with Bell, he had specifically asked about job security and was told that as long as he did his job, he could remain with the company until he reached retirement age. He further indicated that he had been told by Bell that if he came to EcoCare, he would not have to look for another job because she knew of no one ever being discharged. Wayne also told us that a copy of the Supervisory Manual was handed to him during his interview with Bell. He said he specifically recalled reading through the sections of the manual that pertained to discipline and termination procedures at that time (see the Appendix for relevant sections).

At the end of that interview Bell made Wayne a job offer, which he accepted. The Manual is given to all management employees as an aid in supervising persons in their charge and not as a declarative of the contract terms of an employee's hire. Our personnel policy has always been to discharge for just cause only, pursuant to the procedures described in the manual. These procedures apply to all EcoCare employees who have completed their probationary period.

During his five years as assistant to the treasurer, Wayne received above average performance ratings. Last year, he was given the responsibility of administering the company car program. In April of this year, employees began complaining to Bell and Findlay about Wayne's handling of the program. Wayne indicated that he'd had only a brief conversation with Bell about these complaints before the meeting of May 6.

We also spoke with Bell and Findlay about Wayne's employment and subsequent termination. According to Bell, she did tell Wayne during the interview that he would have a job as long as his performance was satisfactory. Bell told us that she made that statement based on her understanding of our company's policies and did not intend her statement as a promise of a permanent job.

Bell and Findlay report that Wayne was fired because of continued personality conflicts with other employees. They report that he was unable to work with other employees and that this was an important job requirement for anyone managing the company car program. After receiving numerous complaints about Wayne's handling of the program, they finally requested from him various reports and documents concerning the odometer discrepancies. Ultimately, they called a meeting with Wayne in an attempt to resolve the problems. During the May 6 meeting, Wayne was reported to have been defensive and insubordinate and unable to provide any satisfactory answers to their questions. At the conclusion of the meeting, they both felt that it would be in the best interest of the company if Wayne were asked to resign. Bell called Wayne into her office the next day and asked for his resignation.

APPENDIX

EXCERPTS FROM SUPERVISORY MANUAL

Section IV. Disciplinary Procedures

(Note: If the unacceptable behavior is repeated between six months and one year, the last disciplinary action will be applied. If the behavior is repeated after one year, it will be treated as a new occurrence for disciplinary purposes.)

A. All discipline shall be administered in a fair, consistent, and reasonable manner within EcoCare.

B. Whenever the work performance or personal behavior of an employee is below department standards, a series of progressive, corrective steps will be taken. Before any of these steps are undertaken, however, the employee shall be counseled about his or her performance discrepancy, what he or she must do to improve the performance, and the action the supervisor will take if the performance is not corrected.

C. Within our discipline system, discipline will be given only for cause. Furthermore, the disciplinary action should fit the problem it is intended to correct.

D. All disciplinary action should be duly documented and reported by the supervisor on Form 29B. The form also requires the employee's signature.

E. The following series of steps shall be followed in administering discipline within EcoCare:

1. Oral Warning: Supervisor should discuss the unacceptable behavior with the employee and document such by completing Section A of Form 29B and obtaining the employee's signature.
2. Written Warning: A written warning should be issued if the unacceptable behavior continues. The supervisor completes Section B of Form 29B and gives the employee the blue copy. The human resource department receives the canary copy.
3. Suspension: If the employee's behavior continues uncorrected, the employee shall be suspended for a given time without pay. Normally, suspension should not exceed five working days. Supervisors should consult with their immediate supervisor and the human resource department before implementing this action. The supervisor shall complete Section C of Form 29B and also include the date the employee should return to work.
4. Discharge: If the employee's behavior is not corrected, the employee shall be terminated. Due to the serious nature of termination, it is recommended that the supervisor review the case with both his or her immediate supervisor and the human resource department before discharging the employee. Examples of reasons for termination without prior corrective discipline are covered in Section V. Note, however, that in such cases the employee should first be suspended according to the following procedures:

Suspension Pending Discharge: (This paragraph applies to all proposed discharges except those which are a result of application of the normal disciplinary procedures.)

a. When an employee's misconduct warrants immediate discharge under Section V, the employee should be first suspended without pay.
b. At the time of suspension, the employee should be informed by the supervisor to leave the premises and that he or she will be notified if and when he or she is to return to work.
c. The supervisor should document the suspension by completing an Employee Discipline Report. The supervisor should consult with the Human Resource Department to determine the appropriate course of action.

Section V. Termination

(Reasons for Immediate Termination.)

1. Misconduct, such as fighting, gambling, or use of profane or abusive language toward others.
2. Furnishing proprietary company information to unauthorized agents or persons.
3. Refusal to obey direct orders from the immediate supervisor (insubordination).
4. Willful damage of company property.
5. Failure to notify supervisor or manager during three successive working days of absence.
6. Engaging in a business likely to conflict with the business of the company without prior permission.

7. Dishonesty, falsification of employee's own or other employee's time cards, company records, employment application, etc.
8. Illegal use or possession of alcohol, drugs, etc.
9. Reporting to work or engaging in company business under the influence of alcohol or drugs.

QUESTIONS

1. Did Wayne have an employment contract, either oral or written, with EcoCare? Why or why not?
2. What problems, if any, do you see with EcoCare's pre-employment process?
3. Can an employer's written human resource policies ever be construed as a contract between an employer and an employee?
4. Was Wayne terminated for just cause? Why or why not?
5. How can companies protect themselves against a claim of wrongful discharge?

16 EXERCISE

The Older Worker Questionnaire

I. OBJECTIVES

A. To familiarize you with typical stereotypes toward older workers and the managerial implications of these stereotypes.

B. To provide you with factual information regarding older workers.

II. OUT-OF-CLASS PREPARATION TIME: 10 minutes to complete the Older Worker Questionnaire

III. IN-CLASS TIME SUGGESTED: 20–30 minutes for group and class discussion of all items on the Older Worker Questionnaire

IV. PROCEDURES

Prior to the class meeting in which this exercise will be discussed, you should read any material on older workers assigned by your instructor and complete the Older Worker Questionnaire (see Exhibit 1.22).

At the start of the exercise, the class will be divided into groups of three to five by your instructor. Your group's task is to discuss each item on the questionnaire and arrive at a consensus regarding the correct answer (20-minute time limit). After all groups have finished, the instructor will present the correct answers along with an explanation. Each group should record these answers alongside the group's own answers and then compare the two to determine the number right and wrong.

EXHIBIT 1.22 *The Older Worker Questionnaire*

Mark the statements "T" for true or "F" for false.

——— 1. Younger workers tend to have higher job satisfaction than older ones.

——— 2. Employees aged 50–65 use on average about an equal amount of healthcare as those in their 30s and 40s.

——— 3. Employers value older workers' loyalty, work ethic, reliability, and experience.

——— 4. About 20 percent of the work force is over 55.

——— 5. Few individuals (less than 10 percent) plan to work after age 65.

——— 6. An important reason older workers retire is that they do not feel valued by the company.

——— 7. The typical unemployment rate for those over 55 has been about 6 percent since 1949.

——— 8. The average retired worker receives over $2,000 a month in Social Security benefits.

——— 9. Older workers generally require less light for performing a task than do younger workers.

———10. All workers are required to collect full Social Security benefits at age 65.

———11. Younger workers are more motivated to exceed expectations than older workers.

———12. Employers view older workers as more productive, at least as attractive in terms of employment, but as more costly than younger workers.

———13. Older employees usually take a longer period of time to learn something new than do younger workers.

———14. The Age Discrimination in Employment Act only applies to workers who are 59 or older.

———15. Younger workers miss more work due to injuries and illness than do older workers.

———16. Ninety percent of Americans over the age of 50 say they learn best by watching and listening.

———17. Older workers who were born between 1946 and 1964 are referred to as "baby boomers."

———18. Older employees tend to react more slowly than younger employees.

———19. Loyalty to a firm among workers over the age of 45 is strong.

———20. One's ability to taste and smell tends to improve with age.

17 EXERCISE

Is This Unlawful Discrimination?

I. OBJECTIVES

A. To help you understand the application of the six major federal laws that regulate equal rights in employment. These laws are Title VII of the Civil Rights Acts of 1964 as amended by the Equal Employment Opportunity Act of 1972, the Civil Rights Act of 1991, the Lilly Ledbetter Fair Pay Act of 2009, the Age Discrimination in Employment Act of 1967, the Vocational Rehabilitation Act of 1973, and the Americans with Disabilities Act of 1990.

B. To help you understand the court's interpretation of these laws.

C. To help you understand the legal definition of discrimination and the burden of proof placed on defendants and plaintiffs.

II. OUT-OF-CLASS PREPARATION TIME: 60 minutes

III. IN-CLASS TIME SUGGESTED: 45 minutes

IV. PROCEDURES

A. Read the exercise and review the major laws before class.

B. The class should be divided into groups of four.

C. Each group should read each of the incidents that follow and answer these questions:

1. What legal statute(s) apply in this case?
2. What issue(s) must the court decide in this case?
3. If you were the judge, how would you rule? Did the employer discriminate unlawfully? Why or why not?

1. Elaine Mobley worked as a social worker with the Virginia Health Department's child abuse program for two years. Mobley was a member of the nonsectarian Unitarian Universalist Church. During her first six months on the job, she divorced her husband of ten years. Her supervisor, a devout Baptist, encouraged her to discuss her marital problems with a Christian psychotherapist. On a number of occasions, the supervisor encouraged other employees in the department who were also Baptists to convert Mobley. Some employees held prayer meetings at her desk while others gave her the silent treatment. Their attempts to convert Mobley did not stop. At one point, the supervisor made her participate in a Christian puppet show. Another time she found a handwritten note on her desk from Jesus that read, "How can you speak of God and reject me? I love you and know all about you." Her attendance at work declined because there were days she did not want to face the stress in her work environment. Mobley filed a complaint with the director of the division stating that she was being constantly bombarded with efforts to convert her to a Baptist. Shortly thereafter, Mobley was fired from her job. Mobley filed a lawsuit claiming that she had been fired because of religious discrimination.

2. Edward Roberts, a black truck driver, applied in person for a tractor trailer truck driver position at a trucking company on March 31, 2005, in response to a newspaper ad. Roberts' application listed 22 months of prior experience as a road driver. He had an

additional 10 years of experience which he did not list on the application due to a lack of space on the form. Roberts was neither interviewed nor contacted by the company about the status of his application. In June 2005, Roberts saw an identical advertisement for tractor trailer truck drivers. Upon inquiry, Roberts learned that eight persons (all white) had been hired as truck drivers between April and June 2005. All of those hired had less than 22 months of driving experience. The company contended that Roberts was not hired because no opening existed when he applied. Roberts filed a discrimination complaint in District Court.

3. Thelma Jones had worked at a large public accounting firm for five years when the partners proposed her as a candidate for partnership. Of the 662 partners in the firm, seven were women. Of the 88 persons proposed that year, Jones was the only woman. Forty-seven were admitted to partnership, 21 were rejected, and 20, including Jones, were held for "reconsideration." Thirteen of the 32 partners who submitted comments on Jones's performance supported her candidacy, three recommended holding her application, eight stated that they had insufficient knowledge to comment, and eight recommended denial. While the partners praised her outstanding performance, both supporters and opponents of her candidacy indicated that she was sometimes overly aggressive, unduly harsh, difficult to work with, and impatient with staff. One partner described her as "macho." In a meeting with a senior partner about her candidacy, she was told that, to improve her chances for partnership, she should "walk more femininely, talk more femininely, dress more femininely, wear make-up, style her hair, and wear jewelry." When the partners refused to reconsider her candidacy the following year, she sued the firm, charging sex discrimination.

4. James McFadden was a transsexual who, while still biologically male, announced to his employer (East Coast Airlines) that he intended to dress and act as a woman in preparation for "surgical sex reassignment." Mr. McFadden was subsequently fired from his pilot's job for refusing to comply with its requirement that he continue to dress and act as a man. McFadden filed a lawsuit in District Court alleging that East Coast Airlines had conspired to discriminate against him on the basis of sex (now to be female) and that he was treated differently from other women employed by the airline.

5. Andrew Johnson, a black maintenance worker, was constantly referred to as "Chicken Little," "Chicken George," "Sparerib Kid," "Boy," and "Watermelon Man" by his white supervisor. These names were used not just during private conversations but in the presence of other workers. Despite several complaints to senior management, the name-calling persisted for several months. When management finally investigated Johnson's claims, the supervisor admitted the comments but argued that he was only kidding. The supervisor was instructed to stop both the name-calling and kidding. A fellow employee warned Johnson that his days were probably numbered because he had gone over the head of his supervisor. Shortly thereafter, Johnson was injured on the job. While he was at home recuperating, his supervisor called to say that he accepted his resignation. Johnson denied resigning and wrote asking for his job back. His request was denied. Johnson filed a lawsuit alleging that he had been a victim of harassment because of his race.

6. Paul Martin had worked 12 years for the Department of Transportation when he applied for a promotion to dispatcher. Martin scored 75 on an interview test. Betty Palmer, another candidate, scored 73 and got the job. Martin sued the county for reverse discrimination. The county said that both Martin and Palmer were qualified and that Palmer had gotten the

job as part of a voluntary affirmative action plan designed to achieve a work force that reflected the race and gender composition of the county. The county pointed out that none of 238 skilled craft worker jobs in the county were held by women.

7. Elnora Williams, a black female teacher with ten years of classroom experience and partial completion of her doctoral degree in education, applied for several vacant middle and secondary principalships in the Knox County school system. Each time she applied, she was told by the superintendent that "the school district believed that a 'male image' is necessary for a middle or secondary school principal." No females had occupied a principal position in the school district. Williams subsequently filed a lawsuit in District Court accusing the school system of discrimination.
8. Frank Poole had been teaching hearing-impaired students in the Jackson County schools for six years when he was hospitalized with *pneumocystis carinii* pneumonia and, subsequently, was diagnosed as having AIDS. Despite the county medical director's report that Poole's condition did not place his students or others in the school at any risk, the Department of Education reassigned Poole to an administrative position and barred him from teaching in the classroom. Poole filed suit, alleging that the Department discriminated against him on the basis of his disability (AIDS).
9. Lauren Hill worked in the plant of Hillbrook Manufacturing Company from 1979 until 1998. During much of this time, salaried employees were given raises or denied raises based on their supervisor's evaluation of their performance. In March 1998, six months before she was to take early retirement, Hill submitted a questionnaire to the EEOC alleging certain acts of sex discrimination, and in July she filed a formal EEOC charge. After taking early retirement in November 1998, Hill commenced a pay discrimination claim under Title VII of the Civil Rights Act and the Equal Pay Act. She alleged that at the time of retirement she was being paid significantly less than any of her male colleagues. Hill also said she had evidence that during the course of her employment with Hillbrook that several supervisors had given her poor evaluations because of her sex and that as a result of these evaluations her pay was not increased as much as it would have been if she had been evaluated fairly. Further, these pay decisions continued to affect her pay throughout her employment with Hillbrook. Therefore, she wanted to be compensated accordingly for the discrimination she had experienced during her employment with Hillbrook.
10. After working as a title clerk for Harrison and Sons Car Dealership for five years, Donna Skeen resigned. At 62 years of age, Donna had decided that she did not want to put up with the treatment she had received at the dealership. She had demanded an end to the teasing she experienced, but to no avail. In a suit she filed in District Court, Skeen alleged that the managers in the dealership referred to her as the "old lady with the sagging boobs." When she forgot something or made an error on a title, she was asked if she had Alzheimer's. If she complained about the temperature in the dealership, she was asked if she was suffering from hot flashes. The owner, Frank Harrison, said that there was lots of informal teasing in the dealership among employees and that Skeen often referred to herself as the "Grandma" of the staff.
11. Officials of a city government charged with discrimination signed a consent decree agreeing to an affirmative action plan with specific promotion and hiring goals for increasing the number of minority firefighters in the city's fire department. Four years later, when faced with severe budget problems, the city implemented a layoff plan aimed at protecting

minority employees who were recently hired. Jerome Atwood, a white firefighter, was laid off even though he had greater seniority than many of the minority firefighters who retained their jobs. Atwood filed a lawsuit charging reverse discrimination.

12. Herbert Fox worked as an office furniture salesman for 25 years with the same company. In his 25th year with the company, he went on leave for clinical depression. When it was time for him to return from leave, he told the company he could not return to work as scheduled. Subsequently, Fox and the company agreed upon a new date for return. However, Fox also requested that he be allowed to miss the first couple of morning sales meetings (a request prompted by the side effects of his antidepressant medicine) or to work on a part-time basis. His request was denied by the company, and they also told Fox that, because of increasing financial pressures, the company would be expecting 110 percent from him on his return to work. Fox did not report to work on the agreed-upon date and filed for disability benefits. The company subsequently terminated him. Fox filed a discrimination suit against the company alleging that the requirements attached to his return to work caused a relapse of his depression.
13. Lia Lee, a Laotian-American, worked for Federal and State Bank for over three years as teller. She had always received outstanding performance reviews from her supervisors. Consequently, when a position became available at the customer service desk that handled customer inquiries and problems, Lia applied for the position. She did not get the promotion. The bank argued that she was not promoted because she did not have sufficient English skills to calm irate customers. Lia Lee filed a lawsuit alleging that Federal and State Bank had overlooked her for a promotion because of her accent.
14. Margaret Reynolds, 5 feet 10 inches, 190 pounds, applied for a job as a fitness instructor teaching aerobics at Slendercise, Inc. She had always been very healthy and fit. She ate healthy foods, worked out five days a week, and could do all of the complicated aerobics steps and exercises. Slendercise, Inc. rejected Margaret's application to teach aerobics because of her size. Reynolds did not look anything like the svelte women on the company's Web site and promotional brochures. The company further argued that an aerobics instructor had to look leaner than the public and that people must believe Slendercise, Inc., will help them improve, not just maintain, their shape. Margaret filed a complaint with the Equal Employment Opportunity Commission alleging weight discrimination.
15. Abdul Mohammed, a Pakistani-American, was employed as a steelworker. As a devout Muslim, Mohammed was obligated to engage in daily prayer. Mohammed, along with five other Muslims working at the plant, asked management to provide a room where they could hold their daily prayers during lunch hour. The plant was located miles from the nearest mosque. Management told the employees that it did not have a room that could be used for such purposes. Consequently, Mohammed and his fellow Muslims were forced to recite their prayers in full view of other employees. Other employees ridiculed the Muslims during their daily prayers and called them derogatory names such as "camel jockey" and "raghead." After being humiliated on several occasions by taunts from other employees, Mohammed and his fellow Muslims once again asked management to provide them with a private space in which to pray. Management again denied their request. Shortly thereafter, Mohammed filed a case with the Equal Employment Opportunity Commission alleging religious harassment and ethnic discrimination.

18 EXERCISE

What Is Sexual Harassment?

I. OBJECTIVES

A. To familiarize you with the EEOC sexual harassment guidelines.

B. To teach you the meaning of these guidelines as they relate to the workplace.

C. To teach you the manager's and organization's role in preventing sexual harassment.

D. To show you the complexities involved in identifying sexual harassment in the workplace and in interpreting EEOC guidelines.

II. OUT-OF-CLASS PREPARATION TIME: 20 minutes to read the EEOC guidelines and complete the sexual harassment questionnaire

III. IN-CLASS TIME SUGGESTED: 45 minutes for group and class discussion of all items on the sexual harassment questionnaire

IV. PROCEDURES

Prior to the class meeting in which this exercise will be discussed, you should read the EEOC Guidelines on Discrimination Because of Sex (see Exhibit 1.23) and any other material related to sexual harassment assigned by your instructor. You also need to complete the 20-item sexual harassment questionnaire shown (Exhibit 1.24).

At the start of the exercise, the instructor will divide the class into groups of three to five students. Your group's task is to discuss each item on the questionnaire and arrive at a consensus regarding whether each item constitutes sexual harassment. More importantly, you need to develop a rationale for your answer (20-minute time limit). After all groups have finished, the class as a whole will discuss the questionnaire items. To facilitate discussion, groups will take turns presenting their analysis. For example, one group will present its analysis regarding Item 1, another group will present Item 2, another Item 3, and so on.

EXHIBIT 1.23 *Code of Federal Regulations [Revised as of July 1, 2006]*

GUIDELINES ON DISCRIMINATION BECAUSE OF SEX

Sec. 1604.11 Sexual harassment.

Harassment on the basis of sex is a violation of section 703 of title VII. Unwelcome sexual advances, requests for sexual favors, and other verbal or physical conduct of a sexual nature constitute sexual harassment when (1) submission to such conduct is made either explicitly or implicitly a term or condition of an individual's employment, (2) submission to or rejection of such conduct by an individual is used as the basis for employment decisions affecting such individual, or (3) such conduct has the purpose or effect of unreasonably interfering with an individual's work performance or creating an intimidating, hostile, or offensive working environment. The principles involved here continue to apply to race, color, religion, or national origin.

In determining whether alleged conduct constitutes sexual harassment, the Commission will look at the record as a whole and at the totality of the circumstances, such as the nature of the sexual advances and the context in which the alleged incidents occurred. The determination of the legality of a particular action will be made from the facts, on a case by case basis.

With respect to conduct between fellow employees, an employer is responsible for acts of sexual harassment in the workplace where the employer (or its agents or supervisory employees) knows or should have known of the conduct, unless it can show that it took immediate and appropriate corrective action.

Source: Equal Employment Opportunity Commission, 2010 Web site.

EXHIBIT 1.24 *Sexual Harassment Questionnaire*

Instructions: Read each situation and circle your answer.

	Situation	**Would it be Sexual Harassment?**		
1.	Mr. (Ms.) X (Supervisor) posts cartoons on the bulletin board containing sexually related materials.	Yes	No	Uncertain
2.	Mr. (Ms.) X (Supervisor) constantly tells sexually-related jokes to female (male) subordinates.	Yes	No	Uncertain
3.	Mr. (Ms.) X (Supervisor) asks a female (male) subordinate for a date, which she (he) willingly accepts.	Yes	No	Uncertain
4.	Mr. (Ms.) X (Supervisor) pats or pinches a female (male) subordinate.	Yes	No	Uncertain
5.	Mr. (Ms.) X (Supervisor) terminates a female (male) subordinate for not complying with his (her) request for sexual favors. He (she) has recently given the subordinate a positive performance appraisal.	Yes	No	Uncertain
6.	Mr. (Ms.) X (Supervisor) sexually assaults a female (male) subordinate.	Yes	No	Uncertain
7.	Mr. (Ms.) X (Supervisor) denies a raise to a female (male) subordinate for failing to go out on a date.	Yes	No	Uncertain
8.	Mr. X (Supervisor) habitually calls all female employees "sweetie" or "honey."	Yes	No	Uncertain
9	Mr. (Ms.) X (Supervisor) asks a female (male) employee how she (he) feels about sex education in schools.	Yes	No	Uncertain
10.	Mr. X (Supervisor) recommends that a female subordinate wear revealing attire at work.	Yes	No	Uncertain
11.	Mr. (Ms.) X (Supervisor) fails to promote a female (male) subordinate for not granting sexual favors.	Yes	No	Uncertain
12.	Mr. (Ms.) X (Supervisor) invites a female (male) subordinate to accompany him (her) on a two-day meeting in another city.	Yes	No	Uncertain
13.	Mr. X (Supervisor) leans and peers over the back of a female employee when she wears a low-cut dress.	Yes	No	Uncertain
14.	Mr. (Ms.) X (Supervisor) tells a female (male) job applicant that she (he) will not be hired unless she (he) agrees to grant sexual favors.	Yes	No	Uncertain
15.	Mr. (Ms.) X (Supervisor) invites a female (male) subordinate to meet him (her) at a bar that features female (male) exotic dancers.	Yes	No	Uncertain
16.	Mr. (Ms.) X (Supervisor) invites a female (male) subordinate to come over to his (her) apartment for a hot tub party.	Yes	No	Uncertain
17.	Male (female) workers whistle every time female (male) employees walk by their work area.	Yes	No	Uncertain
18.	A married female employee and a married male employee are having an affair.	Yes	No	Uncertain
19.	Male (female) employees repeatedly use vulgar language when talking to each other. Two female (male) employees often overhear what is said and find it offensive.	Yes	No	Uncertain
20.	A male (female) repair technician who works for another firm asks female (male) employees for dates whenever he (she) comes to repair equipment.	Yes	No	Uncertain

19 EXERCISE

Understanding the Americans with Disabilities Act

I. OBJECTIVES

A. To help you understand the application of the Americans with Disabilities Act (ADA).

B. To help you understand the court's interpretation of the ADA.

C. To help you understand the meaning of the terms "disability," "qualified individual," and "reasonable accommodation."

II. OUT-OF-CLASS PREPARATION TIME: 45 minutes

III. IN-CLASS TIME SUGGESTED: 45 minutes

IV. PROCEDURES

A. Read the exercise and review the Americans with Disabilities Act's definitions of "disability," "qualified individual," and "reasonable accommodation."

B. The class should be divided into groups of four.

C. Each group should read each of the case incidents that follow and answer these questions:

1. What issue(s) must the court decide in this case?
2. If you were a member of the jury, how would you vote? Did the employer discriminate unlawfully? Why or why not?

1. THE OVERWEIGHT HOSPITAL ATTENDANT

Betty Thomas applied for a position as an attendant for the mentally retarded in a residential facility operated by the Mental Health Retardation Hospital (MHRH). She had previously worked for MHRH in an identical position. She had an excellent work record and left employment with MHRH on good terms. When Thomas reapplied for the position she previously held, she stood 5 feet 2 inches tall and weighed 320 pounds. During her pre-employment physical, it was determined that although Thomas was morbidly obese, no limitations were found that affected her ability to do the job. MHRH refused to hire Thomas because of her obesity, claiming that her weight compromised her ability to evacuate patients in the event of an emergency and put Thomas at greater risk of developing serious ailments that might lead to higher absenteeism, as well as increasing MHRH's exposure to workers' compensation claims.

2. IS ATTENDANCE AT THE WORKPLACE AN ESSENTIAL JOB FUNCTION?

In 1996 Diane worked in the Edmond, Oklahoma Post Office and witnessed the murder of several of her co-workers. She was diagnosed by her doctor with post-traumatic stress disorder and subsequently left her job at the Post Office because working there aggravated her symptoms. In March 2009, while working as a service coordinator at Avaya Communications, Diane became aware of an altercation between two employees where one of the individuals, by the name of Lunsford, had previously threatened to "go postal." Lunsford was suspended from his job. Upon hearing of his return to work, Diane became physically ill and left work. Her current doctors confirmed that she suffered from post-traumatic stress disorder and was unable to work in an environment that she perceived to be unsafe. She eventually was placed on short-term disability leave. After being on short-term disability for two months, Diane requested that her employer either 1) relocate Lunsford, 2) allow her to work out of her home, or 3) allow her to transfer to another position in the Oklahoma City area.

After further investigation by the employer, Diane's requested accommodations were denied. One year later, her request for long-term disability benefits were also denied, and Diane was subsequently discharged because she was unable to return to work. The company maintained that Diane's job required her to be physically present and that her attendance at the job site was an essential function of her job. While her job description did not specifically state that attendance at the work site was an essential function, the company claimed that her presence was required for the appropriate supervision, training, and teamwork required of all coordinators, and that her requested accommodations were not reasonable.

3. The Ultimatum

Joan, a warehouse worker, was diagnosed with carpal tunnel syndrome. She was subsequently assigned to reduced duties. However, the duties were later multiplied, increasing her arm and wrist pain. When Joan presented her employer with a doctor's note advising her to take a six-week leave of absence, the employer gave her an ultimatum—show up for work or lose her job. Joan decided to sue under the ADA, claiming her carpal tunnel syndrome was a disability worthy of accommodation.

4. The Fainting Technician

Jane Flighty was fired after she fainted on the job because the company believed she was suffering from an unknown disability. After the fainting episode, she was sent to a physician. The physician's initial diagnosis was that Jane suffered from syncope, a loss of consciousness caused by a temporary deficiency of blood supply to the brain. Later, the physician determined that the employee was within normal limits and that there was no explanation for the fainting. The company discharged Jane without any further medical examination, concluding that she was a safety risk because she was likely to faint again.

5. The Gun Slinger

John Hitman was fired when he was caught carrying a gun into work. He was hospitalized following the incident and was diagnosed with a mental disorder. His attorney informed the company of his mental status and asked that they delay any decision about his employment status. The company fired John for his clear violation of company rules.

Contributed by Gerald E. Calvasina, Southern Utah University

20 EXERCISE

Group Debate Project

I. Objectives

A. To help you understand both sides of controversial human resource management issues.

B. To allow you to apply human resource management concepts in understanding the policy implications of the issues.

II. Out-of-Class Preparation Time: Equivalent to time required for students to complete a major term paper assignment.

III. In-Class Time Suggested: 45 minutes

IV. Procedures

A. Each debate will consist of two teams: an affirmative team that upholds the proposition and a negative team that opposes it. Debates can be scheduled throughout the semester to coincide with course content. For example, the comparable worth debate should be held after compensation is covered in the course. Alternatively, all debates could be held at the end of the term.

B. Students should be divided into groups of three or four depending on the number of debate topics to be covered during the semester. The number of debaters on each side should be equal and the time allowed for each side should be the same.

C. Each group should be assigned to either the affirmative or negative side of a topic.

D. Each team conducts research on its topic. Because of the current nature of the debate topics, you are encouraged to consult current periodicals (e.g., *Business Index, Business Periodicals Index,* and so on) in addition to academic journals and books. You may want to review the list of journals in the Skill Builders in Part 1.

E. Each team prepares a written paper (8–10 pages) analyzing both sides of the topic in addition to presenting its arguments. The paper should be divided into three major parts: Introduction, Discussion, and Conclusion. (See additional instructions that follow.)

F. The debate is held in class; the two sides present their arguments with the affirmative side opening and closing the debate.

G. A chairperson presides over the debate and keeps time.

H. The debating teams' presentations are evaluated by the rest of the class and by the instructor (see Form 1.4).

Additional Instructions for Debate Teams

Structure of Classroom Debates

First Affirmative	6 minutes
First Negative	6 minutes
Second Affirmative	6 minutes
Second Negative	6 minutes
Rebuttals: Negative	5 minutes
Rebuttals: Affirmative	5 minutes
Audience Cross-Examination	10 minutes

Tips on Oral Presentation

1. All of the speeches in the debate, except the first affirmative speech, should be given extemporaneously by the debaters. They should not be read. Essentially, the debaters' comments must reflect what was presented in the previous speech.
2. The first affirmative speech should be used to build the affirmative case. The affirmative debaters should give an overview of the major arguments they will use to uphold the proposition.
3. The first negative speech must be presented with the content of the first affirmative speech in mind. The aim of the negative speech is to cast doubt on the affirmative's arguments. The second speeches on both sides attempt to elaborate and build arguments as needed.
4. The rebuttal should directly address the arguments made by the other side.
5. Two excellent sources on debating are: Ericson, J. M. 1987. *The Debater's Guide.* Carbondale, IL: Southern Illinois University and Freeley, A. J. & Steinberg, D. L. 2005. *Argumentation and Debate: Critical Thinking for Reasoned Decision Making.* Belmont, CA: Wadsworth.

Suggested Debate Propositions (Your Instructor May Assign Other Topics)

1. Resolved: That the Employee Free Choice Bill be passed by Congress to eliminate secret-ballot union representation elections in the workplace in favor of a card check process.
2. Resolved: That employment-at-will or termination-at-will should remain the basic doctrine governing employee dismissal and should not be subject to legislative control.
3. Resolved: That federal legislation should be passed to prohibit discrimination against homosexuals in the workplace.
4. Resolved: That employee diversity enhances organizational performance.
5. Resolved: That telecommuting enhances employee productivity and morale while reducing turnover.
6. Resolved: That employers should develop and enforce policies prohibiting dating between co-workers.
7. Resolved: That U.S. immigration laws should be changed to allow more immigration by technical specialists from emerging/developing countries.
8. Resolved: That the use of contingent workers is an effective and efficient means of staffing.
9. Resolved: Regulation of stock options and bonuses for high-level executives should be minimized in order to attract and retain high-level executives.

Suggested Paper Format

Your written paper will follow a form known as a "full brief"—a comprehensive analysis of both sides of a given proposition, outlined logically, from which the debater can develop his or her case. Each team should have a minimum of 10 references (in most cases you will have many more). The paper will consist of three parts: Introduction, Discussion, and Conclusion.

Introduction:

a. Statement of the proposition and your group's position.

b. Why is the issue important?

c. Origin and history of the issue—keep it brief.

d. Outline the conflicting arguments—why is there a controversy?

Discussion: (This is the major section of your analysis.)

a. Present arguments to support your position.

b. Back up your arguments with sound reasoning and evidence.

Conclusion:

a. Summarize the main points of the discussion—recapitulate your major points.

b. End with an affirmation or denial of the proposition (depending on whether you have the affirmative or negative position).

FORM 1.4 *Debate Evaluation Form*

Debate:

Use the following scale to write in a rating on each item below for each team.

1	2	3	4
POOR	FAIR	GOOD	SUPERIOR

	Affirmative Team	**Negative Team**
I. Analysis (Was the analysis reasonable, complete, and clear?)		
II. Reasoning and evidence (Were the arguments structured soundly based on research facts and examples? Were arguments logical?)		
III. Organization (Was each speech clearly and cogently organized so that you could follow the structure of the debate?)		
IV. Rebuttal (Were unsupported points and assertions challenged by the opposing team?)		
V. Delivery (Was each speech effectively presented? Consider voice inflection, eye contact, and tone.)		
VI. Questions (Did the team adequately answer audience questions?)		
VII. Overall team rating		

In my opinion, the most effective debating was done by the ______________________ team.
(Affirmative or Negative)

Comments for Affirmative Team:

Comments for Negative Team:

21 INCIDENT

Giving Up Seniority to Accommodate a Disabled Colleague

Jim Martin had been loading and unloading cargo for East Coast Airlines for five years. His job performance ratings had always been above average. One day, Martin injured his back on the job. Because of his injury, he could no longer perform his job as a cargo handler.

The human resource manager, Angela Fisher, suggested that he apply for a transfer to another job appropriate to his skills and qualifications that did not involve physical strain. Transfer requests were governed by East Coast Airlines' seniority policy. Everything being equal, employees with greater seniority were given preference for transfers. Martin requested a transfer to a vacant mailroom position. At the same time, Bryan Beckwith, an employee with greater seniority than Jim, also applied for the vacant position. A position in the mailroom was viewed by many employees as an attractive alternative to some of the other blue-collar positions such as cargo and baggage handling.

After reviewing the transfer requests of the two employees, Angela Fisher awarded the position to Beckwith who had greater seniority at East Coast Airlines than Martin. Her decision was based on East Coast Airlines' seniority policy. In desperation, Martin went to Beckwith and asked him to please withdraw his transfer bid, explaining that he had requested the transfer because of an injury. Martin was hoping that his colleague would understand his plight. Beckwith refused to withdraw his request. Martin went to Fisher and requested an exception to the seniority policy that would allow him, rather than Beckwith, to work in the mailroom. Martin argued that since he was disabled because of his work as a cargo handler, he should be given preference over Beckwith. Fisher said that company policy did not allow her to make any exceptions. Martin lost his job at East Coast Airlines because there were no other vacancies for which he qualified.

QUESTIONS

1. If you were Beckwith, would you have dropped your transfer request to help Martin?
2. Should Fisher have given Martin preference over Beckwith because of his disability? Does seniority override the "reasonable accommodation" as specified in the Americans with Disabilities Act?

22 INCIDENT

"Beautyism" in the Workplace

Harold Hughes is a Professor of Management and Chair of the Department of Management in a College of Business Administration at a major university in the Southeast. Professor Hughes is 52 years old and has been divorced for the past eight years. During that time, he has dated several women for varying periods of time, but is not currently dating or in a relationship.

Recently, Professor Hughes' long-time administrative assistant (Helen Schully) retired from the University at age 60 after 25 years of service. He then put together a committee of three departmental members to assist him in selecting a new administrative assistant. These three committee members were Professors Don Hall and Mike Meyers as well as Pauline Nelson, the department's financial officer. The position was advertised internally within the university as well as externally in the local newspaper.

The committee met, developed a list of selection criteria with appropriate weights, reviewed thirteen applications, and selected four female applicants for interviews. These four were Melissa (a 47-year-old administrative assistant in a local insurance company), Sally (a 38-year-old secretary at the university), Carol (a 52-year-old administrative assistant at the university), and Diane (a 27-year-old secretary at a local bank). Melissa and Carol have BS degrees while Sally is studying for her BA degree at the university. Diane is a high school graduate with no college credits. A college degree (in hand or in process) and/or previous experience as an administrative assistant were two of the selection criteria the committee chose prior to the interviews.

Originally, the committee had selected only Melissa, Sally, and Carol for final interviews. However, Diane had personally brought her application by the office, met briefly with Harold to express her interest in the position, and had received his assurance she would be among those interviewed. He then informed the other committee members that he had added Diane to the group to be interviewed. During the interview process, the other three committee members noticed that Howard seemed quite "taken" with Diane even though (on paper) she seemed to have the least impressive credentials for the position. She was extremely attractive and recently divorced with a four-year-old son. The three other committee members all agreed that Carol seemed to have the education and all the skills, knowledge, and abilities the committee had previously identified (including knowledge of the university bureaucracy).

Despite their consensus, Harold said the person would be working for him, and that he "felt more comfortable with Diane." After the decision was made and Diane was offered and accepted the position, Professor Hall remarked to Professor Meyers "Harold must have been thinking with his ___!" Professor Meyers agreed but added that Diane was "hot" and would definitely "enhance the scenery around here." Pauline Nelson was upset because she felt Harold was sexist since he made the selection decision "based purely on physical attraction."

QUESTIONS

1. What is "beautyism"?
2. To what degree was "beautyism" a factor in this decision? How do you know?

3. Why and to what degree do more attractive male and female job applicants have an advantage in the interview process?
4. What can managers do to eliminate the "beautyism" bias during job interviews?
5. If "beautyism" is frequently used as an informal selection criterion for new employees, what strategies do you suggest to address this issue?

23 INCIDENT

Sexual Orientation Incidents: Bootstrapping Discrimination

1. James Smith, an openly gay man, was employed as a postal worker in Farmingdale, New York for approximately 12 years. He repeatedly received satisfactory to excellent performance evaluations. Smith's sexual orientation was known to his co-workers, who repeatedly assaulted him with sexually derogatory comments and names. He was exposed to frequent threats, obscenities, and nasty letters that referred to his homosexuality. Notes were placed on the wall in the employees' bathroom with Smith's name and the name of celebrities who had died of AIDS. Pornographic photographs were taped to his work area, male dolls were placed in his vehicle, and copies of *Playgirl* magazine were sent to his home. After suffering a heart attack, Mr. Smith resigned from his position. He filed a lawsuit against the post office charging sex discrimination. Mr. Smith argued in his petition that the abuse he endured because of his sexual orientation was so severe that he ultimately suffered a heart attack.

2. John Ortega was employed for five years by Mexicana, Inc., which operates a chain of restaurants in Washington and Oregon. Ortega first worked as a host and then became a food server in one of the Washington restaurants. Throughout his employment with Mexicana, Ortega was subjected to a relentless campaign of insults, name calling, and vulgarities. Ortega had complained to his general manager and assistant manager of the restaurant where he worked, but the abuse did not cease. Male co-workers and one of his supervisors referred to Ortega as a "she" or "her" constantly. He was mocked for walking like a woman, holding a tray like a woman, and having effeminate gestures. Ortega was called sexually derogatory names, such as "faggot" and "female whore."

   Pranks were played on him as well. One such incident ended in a fight between Ortega and a co-worker. Ortega and the co-worker were then called into a meeting with Mexicana's human resources director. The director told Ortega to report any further harassment to the area manager, who would address the issue. The human resources director also promised to do spot checks herself over a two-week period to ensure that the harassment stopped. Mexicana had a clearly stated policy against harassment which stated: "An employee who believes that he or she has been harassed by a co-worker, supervisor, or anyone acting on behalf of the company should immediately report the facts of the incident to the Mexicana EEO officer at the corporate office or to the area manager responsible for the restaurant." The human resources director made one check and Ortega told her that conditions were improving. However, about two weeks later Ortega got into a heated argument with his assistant manager and walked off the job. He was subsequently fired for leaving work in the middle of a shift. A month later, Ortega filed a complaint with the EEOC. Thereafter, he initiated a lawsuit charging he was harassed because of his sex.

3. Delilah Deacon filed a lawsuit against her employer, Hairlocks Preferred in New York City, accusing them of unlawful discrimination because of her sex, sex stereotyping, and/or sexual orientation. Delilah, a lesbian, was employed as a hair assistant at Hairlocks Preferred, a prestigious, high-end hair salon known for its innovative haircutting techniques. Delilah had wanted to move into one of the high-paying haircutting positions

after working as an assistant for several months. Hairlocks Preferred had a rigorous training program that had to be completed before anyone could advance to cutting clients' hair. Only about 10–15 percent of the total number of assistants at the salon completed the difficult and challenging training program. It took successful candidates at least two or three years to complete the training. In addition to its reputation for innovative haircuts, Hairlocks Preferred was known for hiring employees who embodied many different lifestyles and sexual orientations, including a female-to-male transsexual, an openly bisexual man, and both male and female gay employees. It was not uncommon for employees to engage in sexually charged banter in the workplace.

Deacon enrolled in the training program, but according to Hairlocks Preferred, her performance was erratic both in the training program and in her duties as a hair assistant. One of the senior stylists indicated that Deacon was frequently unavailable when needed to assist and that she had been rude to clients or rough with their hair. Other stylists complained she was hostile and disrespectful. Her performance in the basic cutting class was rated inadequate to advance to the next level. Deacon argued that her behavior was a result of the harassment she suffered because of her sexual orientation and gender. While she indicated she had not been at all reticent about her lesbianism while working at the salon, Deacon alleged that on several occasions the owner had told her that females rarely became hair stylists because clients preferred men. Deacon also charged that a range of derogatory comments were hurled at her while she worked at Hairlocks. She was often referred to as "Donald" instead of Delilah, called a "dyke," and was once told by a co-worker that she needed to have sex with a man. In her lawsuit, Deacon alleged the owner of Hairlocks, who was a pre-surgery male-to-female transsexual, informed her that she was being fired because of the way she looked and wore her hair. Hairlocks Preferred countered that she had been fired because of her poor performance.

QUESTIONS

1. What issue(s) must the court decide in each case? What laws, if any, have been violated?
2. If you were the judge, how would you rule? Why?
3. Sexual orientation in the workplace is an increasingly important HR issue. How should companies manage this issue?

24 SKILL BUILDER

Data Analysis for Affirmative Action Plans

I. OBJECTIVES

A. To enhance your understanding of how to prepare a utilization/availability analysis for Affirmative Action Plans.

B. To teach you the data analysis requirements under affirmative action guidelines.

II. TIME REQUIRED TO COMPLETE: Two to three hours

III. INSTRUCTIONS

You work for a manufacturing firm located in Charlotte, North Carolina, and your company has just been awarded its first federal contract of $250,000. This contract is to supply, over a two-year period, one of your major products to the Department of Defense. You have been asked by your boss, the plant manager, to perform the utilization/availability analyses required under Executive Order 11246 as input in developing an Affirmative Action Plan (AAP) for the Office of Federal Contract Compliance Programs (OFCCP).

You have reviewed the guidelines from the OFCCP on the requirements (see Exhibit 1.25). You have also pulled together labor market data in addition to compiling a detailed breakdown of the company's workforce by job category, sex, and race (see Exhibits 1.26, 1.27, 1.28, and 1.29).

REQUIRED

Using the relevant data, complete Form 1.5. You may need to generate additional forms for your use. It is easier to set this up in spreadsheet form. This is the first step toward developing an Affirmative Action Plan. Be sure to list any assumptions you make about the relevant labor market for each job category. Also be sure to indicate the job categories in which women and minorities are underutilized. Make any other recommendations you deem necessary to the plant manager.

EXHIBIT 1.25 *Summary of OFCCP/AAP Guidelines*

Definition

An affirmative action program is a management tool designed to ensure equal employment opportunity. A central premise underlying affirmative action is that over time and absent discrimination, a contractor's work-force will generally reflect the gender, racial, and ethnic profile of the labor pools from which the contractor recruits and selects. Affirmative action programs contain a diagnostic component, which includes a number of quantitative analyses designed to evaluate the composition of the workforce of the contractor and compare it to the composition of the relevant labor pools. Affirmative action programs also include action-oriented programs. If women and minorities are not being employed at a rate to be expected given their availability in the relevant labor pool, the contractor's affirmative action program includes specific practical steps designed to address this underutilization. Effective affirmative action programs also include internal auditing and reporting systems as a means of measuring the contractor's progress toward achieving the workforce that would be expected in the absence of discrimination.

Utilization Analysis

An AAP must contain a utilization analysis—a comparison of the percentages of women and minorities in each job category within the company (organizational profile or a workforce analysis) with the percentages available in the relevant labor market (availability analysis). An organizational profile is a depiction of the staffing pattern within an establishment. It is one method contractors can use to determine whether barriers to equal employment opportunity exist in their organizations. The profile provides an overview of the workforce at the establishment that may assist in identifying organizational units where women or minorities are underrepresented or concentrated.

The contractor must use either the organizational display or the workforce analysis as its organizational profile: An organizational display is a detailed graphical or tabular chart, text, spreadsheet, or similar presentation of the contractor's organizational structure. The organizational display must identify each organizational unit in the establishment, and show the relationship of each organizational unit to the other organizational units in the establishment. An organizational unit is any component that is part of the contractor's corporate structure. In a more traditional organization, an organizational unit might be a department, division, section, branch, group, or similar component. In a less traditional organization, an organizational unit might be a project team, job family, or similar component. The term includes an umbrella unit (such as a department) that contains a number of subordinate units, and it separately includes each of the subordinate units (such as sections or branches). For each organizational unit, the organizational display must indicate the following:

i. The name of the unit;
ii. The job title, gender, race, and ethnicity of the unit supervisor (if the unit has a supervisor);
iii. The total number of male and female incumbents; and
iv. The total number of male and female incumbents in each of the following groups: Black, Hispanic, Asians/Pacific Islander, and American Indians/Alaskan Native.

Alternatively, a company may use a workforce analysis approach. A workforce analysis is a listing of each job title as appears in applicable collective bargaining agreements or payroll records ranked from the lowest paid to the highest paid within each department or other similar organizational unit including departmental or unit supervision. For each job category, the total number of male and female incumbents in each of these groups (Black, Hispanic, Asian/Pacific Islander, and American Indians/Alaskan Native) is indicated (see Exhibit 1.29). An analysis of all major job groups and the extent to which minorities or women are underutilized is also requested. Underutilization is having fewer minorities or women in a particular job category than would reasonably be expected, according to their availability in the relevant labor market. Two factors must be considered in determining availability:

1. The percentage of minorities or women with requisite skills in the reasonable recruitment area, defined as the geographical area from which the contractor usually seeks or reasonably could seek workers to fill the positions in question; and
2. The percentage of minorities or women among those promotable, transferable, and trainable within the contractor's organization.

Based on Revised 41 C.F.R. Chapter 60, Office of Federal Contract Compliance Programs, Department of Labor. The new guidelines became effective in 2000.

EXHIBIT 1.26 *Workforce Analysis*

		Number of Male Employees					Number of Female Employees				
	Overall Totals (Sums of Columns B thru K)	White (Not of Hispanic Origin)	Black (Not of Hispanic Origin)	Hispanic	Asian or Pacific Islander	American Indian or Alaskan Native	White (Not of Hispanic Origin)	Black (Not of Hispanic Origin)	Hispanic	Asian or Pacific Islander	American Indian or Alaskan Native
Job Categories	**A**	**B**	**C**	**D**	**E**	**F**	**G**	**H**	**I**	**J**	**K**
Officials and managers*	154	138	2	0	0	0	13	1	0	0	0
Professionals	137	126	1	0	0	0	10	0	0	0	0
Technicians	76	61	2	1	1	0	6	2	0	3	0
Sales workers	77	65	4	0	0	0	7	1	0	0	0
Office and clerical	188	21	3	0	1	0	144	17	2	0	0
Craft workers (skilled)	150	120	15	1	2	0	9	3	0	0	0
Operatives (semiskilled)	294	200	58	2	10	2	16	4	0	2	0
Laborers (unskilled)	655	504	82	5	10	1	38	10	3	2	0
Service workers	89	17	49	5	1	2	2	9	2	0	2
TOTALS	1,820	1,252	216	14	25	5	245	47	7	7	2

*Includes supervisors

EXHIBIT 1.27 *Civilian Labor Force by Sex and Race, Charlotte, Gastonia, Rock Hill, NC-SC, SMSA, 2000*[1]

Sex and Race	Civilian Labor Force	Employed	Unemployed
Both Sexes			
TOTAL	514,796	489,574	25,222
White	417,540	400,260	17,280
Black	90,270	82,710	7,560
American Indian, Eskimo, and Aleut	1,093	1,048	45
Asian and Pacific Islander	2,193	2,066	127
Hispanic	3,700	3,490	210
Female			
TOTAL	233,298	220,545	12,753
White	184,190	175,420	8,770
Black	45,970	42,150	3,820
American Indian, Eskimo, and Aleut	495	467	28
Asian and Pacific Islander	993	938	55
Hispanic	1,650	1,570	80

[1] *Numbers are fictionalized based on North Carolina Census Data.*

EXHIBIT 1.28 *Occupations of the Civilian Labor Force by Sex and Race, 2000, Charlotte, Gastonia, Rock Hill, NC-SC SMSA*[1]

Occupation	Total[2]	Total White	Total Black	American Indian	Asians	Hispanic	White Not Hispanic	Black Not Hispanic	Total Minority
TOTAL									
All industries	447,254	364,832	78,955	1,348	1,837	3,165	362,595	78,302	84,659
Managerial and professional specialty	87,018	77,673	8,482	119	689	589	77,211	8,410	9,807
Technicians	10,077	8,557	1,415	20	80	53	8,517	1,407	1,561
Sales occupations	45,837	42,341	3,241	84	141	287	42,115	3,203	3,772
Administrative support, including clerical	72,927	62,762	9,857	115	173	387	62,438	9,814	10,489
Service workers	47,097	29,970	16,627	225	249	429	29,765	16,429	17,332
Farming, forestry, and fishing	5,483	4,301	1,103	53	19	26	4,282	1,103	1,201
Precision production and craft	59,987	51,716	7,830	282	130	477	51,341	7,757	8,646
Operators and fabricators	92,707	69,331	22,678	344	251	713	68,884	22,515	23,823
Handlers, equipment cleaners, helpers, and laborers	26,121	18,181	7,722	106	105	204	18,042	7,664	8,079

[1] *North Carolina portion only.*

[2] *Racial and ethnic group columns may not be additive to total due to "race or ethnic group not classified" in census response.*

EXHIBIT 1.29 *Occupations of the Female Civilian Labor Force by Sex and Race, 2000, Charlotte, Gastonia, Rock Hill, NC-SC SMSA*[1]

Occupation	Total[2]	Total White	Total Black	American Indian	Asians	Hispanic	Not Hispanic	Not Hispanic	Total Minority
TOTAL									
All industries	202,039	160,509	40,184	524	702	1,436	159,524	39,821	42,490
Managerial and professional specialty	36,447	30,864	5,346	48	167	260	30,682	5,290	5,765
Technicians	4,667	3,716	923	7	16	23	3,706	915	961
Sales occupations	20,006	17,652	2,211	53	71	170	17,524	2,181	2,482
Administrative support, including clerical	55,628	48,504	6,928	86	95	280	48,269	6,898	7,359
Service workers	28,122	17,269	10,557	134	143	261	17,159	10,425	10,963
Farming, forestry, and fishing	1,166	877	278	6	5	0	877	278	289
Precision production and craft	5,778	4,488	1,256	13	14	51	4,450	1,250	1,328
Operators and fabricators	43,556	32,601	10,588	169	165	344	32,375	10,503	11,181
Handlers, equipment cleaners, helpers, and laborers	6,669	4,538	2,097	9	26	47	4,507	2,081	2,162

[1] *North Carolina portion only.*

[2] *Racial and ethnic group columns may not be additive to total due to "race or ethnic group not classified" in census response.*

FORM 1.5 *Utilization/Availability Analysis*

	Sex		Race				
Job Category	**Male**	**Female**	**White**	**Black**	**Hispanic**	**Asian**[1]	**American Indian**[2]
Number of employees							
Percentage of employees (utilization)							
Percent available							
Underutilized							

[1] *Asian/Pacific Islander*
[2] *American Indian/Alaskan Native*

Note: A table will be needed for each job category.

PART

2

Meeting Human Resource Requirements: Job Analysis/ Design, Planning, Recruitment, and Selection

Analysis/Planning/Outsourcing/ Mergers/Layoffs

25 CASE

Employee Layoffs at St. Mary's Hospital

St. Mary's Hospital is a medium-sized, 400-bed hospital in a northwestern city. It was established in 1908 by the Sisters of the Sacred Heart, an order of Catholic sisters. The facility has grown gradually over the years and is now the third largest hospital in the city. It is entirely nonunion and has never experienced an employee layoff since its inception.

Robert Barry has been the CEO of the hospital for 11 years. Eight years ago, he hired Sharon Osgood as director of Human Resources. Osgood has an MA in Human Resource Management and has been instrumental in formalizing the institution's human resources' policies and procedures.

Occupancy rates in the hospital had run between 76 and 82 percent from 1990 to 2002. However, since then, occupancy has fallen to 57 percent. This decline has been experienced throughout the industry and is the result of changing reimbursement policies, emphasis on outpatient services, increasing competition, and the financial meltdown of 2008–2010. The declining occupancy rate has affected this hospital's revenues to such an extent that it ran a deficit for the first time last year. The only response to these changes thus far has been a tightening of requirements for equipment or supply purchases.

At the most recent quarterly meeting of the Board of Directors, Barry presented the rather bleak financial picture. The projected deficit for the coming year was $3,865,000, unless some additional revenue sources were identified or some additional savings were found. The Board's recommendation, based on the immediate crisis and the need to generate short-term savings, was to lay off employees. They recommended that Barry consider laying off up to 10 percent of the hospital's employees with an emphasis on those in "nonessential" areas.

Barry responded that the hospital's employees had never been laid off in the history of the institution. Moreover, he viewed the employees as "family" and would have great difficulty implementing such a layoff. Nevertheless, since he had no realistic short-term alternative for closing the "revenue gap," Barry reluctantly agreed to implement a layoff policy that would be as fair as possible to all employees, provide a guarantee of reemployment for those laid off, and find additional revenue sources so that layoffs would be unnecessary in the future.

Barry then called Sharon Osgood into his office the next morning, shared his concerns, and asked her to prepare both a short-term plan to save $3 million over the next year through staff layoffs, as well as a long-term plan to avoid layoffs in the future. Osgood's concerns were that the layoffs themselves might be costly in terms of lost investment in some of the laid-off employees, higher turnover costs, lost efficiency, potential lawsuits, and lower morale. She was concerned that the criteria for the layoffs not only *be* equitable, but also *appear to be* equitable to the employees. She also wanted to make sure that those being laid off received "adequate" notice so they could make alternative plans or so the hospital could assist them with finding alternative employment. Since the hospital had no previous experience with employee layoffs and no union contract constraints, her feeling was that both seniority and job performance should be considered in determining who would be laid off.

Osgood knew the hospital's performance appraisal system was inadequate and needed to be revamped. While this task was high on her "to do" list, she also knew she had to move ahead with her recommendations on layoffs immediately. The present performance appraisal system uses a traditional checklist rating scale with a summary rating. Since there is no forced distribution, the average ratings of employees in different departments vary widely.

Exhibit 2.1 shows the summary ratings of employees in each department. Most supervisors across all departments rate many of their subordinates either "satisfactory" or "outstanding." Osgood has done a quick review of those employees whose overall ratings were "unsatisfactory" or "questionable." Most are employees with less than three years of seniority, whereas the "satisfactory" employees have worked an average of seven years for St. Mary's Hospital. Osgood is preparing to submit her recommendations to Barry and has come to you for advice. Exhibit 2.2 provides a summary of the distribution of employees and payroll expense by department for the most recent year.

QUESTIONS

1. Identify the major problem or problems at St. Mary's Hospital and the causes.
2. What are some alternatives for dealing with these problems? For example, is it possible to avoid employee layoffs through the use of attrition?
3. Develop a plan for implementing employee layoffs over the next year that will generate $3 million in savings. Give specific details concerning departments affected, the use of seniority versus merit, the amount of notice, and out-placement activities. What additional information (if any) will you need? Provide a rationale for each recommendation, together with reasons why other alternatives were not chosen.
4. What might be the effects of a layoff plan on "survivors" in terms of morale, job security, organizational commitment, productivity, and career planning? How could you avoid or minimize any potential problems in these areas?
5. What long-term solutions do you see for St. Mary's Hospital once it gets its cash flow problems under control and eliminates its deficit? What can it do to increase revenue so that future layoffs will not be necessary?
6. What difficulties exist in using performance as a criterion for layoffs? How can such difficulties be overcome?

EXHIBIT 2.1 *Percentage Distribution of Performance Appraisal Summary Ratings by Department at St. Mary's Hospital*

Department	Unsatisfactory: Needs to Improve Substantially	Questionable: Needs Some Improvement	Satisfactory: Meets Normal Expectations	Outstanding: Substantially Exceeds Norms
Nursing	6.4	6.4	54.2	33.0
Allied Health	5.7	6.2	47.8	40.3
Central Administration	2.7	3.1	67.5	26.7
Dietetics/Nutrition	2.1	6.2	68.3	23.4
Housekeeping/Maintenance	7.8	12.4	54.6	25.2
Medical Staff	1.1	6.2	63.8	28.9

EXHIBIT 2.2 *The Distribution of Employment and Payroll Expenditures at St. Mary's Hospital*

Department	Number of Employees	Payroll ($)	Annual Turnover Rates (%)*
Nursing	602	$15,050,000	12.2
Allied Health Departments	261	5,742,000	8.7
Central Administration	154	6,160,000	3.5
Dietetics/Nutrition	65	1,430,000	7.3
Housekeeping and Maintenance	36	540,000	8.4
Medical Staff	32	1,680,000	2.1
TOTAL	1,150	$30,602,000	9.5*

**Represents weighted average turnover for all employees.*

26 Case

Strategic Human Resource Management

The School of Business Administration at Old State University is one of 12 state-supported collegiate business schools in a midwestern state. It is located in a city with a population of 400,000 and a diversified industrial base. Old State University is the only state-supported institution in town. One small private college provides competition to the university's business school.

Recently, the university experienced leadership transition when Dr. George Barnes, dean of the College of Business Administration since 1988, retired. During his administration, enrollment increased from 1,792 undergraduates and 142 MBA students in the 1988–1989 academic year to 2,284 undergraduates and 233 MBA students in the most recent academic year.

Dean Barnes was well-liked by students, faculty, and the central administration of Old State University. However, he had not led the School of Business in any new directions and had basically concentrated on "doing the same things better." The "same things" meant an emphasis on traditional programs (accounting, marketing, finance, and so on), teaching undergraduate students in the age range of 18–22 in daytime programs, and teaching a small number of full-time MBA students. The latter have been mostly graduates of the school's undergraduate program who decided they were willing to spend two more years on campus to obtain the second degree.

Dean Barnes has also successful in upgrading the proportion of faculty with terminal degrees from 75 percent in 1988 to 90 percent in the most recent year. Exhibit 2.3 provides faculty and student enrollment data for the university for selected years during Barnes's tenure.

During the most recent academic year, the dean's search committee (consisting of faculty, students, alumni, central administration, and local business representatives) met frequently, screened over 100 applicants, and personally interviewed six. While the committee arrived at no consensus, the majority supported Jack Blake for the deanship. An offer was made and, after several weeks of negotiation, Blake accepted the deanship. His background consisted of an MBA from a prestigious Ivy League business school and executive leadership positions in a variety of U.S. corporations in marketing. He left the position of vice president of marketing at a Fortune 500 company to accept the deanship.

During the screening interviews with the search committee, Blake made it clear that if he were selected, the College of Business would be "moving in new directions and exploring new markets." Blake made it clear that he did not want to be a "paper pusher," but rather an innovator and entrepreneur. When pressed for specifics, he indicated he "would have to study the situation in more detail."

When the new dean arrived on campus in the fall, he immediately convened a Strategic Planning Committee to 1) evaluate the university's external environment, opportunities, threats, competitive advantages, and internal strengths and weaknesses, and 2) recommend a new long-term mission, goals, objectives, and programs. The committee consisted of two senior professors, the university's vice president for academic affairs, one graduate student, one undergraduate student, two prominent alumni, and two local business leaders.

The committee recommended that the school focus on the adult learner since demographic analysis suggested the age group 18–22 in the state was shrinking and would be a declining market over the next decade. Specific recommendations included 1) offering more

EXHIBIT 2.3 *Faculty and Student Enrollment Data for the College of Business Administration in Selected Years, 1988–2007*

Academic Year	Faculty	Faculty with PhD	Student Enrollment BS	MBA	Total
1988–1989	69	52	1,792	142	1,934
1995–1996	74	57	1,913	154	2,067
2000–2001	78	66	2,065	221	2,286
2006–2007	85	76	2,284	233	2,517
2010–2011	90	81	2,587	248	2,837

evening courses for both undergraduate and graduate students; 2) structuring the schedule so that both degrees could be earned entirely in the evening; 3) offering credit courses in some suburban locations; 4) offering requested noncredit practitioner courses at the school, at the employer's worksite, and in various underserved small cities around the state; 5) exploring possibilities of offering degree programs at these locations; 6) offering new MBA degree concentrations in such areas as management of the arts, healthcare management, and public sector management, and 7) offering a new "executive" MBA.

The new dean enthusiastically endorsed the report and distributed copies at the last faculty meeting of the fall semester. Several questions were raised, but it did not appear that serious opposition existed. However, at a following meeting of department chairs, the dean indicated that his top priority for the next academic year was to fill five vacant positions with new faculty who would be supportive of the new directions in which the school was moving. Specifically, he asked them to keep several criteria in mind while recruiting and selecting new faculty. These included previous managerial work experience, a willingness to teach night courses, a willingness to travel to other cities to offer coursework, an ability to work with management practitioners on continuing education training and special projects, and previous experience in teaching executives.

In addition, Dean Blake suggested that the chairs consider those criteria when evaluating the performance of existing faculty and recommending salary increases. Finally, he indicated that one of the faculty positions would be used to recruit a new assistant dean for external affairs who would become his link to the practitioner community. This person would be involved with helping practicing managers identify their needs, working with faculty to meet these needs, and negotiating contracts for these services.

When word of the dean's faculty recommendations spread through the rumor mill, the reaction was swift and negative. Many of the "old-guard" faculty felt they were hired primarily to teach full-time students on campus during the day. Consequently, they were threatened by the new evaluation criteria. They were also concerned that the dean was interjecting non-academic criteria into their departmental faculty recruitment processes and diverting resources to nonacademic activities. These faculty felt the inevitable result would be a declining quality of education in the school.

A group of these faculty has asked to meet with the dean to discuss his proposals. The dean is preparing a justification for both his strategy and his human resource management (faculty) recommendations.

QUESTIONS

1. How and why do strategic decisions affect human resource management policies? Can human resource policies or constraints ever affect strategy? Why or why not?
2. Identify the problem and causes of the problem in this case.
3. Evaluate Dean Blake's strategy and human resource policies. Did the strategy make sense in terms of the internal and external environment of the school? Do the human resource strategies support and reinforce the organizational strategy? Why or why not?
4. Evaluate the process by which Dean Blake implemented the strategic and human resources changes. Can you suggest any improvements?
5. How can resistance to his plans and strategies be overcome?

27 CASE
The Alternative Work Schedule

BACKGROUND

March 13 marked an important day in the history of Building Products, Inc. The planning committee was meeting to determine the work schedule for all of the production workers at its new plant. Attending the meeting was the human resource director, the plant manager, and the production manager. The plant was scheduled to open in a few months, and it was time to begin hiring new employees.

The committee knew that the new work schedule would need to meet specific parameters. First, the plant's production process would require that chemicals and materials be heated to high temperatures, so the plant would have to operate 24 hours a day, seven days a week, 363 days a year. On Christmas Day and the day before Christmas, the plant would shut down with only two employees needed—a production operator and a maintenance technician. Second, workers would not be able to take breaks all at one time. Rather, they would need to stagger the breaks and cover for each other. Third, having the standard 8-to-5 work schedule would not be possible, given the need for 24-hour coverage. Likewise, a work schedule that entails three shifts, each working eight-hour days would not work because coverage is needed seven days a week, and employees need time off to rest.

After much discussion, the human resources director suggested that the firm try a schedule that she had heard about at another firm. The schedule entailed dividing workers into four crews, with each crew working 12-hour shifts on either three or four consecutive days or nights. It also meant that employees would switch between day shifts and night shifts. More specifically, the schedule of rotation for one crew would be as follows:

4 night shifts—12 hours per night (7 PM to 7 AM)

2 days/nights off

3 day shifts—12 hours per day (7 AM to 7 PM)

2 days/nights off

3 night shifts—12 hours per night (7 PM to 7 AM)

2 days/nights off

4 day shifts—12 hours per day (7 AM to 7 PM)

8 days/nights off

Repeat sequence throughout this and future years

A typical schedule over a 28-day period for each of the four crews would be:

	Week 1	Week 2	Week 3	Week 4
Crew	S M T W T F S	S M T W T F S	S M T W T F S	S M T W T F S
A	O N N N O O D	D D D O O O O	O O O O N N N	N O O D D D O
B	N O O D D D O	O N N N O O D	D D D O O O O	O O O O N N N
C	O O O O N N N	N O O D D D O	O N N N O O D	D D D O O O O
D	D D D O O O O	O O O O N N N	N O O D D D O	O N N N O O D

Key: N night shift; O off work; D day shift

The human resources director noted that by dividing all of the workers into four crews, the schedules for the crews could be integrated in such a way that only one crew would be working, yet all hours could be covered (see schedule above). Each crew would consist of 17 production operators, two warehouse/forklift truck workers to take product off the line, and one production supervisor. Also, she suggested that overtime pay be granted to employees when they work more than 40 hours per week. An employee who works a 48-hour week would receive straight pay for 40 hours and time-and-one-half for eight more hours. This equates to 52 hours of straight pay. Thus, in the course of a 28-day period, employees would work shifts totaling 168 hours, but be paid for 176 hours. In addition, she recommended that employees who work over a holiday receive double pay for those hours, but that no additional overtime pay be provided for working Saturday or Sunday.

After hearing the human resources director's recommendations, the plant manager and the production manager sat quietly, trying to digest the plan. The schedule was completely unlike anything they had ever experienced, and it struck them as bizarre. They could not help but question whether the plan would actually work. They also wondered if there might not be a better production schedule.

QUESTIONS

1. What do you see as the strengths and weaknesses of the human resources director's work schedule from (a) the employees' perspective, and (b) the firm's perspective?
2. Would you recommend the firm use the new work schedule? Why?
3. What alternative work schedule could be used?

28 EXERCISE

Which Employee Should Be Terminated?

I. OBJECTIVES

A. To make you aware of the difficulties involved in making termination decisions.

B. To familiarize you with possible criteria a manager can use in making termination decisions.

C. To give you practice in conducting termination interviews.

II. OUT-OF-CLASS PREPARATION TIME: 10 minutes to read exercise and decide which employee should be terminated

III. IN-CLASS TIME SUGGESTED: 40–50 minutes

IV. PROCEDURES

Either at the beginning of or before class, you should read the exercise and determine which title examiner should be terminated. This exercise requires that groups determine which company employee should be terminated. To start the exercise, the instructor will ask five students to play the role of title examiners. One will play the role of Rick Feinberg, another the role of Jeff Simon, and so on. These individuals will be asked to leave the classroom and prepare to play their roles. They should study carefully the material contained in this exercise and determine how to respond if, in fact, they are the one chosen to be terminated.

The instructor will divide the remaining students into groups of four to six. Each group should develop a list of criteria for layoffs/termination, and rank the title examiners from first to go to last to go. After the group has reached a consensus, it should select one spokesperson to communicate the decision to the title examiner who is to be terminated.

After all groups have finished performing the preceding tasks, the role play begins. One at a time, each group's spokesperson announces to the class which title examiner his or her group believes should be terminated. The instructor then brings that person into the room and asks him or her to sit down at the front of the class. The spokesperson sits down opposite the title examiner, tells that person that he or she is terminated, and gives the rationale behind the decision. The title examiner then responds in any realistic way that he or she deems appropriate. This process continues until all groups' spokespersons have had an opportunity to present their decision. A critique of the role plays and a discussion of the difficulties involved in terminating an employee should then follow.

SITUATION

The Stanton Title Insurance Company was founded in 1964 by Harvey Stanton to sell title insurance policies to buyers of real estate. The company works closely with a group of about 35 lawyers who, although they do not actually buy the title insurance policies, encourage their clients (the property purchasers) to do so. When the company was originally established, Stanton was its only employee. As company sales increased, new employees were hired, and now 23 individuals are working in various capacities for the firm. Stanton has always followed the policy of making all major decisions himself. This includes all personnel decisions such as determining who should be hired and how much they should be paid.

EXHIBIT 2.4 *Harvey's Evaluation of Individual Job Performance for Title Examiners for Last Year*

Title Examiner	Current Salary	Work Quality	Work Quantity	Knowledge of Job	Dependability	Cooperativeness
Rick Feinberg	$56,500	Excellent	Good	Excellent	Good	Poor
José Sanchez	$32,000	Good	Good	Fair	Excellent	Excellent
Kathy Wallace	$36,500	Good	Fair	Good	Fair	Excellent
Doris Matthews	$45,000	Poor	Good	Excellent	Good	Good
Anthony Pope	$50,200	Good	Poor	Excellent	Excellent	Excellent

Five of the employees work primarily on examining titles at local government offices. In recent weeks, Stanton has noticed that the workload of these five employees has declined considerably. In part, this is due to the recent election of three "no-growth" candidates to the city council. In addition, a competing firm has recently opened an office in town and is successfully taking away business. Stanton has reluctantly decided that he must terminate the employment of one of the title examiners. He simply cannot transfer one of them to a new position. His only question is, which one?

A summary of Harvey's evaluation of each title examiner is in Exhibit 2.4; a profile of each of the five title examiners appears below.

Rick Feinberg: 45 years old; white; married with three children; 20 years with the company; graduated from a community college; knows how to resolve difficult title policies due to his extensive experience; is difficult to get along with; antagonizes other employees at main office; hates to fill out company reports not related to title examination and refuses to do so on occasion; will not work overtime under any condition, which puts a burden on others.

José Sanchez: 23 years old; Latino; married; attending college; one year with the company; wife works at main office as a computer programmer; works very hard and is eager to learn; well-liked by all employees and is highly dependable; is never absent and will gladly work overtime to meet emergencies; with more experience, he should be an outstanding title examiner; is highly loyal and dedicated; moved recently to a new apartment across the street from the government office where he works.

Kathy Wallace: 24 years old; single; college degree; African-American; working on MBA at night; three years with company; well-liked by employees; very active in community affairs; capable of moving up to a top management position with the company; often misses work due to school and community activities.

Doris Matthews: 36 years old; married; white; attended community college but did not graduate; ten years with company; niece of Harvey Stanton; has had eye problems and headaches, which affected work quality this year and may continue to do so; has been very helpful in getting new business for the company; is well-known and highly respected by law firms.

Anthony Pope: 63 years old; white; 15 years with company; no college; hard working and well-liked by employees; three children in college; a solid, stable employee who is able to remain calm and solve problems in crisis situations; excellent at resolving conflicts between employees; well-known to local government officials; very slow but highly accurate worker.

29 EXERCISE

Outsourcing the Human Resource Management Functions

I. OBJECTIVES

A. To familiarize you with the potential costs and benefits of human resource management outsourcing.

B. To familiarize you with the degree to which various human resource management functions are being successfully outsourced.

II. OUT-OF-CLASS PREPARATION TIME: 50 minutes

III. IN-CLASS TIME SUGGESTED: 30 minutes

IV. INSTRUCTIONS

A. In groups of three to five students, read the "Situation" below, as well as Forms 2.1 and 2.2.

B. Each group will complete Forms 2.1 and 2.2, as well as Question 1. List as many outsourcing benefits and costs for both employers and employees as you can on Form 2.1. Put an X beside your group's assessment of the corporate benefits (Form 2.2) of outsourcing each HR function.

C. One person in each team will report the group's assessment and recommendations (Question 1) to the class.

SITUATION

Sharon Osmond is the vice president of human resources for Silicon Electronics, a small electronics company in the Silicon Valley area outside of San Francisco. She has been concerned that their patched-together human resource information system uses a software program so outdated that Peoplesoft will no longer support it. This morning she met Edward Cutter, the CEO of her company, in the parking lot as they were both coming to work.

Cutter told her of a conversation he had with a consultant from Hewitt Associates, Inc., a human resource management consulting company. The consultant said that when the entire human resource management function was outsourced to Hewitt, they had saved a company similar to his almost $400,000 in human resource management costs last year. The consultant also told Cutter that a number of blue-chip companies have joined the HR outsourcing bandwagon including AT&T, Motorola, American Express, and Prudential. Based on that conversation, Cutter then asked Osgood to do some research and let him know whether it made sense to consider outsourcing some or all of the current human resource management functions at Silicon Electronics to Hewitt or a similar firm.

Osgood was quite upset after the conversation because she knew her own position, as well as positions of her subordinates, might be in jeopardy. However, after recovering from her initial shock, she called Mary Gannon, her former professor of Human Resources Management at California State University, to solicit her input. Professor Gannon told Osgood she would get back to her in a week after giving this assignment to one of the student groups in her Human Resources Management class.

Your group has been given this assignment. Professor Gannon has asked your group to do the research necessary to complete Forms 2.1 and 2.2 and then answer the questions below.

QUESTIONS

1. Complete Forms 2.1 and 2.2 using information gathered from the various human resource Web sites listed throughout this book. Identify as many benefits and costs from both the employer and employee perspective as you can as a result of outsourcing the entire human resource function (Form 2.1). Also consider which human resource functions have the greatest potential to be outsourced based on what other companies are doing and why (Form 2.2). On the basis of these assessments, which of the three strategies should Osmond recommend to Cutter and why? Circle either a, b, or c and be prepared to explain your reasons based on Forms 2.1 and 2.2.

   a. Do not outsource any of the human resource functions.

   b. Outsource only the following human resource functions:____________

   c. Outsource all of the human resource functions.

FORM 2.1 *Benefits and Costs Associated with Outsourcing Human Resources Functions*

Employer
Benefits
Costs

Employee
Benefits
Costs

FORM 2.2 *The Potential Expected Corporate Benefits Associated with Outsourcing Specific Human Resource Functions*

	Potential Expected Benefits			
HR Functions	**Uncertain**	**Very Low**	**Moderate**	**Very High**
1. Payroll and benefits				
2. Recruitment				
3. Selection				
4. Information technology				
5. Training				
6. Performance management				
7. All HR functions				

30 EXERCISE

Job Analysis: Writing Job Descriptions

I. OBJECTIVES

A. To familiarize you with the job analysis process and with job descriptions.

B. To give you practice writing job descriptions.

II. OUT-OF-CLASS PREPARATION TIME: 30 minutes

III. IN-CLASS TIME SUGGESTED: 45 minutes

IV. PROCEDURES

A. Before beginning this exercise, you should (a) review carefully, if you have not already done so, the different methods organizations use to conduct job analyses, and (b) review the Job Analysis Questionnaire (Exhibit 2.5).

B. Students should be divided into pairs. Each person should then interview his or her partner with reference to a job about which the partner is very familiar. Use the Job Analysis Questionnaire for the interview. The questionnaire can be used to help determine the major responsibilities and tasks of the job and the required knowledge, skills, abilities, and personal characteristics needed to perform the job.

C. After each student has interviewed his or her partner, write a job description covering your partner's job. Remember to use action verbs when describing the employee's tasks, duties, and responsibilities. It is also important that specific duties be grouped and arranged in descending order of importance. The completed job description should follow the format shown in Exhibit 2.6. The completed job description should be shown to the partner to determine whether additional information is required or whether changes should be made. Your instructor may require that you turn in a final copy of the completed job description for the next class.

D. If time permits, the entire class should discuss the various uses of job descriptions and the effectiveness of the interview as a method of job analysis.

EXHIBIT 2.5 *Job Analysis Questionnaire*

A. Job Responsibilities and Duties

1. Job title
2. Department title and/or division title
3. Title of immediate supervisor
4. Description of duties (Describe the duties in enough detail to provide a complete and accurate description of the work.)
   a. Provide a general overall summary of the purpose of your job.
   b. What are the major results or outputs of your job?
   c. Describe the duties and tasks you perform daily; weekly; monthly.
   d. Describe duties you perform irregularly.
5. List any machines, instruments, tools, equipment, materials, and work aids used in your job. Indicate percent of time used.
6. Describe the nature of your responsibility for nonhuman resources (money, machinery, equipment, and so on). What monetary loss can occur through an error?
7. What reports and records do you prepare as part of your job? When are they prepared?
8. What is the source of instructions for performing your job (e.g., oral or written specifications)?
9. Describe the nature and frequency of supervision received.
10. How is your work reviewed, checked, or verified?

B. Reporting Relationships

11. How many employees are directly under your supervision? What are their job titles?
12. Do you have full authority to hire, terminate, evaluate, and transfer employees under your supervision? Explain.
13. What contacts are required with other departments or persons other than your immediate department in performing your job? Describe the nature and extent of these contacts.

C. Working Conditions

14. Describe the working conditions present in the location and environment of your work such as cold/heat, noise, fumes, dust, and so on. Indicate frequency and degree of exposure.
15. Describe any dangers or hazards present in your job.

D. Job Qualifications (Be certain not to list the incumbent's qualifications, but what is required for performance by a new employee.)

16. Describe the kind of previous work experience necessary for satisfactory performance of this job.
17. What is the amount of experience required?
18. What kinds of knowledge, skills, and abilities (KSAs) are needed to perform the job?
19. What is the minimal level of education (grammar, high school, two-year college, four-year college, etc.) required?
20. Are any special physical skills and/or manual dexterity skills required to perform the job?
21. Are there any special certification, registration, license, or training requirements?

EXHIBIT 2.6 *Sample Job Description*

Job Title: Shift Supervisor

Position Purpose: The purpose of this position is to maintain a safe and efficient plant operation through directing the activities of the operation's personnel and providing a management support function for the plant superintendent.

Typical Job Duties:

1. Directs the activities of the operations personnel and coordinates the activities of the maintenance personnel.
2. Issues written communication to employees concerning personnel policies and operational concerns.
3. Administers a maintenance request program through collecting requests, scheduling, and recording maintenance activities.
4. Administers the plant tagging procedure.
5. Conducts the training and safety programs for shift employees.
6. Schedules shift assignments to reflect workload and vacation schedules.
7. Performs administrative tasks such as recording workers' time, maintaining records concerning operational activities, and updating written procedures.
8. Prepares annual budget for assigned plant area and maintains the inventory level on these items.
9. Appraises performance of shift employees annually.
10. Counsels employees on disciplinary problems and job-related performance.
11. Assumes plant superintendent's duties when assigned.

Physical Requirements: Walking and climbing stairs

Working Conditions: Good, some noise

Equipment and Machines Used: CRT, spectrometer, PH meter, conductivity meter

Reporting Relationships: The shift supervisor reports directly to the plant superintendent. The shift supervisor directs the control room operator, two or more utility operators, trainees, and other assigned personnel, and coordinates the activities of the maintenance personnel present on shift.

Qualifications:

Education: Associate degree or equivalent training (e.g., management training classes) OR five (5) years of management experience.

Related Experience: Minimum of three (3) years as a control room operator for a coal-fired boiler operation.

Job Knowledge/Skills Required:

1. Comprehensive understanding of plant systems.
2. Fundamental understanding of electrical systems and motor control centers.
3. Thorough knowledge of boiler chemistry.
4. Comprehension of flow, logic, and electrical prints.
5. Ability to perform elementary mathematical and algebraic calculations.
6. Communication and human relations skills.
7. Ability to operate CRT, spectrometer, PH meter, and conductivity meter.
8. Managerial skills.

31 Exercise

Work and Family Issues

I. Objectives

A. To understand the conflicts that sometimes arises between the individual's work and family responsibilities.

B. To analyze the advantages and disadvantages of alternative policies and programs that attempt to reconcile the sometimes conflicting demands of work and family.

II. Out-of-Class Preparation Time: 1 hour

III. In-Class Time Suggested: 45 minutes

IV. Procedures

A. Read the entire exercise before class. Students may want to conduct research on the topic prior to class.

B. Develop a list of possible policies and programs for this company to better reconcile work and family life before class.

C. Share your group's recommendations with the rest of the class.

Form groups of three to five students, share your ideas with one another, and write out your group recommendations for policies and procedures to better reconcile employee work and family responsibilities on Form 2.3. Form 2.3 should also be used to provide details of your recommendations as well as a time frame for implementation. This time frame will depend upon how high a priority the group assigns to a particular recommendation and how much time will be required to work out the details of the proposal. In preparing your recommendations, consider the pros and cons of responding to the needs of nurses with small children without alienating other nurses who do not have small children.

D. Present your group's recommendations to the instructor and to other class members.

Background

Sunshine Health Services provides home healthcare services to a metropolitan area of 1.5 million in Florida. Patient visits are primarily based on referrals from physicians and health systems. The company currently offers services in eight different locations in the area and served 11,000 patients in their homes over the past year. Sunshine is a for-profit facility that generated revenues of $10,400,000 dollars and a net profit of $430,000 dollars in the most recent fiscal year. The company currently employs a total of 243 staff, of which 186 are nurses.

Most of the home visits are conducted by home health nurses. However, the nursing shortage has negatively impacted the company's ability to recruit and retain the number and quality of nurses needed to service the existing volume of patient visits, much less staff up for the four percent annual growth in patient visits per year expected through 2015.

Home health care has had a difficult time competing for new nursing graduates because pay rates are lower than those in hospitals. The 18 percent turnover rate of nurses at Sunshine exceeds the area nurse turnover rate of 12 percent. In addition to salary, some nurses prefer the hospital environment to home health care and others feel hospitals offer more "family friendly" benefits as compared to home health care. Currently Sunshine provides either part-time (20 hours per week) or full-time (40 hours per week) employment options. However, they do not offer any type of flex time.

The company has taken the position that the individual's family and work life are, and should be, separate. Both require time and effort, but should never interfere with each other. The company's philosophy has been that each individual has a responsibility to hire or otherwise provide child-care service or whatever other services are necessary for the proper functioning of the family. The company's responsibility has been only to provide part-time and full-time jobs for employees while serving customer needs.

Recently, that philosophy has been challenged by several employees who claim the company is insensitive to employees who have family responsibilities. In particular, they cite the lack of any child-care facilities and family-leave policies. They argue that uniform personnel policies applied rigidly to all employees (irrespective of their family situation) are inherently unfair. If the company really viewed their employees as family members, it would be more flexible in accommodating the employee's family responsibilities.

The company CEO, Renee Brent, recently read an article in *BusinessWeek* identifying the best companies for women. This article identified a number of family-oriented policies and programs followed by 24 leading companies. Among the most significant of these were modifications in the company culture, executive development to enhance sensitivity, subsidized babysitting, child care, sick-child care, telecommuting, on-site take-home meals, elder care, job sharing, mentorship programs, women on the Board, career development policies, family leave policies, maternity leave with partial pay, modified work and family benefits, flexible benefits, hiring a pluralistic workforce, job sharing, mentoring programs, and part-time professional and/or executive positions. Some of the 24 corporations identified in the *BusinessWeek* article were in health services.

A potential major source of nursing staff for the company is the large number of nurses in the area who are out of the labor force. While some of these have left the field permanently to pursue other opportunities, others have left the field on a temporary basis to raise children or for other reasons. If a substantial number of these nurses could be enticed back into the labor force through the development of attractive job options at Sunshine, the nurse staffing issue might be elevated. Such options would need to meet the needs of a largely female work force to help them balance their work and family responsibilities.

FORM 2.3 *Recommendations for Reconciling Work and Family Life at Sunshine Health Services*

Policy or Program	Specific Details	Time Frame for Implementation*
1.		
2.		
3.		
4.		
5.		
6.		
7.		
8.		
9.		
10.		
11.		
12.		

**short-term within the next year; intermediate term one to two years; long-term more than two years.*

32 SKILL BUILDER

Human Resource Forecasting Assignment

I. OBJECTIVES

A. To give you practice in forecasting an organization's human resource needs.

B. To familiarize you with some of the factors that affect an organization's future human resource needs (growth, automation, turnover).

C. To familiarize you with the complexities involved in making human resource forecasts.

D. To point out that all human resource forecasting is based on assumptions and that these assumptions are critical to the accuracy of the forecast. Incorrect assumptions lead to erroneous forecasts.

II. TIME REQUIRED TO COMPLETE: One to two hours

III. INSTRUCTIONS

You have been given the assignment of forecasting the human resource needs of the National Bank and Trust Company which currently employs approximately 1,100 people. The bank presently has 50 branch offices located throughout the metropolitan area, each of which employs approximately 14 individuals. The bank expects to add 38 branches during the next three years. Branches within the bank differ considerably in size, so the figures given represent averages.

During the past month, the bank has placed an order for 30 automated teller machines to be placed in its former branch offices. These machines are scheduled to be in operation December 31, one year from now. The bank has found that for each new machine purchased, one less teller is needed, on average. A breakdown of the bank's current staffing is shown in Table 2.1.

The bank has asked you to perform three human resource forecasting tasks. First, based on the assumptions given below, you are required to determine employee turnover for the main office, the former branches, and the new branches. Your boss would like to know this information for each of the next three years and for each of the major personnel categories (i.e., supervisors, tellers/clerical, and main office). Your job is to complete Table 2.2.

Second, your boss would like to know the number of new employees the bank will need to hire for each major personnel category for each of the next three years. Your job is to complete Table 2.3.

Table 2.1 *Present Staffing*

Total Employees	**1,100**
Number of Branches	50
Supervisors per Branch	4
Number of Supervisors	200
Tellers per Branch	10
Number of Tellers	500
Branch Employees	700
Main Office Employees	400

Table 2.1 *Turnover*

Employee Category	Year 1	Year 2	Year 3
Former Branch Supervisors			
Former Branch Tellers			
Main Office			
New Branch Supervisors			
New Branch Tellers			

Table 2.3 *Number of Employees to be Hired*

Employee Category	Year 1	Year 2	Year 3
Former Branch Supervisors			
Former Branch Tellers			
Main Office			
New Branch Supervisors			
New Branch Tellers			
Totals			

Table 2.4 *Year-End Employment*

Employee Category	Year 1	Year 2	Year 3
Former Branch Supervisors			
Former Branch Tellers			
Main Office			
New Branch Supervisors			
New Branch Tellers			
Totals			

Finally, your boss would like to know the total number of employees who will be working for the bank as of the end of each of the next three years. Your job is to complete Table 2.4.

In order to complete your assignment, your boss has told you to make a number of assumptions. They are:

A. You are making all projections in December for subsequent years ending December 31.

B. With regard to former branches, assume

1. The 50 former branches employ four supervisors and ten clerical personnel/tellers each.
2. On December 31 (one year hence), 30 teller machines are placed in operation and replace 30 tellers.
3. The bank does not terminate any employees because of the new teller machines. Rather, as tellers quit throughout the year, 30 are not replaced.
4. Turnover is 30 percent for tellers/clerical personnel, and 20 percent for supervisors.

C. With regard to new branches, assume

1. New branches are added as follows: 10 in Year 1, 12 in Year 2, and 16 in Year 3.
2. Each new branch employs 14 individuals (four supervisors and ten tellers/clerical).
3. New branches are added evenly throughout the year. Thus, for the purpose of calculating turnover, on average, there are five new branches in Year 1 (50% 10); 16 in Year 2 [10 in Year 1 plus 6 (50% 12)]; and 30 in Year 3 [22 plus 8 (50% 16)].
4. Turnover is 30 percent for tellers/clerical personnel, and 20 percent for supervisors.

D. With regard to the main office, assume that turnover will be 10 percent per year.

33 Skill Builder

Phased Retirement Options

I. Objectives

A. To give you practice in using the Internet to generate information relevant to solving human resource problems.

B. To familiarize you with the various options to traditional employee retirement.

II. Time Required to Complete: One to two hours

III. Instructions

Read the "Situation" below and then search the Internet for the following: 1) phased retirement options; 2) advantages or benefits of each option for employees and the employer; and 3) disadvantages or costs of each option.

Possible Web sites are:

http://www.magicnet.net/benefits.index.html

http://www.vcn.bc.ca/timework.worksite.htm

http://www.insword.com/newsletter/index.html

Then, fill in Form 2.4 by identifying three phased retirement options and provide at least one advantage and disadvantage for each of the three listed options. Be prepared to present your findings and recommendations to the class.

Situation

The Owens Engineering Company provides a full range of engineering services to a wide variety of governmental and private organizations in the Denver metropolitan area. Ron Owens, the company president, has become increasingly concerned about his company's demographics. Two-thirds of their 82 engineers range in age from 50 to 67 years old. The company's current retirement policy is to offer retirement to all employees who reach age 55 or more, with 25 or more years of service.

Within the next few years, Owens has determined that 42 percent of the engineers will be eligible for retirement, and based on past company data, 70 percent will retire within two years of their actual eligibility. This means he expects to lose 29 out of 82 engineers to retirement over the next four years. In addition, the "normal" annual turnover rate among engineers has been 8 percent. This would reduce the company's pool of engineers by another seven per year, or 28 over the next four years.

After discussing the situation with Susan Barber, the human resources manager, Owens concludes that most voluntary turnover is unavoidable. While the company provides competitive salaries and benefits for the Denver area, the local unemployment rate is relatively low (averaging 7.8 percent), and there are few unemployed engineers in the area. Future forecasts are for a continued tight labor market for engineers in Denver.

Owens and Barber determined that the best way to deal with their potential engineer shortage is to retain older engineers as they become eligible for retirement. This decision is not only based on the numbers, but also on the qualities and qualifications the company anticipates losing. For example, when four senior civil engineers retired during the past year, the company lost their contacts and influence, their knowledge of their customers, special

FORM 2.4 *Phased Retirement Options*

Option 1	
Advantages/Benefits to the Company	**Advantages/Benefits to the Employee**
1.	1.
2.	2.
3.	3.
Disadvantages/Costs to the Company	**Disadvantages/Costs to the Employee**
1.	1.
2.	2.
3.	3
Option 2	
Advantages/Benefits to the Company	**Advantages/Benefits to the Employee**
1.	1.
2.	2.
3.	3.
Disadvantages/Costs to the Company	**Disadvantages/Costs to the Employee**
1.	1
2.	2.
3.	3.
Option 3	
Advantages/Benefits to the Company	**Advantages/Benefits to the Employee**
1.	1.
2.	2
3.	3.
Disadvantages/Costs to the Company	**Disadvantages/Costs to the Employee**
1.	1.
2.	2.
3.	3.

requirements in the contract bidding process, and their knowledge about who to see and how to get things done internally.

Barber is a friend of your human resource management instructor this term. Your instructor has assigned your student team the term project of assisting Owens Engineering in assessing its options for retaining its older engineers.

Recruitment and Selection

34 CASE

Recruiting Recreational Vehicle Surveyors

Liberty Engineering Company is located in a large suburb of Cleveland, Ohio. The company was founded during the 1940s and does a considerable amount of drafting and design work for the major automotive companies and their suppliers. When sales in the auto industry are high, Liberty Engineering experiences a significant volume of work. However, when recessions hit the automotive marketplace, work at Liberty also sharply decreases.

In an attempt to stabilize revenues, the president of Liberty Engineering decided it would be prudent to diversify the company by bidding on government contracts. The company had little experience in these areas, but the president felt that this would not preclude it from bidding on contracts and obtaining them.

Within a six-month period, the company had bid on and lost two contracts. However, a third bid pertaining to the safety and use of recreational vehicles proved to be successful. The contract was for several hundred thousand dollars and was granted on a cost-plus basis. The government was interested in obtaining information regarding how people actually use recreational vehicles such as pick-up truck campers, motor homes, and various kinds of camping trailers. Ultimately, the purpose of the study was to determine what additional safety rules, if any, should be established relating to the manufacture and use of recreational vehicles. Among the pieces of information desired by the government were how much weight citizens place in their recreational vehicles, what kinds of trailer hitches are in use, whether recreational vehicles have proper suspension systems, and to what extent citizens are aware of the safety features of their recreational vehicles.

In Liberty Engineering's proposal to the government, the company stated that it would recruit, select, and train qualified individuals to survey over 1,000 recreational vehicles. The surveying would be done at three different sites: in the desert, at the seashore, and in the mountains. At a meeting with government officials, three locations were selected: Lake Mead, Nevada; Cape Hatteras, North Carolina; and Smoky Mountains National Park, Tennessee. Two other important decisions were also made at the meeting. First, to ensure consistency of data collection, all surveyors would be trained together at a campground at Smoky Mountains National Park. Second, the employees would then be divided and sent to their respective job sites. It was also decided that each survey crew would consist of one leader and four surveyors, and that two crews would be sent to each data collection site.

All responsibility for recruiting and training the 30 employees (6 leaders and 24 surveyors) fell upon the shoulders of Bob Getz, the new human resource director. Getz had worked as a designer for Liberty Engineering for 20 years before being transferred to human resources. At the same time that a project Getz had been working on for two years ended, the then-current human resource director resigned, so he was a logical choice. In addition, Getz was well-liked by most of Liberty's older employees and knew a great deal about the company's policies and procedures. Getz's major shortcoming was that he knew little about staffing activities.

Before recruiting potential job applicants, Getz knew that he would first need to develop a set of job descriptions for all 30 employees. Since crews would be doing essentially similar jobs, albeit at different locations, he needed only to develop job descriptions for each of four survey positions and that of the leader. Hence, he obtained the list of data that was to be collected on each vehicle, determined the tasks required to collect the data, and divided the tasks into four job positions. Getz realized that the job duties of each surveyor would ultimately need to be changed based on actual experience. Nonetheless, he sketched out the following job descriptions:

Surveyor I: Take pictures of recreational vehicle with a camera. Interview driver and record information received.

Surveyor II: Read and record scale weights for each recreational vehicle tire. Take tire pressures and measure tread depth. Record make, size, and air capacity of each tire.

Surveyor III: Unhook trailer hitch, if present, and record make of hitch, ball diameter, and whether levelers are present. Determine type of suspension on recreational vehicle and count number of leaf springs, if present.

Surveyor IV: Stop recreational vehicle as it enters campground, explain to driver the purpose of the study, ask the driver to participate in study. When survey of recreational vehicle is complete, discuss the findings with the driver.

The leader's responsibilities would be to plan daily work activities, motivate the employees to do the surveying, complete all forms, and do occasional troubleshooting.

With job descriptions in hand, Getz met with Norm Larson, vice president of Liberty Engineering Company, who was ultimately responsible for conducting the recreational vehicle surveys. During the meeting, Getz learned that all 30 employees were to meet at Smoky Mountains National Park on June 10. They were to be trained on the job for four days, and the company would provide them with lodging and food while they were there. All employees were to provide their own transportation to the park, to their subsequent job sites, and then back home. The company would pay them for travel time but would not provide any mileage allowance, lodging, or food. Upon arrival at the job site, employees would need to find accommodations for July and August, and would receive no lodging or food allowance from the company during their stay. Once work commenced at each job site, employees would be responsible for providing their own transportation to and from the campground.

All employees were to be paid $11.15 per hour. No vacation benefits, sick days, or other major benefits would be provided. The company would, however, provide benefits mandated by law such as Social Security and workers' compensation. No one under the age of 18 would be hired because of safety reasons.

After the meeting with Larson, Getz decided he should check with the campground management at the different job sites. He learned that most recreational vehicles leave campgrounds early in the morning and enter late in the afternoon. Few arrive or depart between 10 AM and 4 PM. In order to survey a maximum number of vehicles, crews would need to work from 6 AM to 11 AM and from 3 PM to 8 PM, a total of ten hours a day. Therefore, each crew could work a four-day-on and a four-day-off schedule. Getz was told that temperatures at Cape Hatteras would range between 65 and 95 degrees Fahrenheit, while at Lake Mead they would range between 85 and 115 degrees Fahrenheit. Neither of these locations would provide employees with any shade; hence, employees at these sites would need to work in the sun and wear uniforms, including hats. The Smoky Mountains National Park location would be cooler than the others and surveying could be done in shaded areas. When Getz asked the campground managers whether they knew of any people who would be interested in working on the survey project, their response was, "You've got to be kidding." The manager at Lake Mead campground flatly told Getz that he could not conceive of any person being willing to drive from Lake Mead to Tennessee and back under the conditions he outlined. He suggested that Getz put a want ad in the Cleveland newspaper.

After talking with the campground managers, Getz was quite depressed. He knew that he had to hire 30 employees within the next few weeks. He knew that six of them had to have sufficient leadership skills to get the job done while not antagonizing the employees so much that they would quit. He further realized that the 24 surveyors would have to enjoy the outdoors and be willing to tolerate extreme heat. He realized, too, that the ideal surveyor would be one who had above-average knowledge of auto mechanics, legible handwriting, reasonable communication skills, and an ability to work well with others under adverse conditions. What Getz did not know was how he could recruit and hire 30 people who fit this description.

QUESTIONS

1. If you were Bob Getz, how would you recruit the needed employees?
2. Evaluate the Lake Mead campground manager's suggestion that Getz recruit employees by placing a want ad in the Cleveland newspaper.
3. What should the firm do if they are unable to recruit sufficient employees for the job?

35 CASE

Recruiting and Selecting High-Level Managers through the Internet

Michael Jackson is the president and CEO of a small hotel corporation (Jackson Hotels, Inc.) which caters to high-end vacationers in resort communities. The company currently employs 2,144 staff members at its corporate headquarters in Palm Springs, CA and its other hotels in Scottsdale, AZ; Aspen, CO; Orlando, FL; Santa Fe, NM; Sea Island, GA; and Charleston, SC. Recently, the company underwent a strategic planning process. The plan envisions adding ten new locations and tripling its workforce over the next five years. The human resource challenge is to recruit experienced and high-quality managers for its corporate headquarters, recruit managers for new hotels, and manage existing and expansion hotels in a variety of managerial roles.

Up to the present, Jackson has relied on his contacts in the hotel industry to recommend candidates for these positions. Some have been hired and some have not, and many of those hired have not performed as well as Jackson had hoped and expected. During an informal discussion with Carol Cross, one of his hotel managers, Cross suggested most of the larger hotel chains now recruit their managers and other professionals through the Internet. She suggested that Internet recruitment might enhance both the quantity and quality of the applicant pool.

Jackson then asked his vice president of human resources, Shirley Gomez, to research online recruiting and make recommendations to him. She reported the following:

- Finding qualified and motivated employees was one of the top three business worries among small companies like his own.
- Almost all large companies and many small companies now provide online recruiting and some only accept online applications.
- Almost all applicants for professional and managerial positions now use the Internet.
- Another trend is the use of online prescreening tools to separate the qualified applicants from the unqualified.
- Some hotel chains are now tapping into skilled foreign labor through the Internet.
- There are more than 2,500 Web sites that contain job postings and among the most prominent generic Web sites are:

  http://www.monster.com
  http://www.careerpaths.com
  http://www.careerbuilder.com
  http://www.careermosaic.com
  http://www.hotjobs.com
  http://www.flipdog.com
  http://www.jobtrak.com
  http://www.spherion.com

- The latest generation of Web tools includes online job fairs in which companies can meet candidates in a virtual environment and can chat with them online.
- All approaches to online recruitment and selection seem to be cost effective relative to alternatives.
- The three main approaches to Internet recruiting are job boards (like the Web sites above), professional/career Web sites, which focus on particular occupations and professions, and employer Web sites.

Gomez has asked your professor of Human Resources Management (Dr. Martin Cannon) to help her formulate recommendations for Jackson. Dr. Cannon has asked your class to meet in small groups of two to four students each to address her questions and report to the class. These questions are outlined below.

QUESTIONS

1. What are the advantages and disadvantages of Internet recruitment and selection for a small, but expanding company like Jackson Hotels? How would you minimize the disadvantages?
2. Which of the above three approaches to online recruiting and selection (if any) makes the most sense in this case and why?
3. What prescreening hurdles would you impose in your Internet recruitment in order to pre-qualify a small number of truly qualified applicants? Why?
4. Based on your knowledge of other companies' Web sites, what information should Jackson Hotels provide to job applicants and what steps should follow Internet recruitment to identify the most qualified applicants?

36 CASE

Recruiting and Selecting Low-Level Workers among Seniors

Jackson Hotels, described previously in Case 35, also has a challenge in recruiting and selecting lower-level employees in their resort hotels for such jobs as desk clerk, night manager, reservations, maid service, food service, and maintenance. In many cases, the labor pool of qualified candidates found in larger cities is simply not available or adequate in or near resort communities.

Shirely Gomez, vice president for human resources, has determined that senior citizens might be the best recruitment option for Jackson Hotels given the high-income customers the hotel chain seeks to serve. Her rationale is they have a vast amount of experience, lower accident rates, lower absentee rates, and higher job satisfaction scores than younger workers. As a result of changing attitudes of both employers and employees as well as the increasing availability of seniors in resort areas, she noted that many other companies have begun to target seniors for recruitment. These organizations realize seniors usually have proven employment experience, job savvy, reliability, interpersonal skills, and commitment to the employer. She believes these qualities are important determinants of success in the hotel jobs she hopes to fill in the future. She is also aware that many seniors gravitate toward independent contracting, on-call work, and temporary assignments rather than full-time employment.

Gomez is concerned that some hotel chains have been successfully sued for failure to do adequate background checks on all new employees. In some cases, this failure resulted in the theft of personal property or worse. Consequently, she is aware that whatever processes of recruitment and selection she initiates will need to incorporate some type of background investigation. Up to the present, she has relied on local newspaper advertisements and applicant interviews with hotel managers to recruit and screen applicants. Results have been unsatisfactory thus far due to high turnover and mixed performance among the newly hired employees. She expects present recruitment approaches to be even more inadequate as the hotel chain expands over the next five years. She has asked your professor, Dr. Martin Cannon, to help her focus her recruitment and selection strategies for the years ahead. More specifically, she has asked him to help her answer the questions below. Dr. Cannon, in turn, has asked your class to form groups of two to four students each to discuss these questions and report to the class.

QUESTIONS

1. What recruitment sources do you recommend Jackson Hotels use to recruit seniors for the kinds of positions they are planning to utilize? Why?
2. What background investigations, if any, would you recommend to differentiate acceptable from unacceptable job candidates? Why?
3. What selection criteria and processes would you recommend to identify the best candidates? Why?

37 CASE

Selecting Patient Escorts

City Hospital is located in the heart of a large midwestern city. It is one of five major hospitals in the area and has recently built a small addition for treating well-known patients, such as professional football players, top company executives, and singing stars. Visiting or local celebrities always choose City Hospital if they need treatment.

City Hospital has about 1,200 hospital beds and employs 4,500 individuals, including about 40 patient escorts. The job of patient escort is a rather simple one, requiring only minimal training and no special physical talents. When patients need to be moved from one location to another, patient escorts are summoned to assist in the move. If the move is only a short distance, however, a nurse or orderly can move the patient. Of particular importance is the fact that patient escorts almost always take patients who are being discharged from their hospital room to the front door of the hospital. A wheelchair is always used, even if the patient is able to walk unassisted. Thus, the typical procedure is for the nurse to call for a patient escort. The escort then gets a wheelchair and goes to the patient's room, assists the patient into the wheelchair, picks up the patient's belongings, wheels the patient down to the hospital's front door or to his or her car in the parking lot, and returns to the work station.

The job of patient escort is critical to the hospital since the escort is always the last hospital representative the patient sees, and hence has a considerable influence on the patient's final perception of the hospital. Of approximately 40 escorts, about three-fourths are men and one-fourth are women. Most are high school graduates in their early twenties. Some, particularly those on the early morning shift, are attending college at night and working for the hospital to earn money to pay college expenses. Four of the escorts are older women who had previously served as hospital volunteers and then decided to become full-time employees instead. Turnover among patient escorts is quite high and has averaged 25 percent in recent years. In addition, upward mobility in the hospital is quite good, and as a result, another 25 percent of the escorts typically transfer to other jobs in the hospital each year. Thus, about half of the patient escorts need to be replaced annually.

The hospital follows a standard procedure when hiring patient escorts. When a vacancy occurs, the human resource department reviews the file of applications of individuals who have applied for the patient escort job. Usually the file contains at least 20 applications because the pay for the job is good, the work is undemanding, and few skills are required. The top two or three applicants are asked to come to the hospital for interviews. Typically, the applicants are interviewed first by the human resource department and then by the patient escort supervisor. The majority of those interviewed know some other employees of the hospital, so the only reference check is a call to these employees. Before being hired, applicants are required to take physical exams given by hospital doctors.

Every new escort attends an orientation program the first day on the job. This is conducted by a member of the hospital's human resource department. The program consists of a complete tour of the hospital; a review of all the hospital's HR policies, including a description of its promotion, compensation, and disciplinary policies; and a presentation of the hospital's mission and philosophy. During this orientation session, employees are told that the hospital's image in the community is of major importance and that all employees should strive to maintain and enhance this image through their conduct. After orientation, all patient escorts receive on-the-job training by their immediate supervisor.

During the last two years, the hospital has experienced a number of problems with patient escorts, which have had an adverse effect on the hospital's image. Several patients have complained to the hospital administration that they were treated rudely, or in some cases roughly, by one or more patient escorts. Some complained that they were ordered around or scolded by an escort during the discharge process. Others stated that their escorts were careless when wheeling them out of the hospital to their cars. One person reported that an escort carelessly tipped him over. All escorts are required to wear identification tags, but patients usually cannot remember the escort's name when lodging a complaint to the hospital. Additionally, the hospital usually has difficulty determining which escort served which patient because escorts often trade patients. Finally, even when the hospital can identify the offending escort, the employee can easily deny any wrongdoing. He or she often counters that patients are generally irritable as a result of their illness and, hence, are prone to complain at even the slightest provocation.

At the hospital administrator's request, the human resource manager asked the chief supervisor of patient escorts, the head of the staffing section within the human resource department, and the assistant human resource director to meet with her to review the entire procedure used to select patient escorts. It was hoped that a new procedure could be devised that would eliminate the hiring of rude, insulting, or careless patient escorts.

During the meeting, a number of suggestions were made as to how the selection procedure might be improved. Criticisms of the present system were also voiced. The chief supervisor of patient escorts argued that the problem with the hospital's present system is that the application form is void of any useful information. He stated that the questions that really give insights into the employee's personality are no longer on the application form. He suggested that applicants be asked about their hobbies, outside activities, and their personal likes and dislikes on the application form. He also suggested that each applicant be asked to submit three letters of recommendation from people who know the applicant well. He wanted these letters to focus on the prospective employee's personality, particularly the applicant's ability to remain friendly and polite at all times.

The assistant human resource director contended that the hospital's interviewing procedure should be modified. He observed that, during the typical interview, little attempt is made to determine how the applicant reacts under stress. He suggested that if applicants were asked four or five stress-producing questions, the hospital might be in a better position to judge their ability to work with irritable patients.

The head of the staffing section noted that patient escorts require little mental or physical talent and agreed that the crucial attribute escorts need is the ability to always be courteous and polite. He wondered whether an attitude test could be developed that would measure the applicant's predisposition toward being friendly, helpful, sensitive, and so on. He suggested that a job analysis could be done on the patient escort position to determine those attitudes that are critical to being a successful patient escort. When the job analysis was complete, questions could be developed that would measure these critical attributes. The test questions could be given to the hospital's present patient escorts to determine whether the test accurately distinguishes the best escorts from the worst. The head of the staffing section realized that many of the questions might need to be eliminated or changed, and if the test appeared to show promise, it would probably need to be revalidated in order to meet government requirements. He felt, however, that a well-designed test might be worth the effort and should at least be considered.

The meeting ended with all four participants agreeing that the suggestion of trying to develop an attitude test was probably the most promising. The assistant human resource director and chief supervisor of patient escorts stated that they would conduct a thorough job analysis covering the patient escort position and develop a list of attitudes that are critical to its success. A second meeting would then be scheduled to prepare the actual test questions.

QUESTIONS

1. Critique each of the alternative approaches suggested for solving the problem of selecting patient escorts at City Hospital.
2. Recommend a procedure for recruiting and hiring patient escorts.
3. Besides improving its selection procedures, what other actions could the hospital potentially take to improve the behavior of the patient escorts?

38 CASE

A Solution for Adverse Impact

A federal government agency was in need of assistance regarding its staffing practices. Recently, some of the job applicants had complained that the selection procedures for one of the entry-level law enforcement jobs were discriminatory. The personnel specialists, who had previously ignored this possibility, were now alerted to the potential problem of adverse impact against women and minorities.

Bob Santos was a personnel specialist for the agency and had been employed with the staffing division for almost three years. He kept up with the laws and regulations on discrimination and equal employment opportunity. About two months ago, he attended a training seminar on the Uniform Guidelines on Employee Selection Procedures. Upon returning to the agency, Santos decided that an evaluation of their current staffing practices was necessary because they were developed prior to the adoption of the Uniform Guidelines in 1978. These Guidelines were designed to provide a framework for determining the proper use of selection procedures. They indicated how organizations should evaluate their selection rates using the four-fifths rule, and also specified the standards that organizations should use to validate their procedures.

THE SELECTION PROCESS

The selection of entry-level agents for the law enforcement job involved a two-step, multiple-hurdle process. Applicants were first required to pass a cognitive ability test, a similar but somewhat easier test than the Scholastic Aptitude Test (SAT). The exam was made up of 25 verbal items and 25 quantitative items. A candidate was required to receive a passing score of 70 (35 of the items correct) in order to be eligible for the second step of the selection process, an interview. A three-member panel of supervisors asked each applicant questions on how they would deal with various hypothetical job situations. After an initial period of questions regarding the applicant's education and experience, the applicant was given a situation and then asked to respond to the situation. Typically, after each candidate's initial response, further questioning would ensue from the panel to determine the full response of the candidate. The interview would last about a half hour. At the end of the interview, the three interviewers would rate the candidate on ten dimensions, including attitude, motivation, communication, and so on. Candidates receiving high scores on most of the dimensions would pass the interview. After a physical examination and a security check, the candidate would be hired and asked to report to training.

THE DETERMINATION OF ADVERSE IMPACT

Santos knew that the guidelines required employers to make adverse impact determinations at least once a year. Although records had been kept, the agency had not calculated the selection rates over the past three years. Santos thought that it was long overdue and decided to have this done as soon as possible. A week later, the selection rates were tabulated. The data are presented in Exhibit 2.7.

After calculating the adverse impact for both the test and the interview, he decided that a discussion with the personnel psychologist in the agency would be necessary. A meeting was arranged between Santos, his supervisor and head of the staffing division, and the personnel

This case was prepared by Ronald J. Karren, Isenberg School of Management, University of Massachusetts.

EXHIBIT 2.7 *Tabulation of Selection Rates*

Group	Number Who Took Test	Pass Rates for the Test Number Who Passed	Pass Rate %
Whites	282	134	47.5
Blacks	36	10	27.8
Hispanics	102	44	43.1
Asians	0	0	0
Native Americans	0	0	0
Men	385	170	44.2
Women	35	18	51.4
Total	420	188	44.8

Group	Number Who Interviewed	Pass Rates for the Interview Number Who Passed	Pass Rate %
Whites	112	87	77.7
Blacks	8	5	62.5
Hispanics	40	22	55.0
Men	148	109	73.6
Women	12	5	41.7
Total	160	114	71.2

Note: The number interviewed for each group is less than the number who passed the test. The difference represents individuals who did not wish to continue through the second part of the selection process.

psychologist for the agency, Ron Burden. A discussion ensued regarding the validation requirements of the Uniform Guidelines. It was decided that the original job analysis was poorly done and that very little documentation had been retained by the agency. Although there was a task inventory, the major tasks or job duties had not been rated for importance, frequency, difficulty, and trainability. Burden pointed out that this documentation would be critical if they ever needed to defend the selection procedures in court. By the end of the meeting, the group decided that it would probably be a good idea to do another job analysis that was in accordance with the new Uniform Guidelines. Burden felt that the selection procedures would have to be modified to fit the results of the job analysis. He was asked to determine how the job analysis would be done, while Santos would coordinate the project in the field.

JOB ANALYSIS

The Uniform Guidelines recognize that there is not a single best way to analyze the job. Since there was little documentation available, Ron Burden had to decide on a method or technique that would generate from the agents and supervisors the important work responsibilities and the tasks associated with them. After much deliberation, he decided to use the critical-incident technique. Burden knew that if the agency wanted to continue using situational questions in the interview, the critical-incident job analysis technique readily lends itself to the development of this type of question. The method involves collecting reports of behaviors that are critical, in that they distinguished between successful and unsuccessful work performance. Instructions to the agents and supervisors were to include

1) the circumstances that preceded the incident, 2) the setting in which the incident occurred, 3) what the agent did that was effective or ineffective, and 4) the consequences of the incident.

Burden asked a sample of agents to develop three critical incidents and to indicate the task associated with each critical incident. Upon receipt of the critical incidents, Burden and Santos derived an inventory of work behaviors. This list of work behaviors was then sent back to the agents, and they were asked to rate the importance of the behavior, how frequently it was performed, and the amount of training that was required to learn that behavior.

When this information was collected, Burden and Santos generated a list of major job tasks or job duties. They assigned all the important work behaviors to their associated tasks. This list of tasks and work behaviors was then sent out to a group of supervisors who were asked to review the list. This same group of supervisors were also asked to meet for a two-day conference later in the month to determine the important knowledge, skills, abilities, and other characteristics (KSAOs) required to perform these work behaviors. Burden also planned for these experts to select the critical incidents to be used for the new interview.

Supervisory Conference

At the conference, the supervisors were given the inventory of tasks and their corresponding work behaviors. They were asked to derive the KSAOs and then rate how important the skill or ability was for the performance of the work behaviors. The most important knowledge, skills, abilities, and other characteristics are shown in Exhibit 2.8.

The job experts were asked to evaluate the current staffing practices in light of this list of KSAOs. Burden, Santos, and the supervisors agreed that the content of the exam would have to be changed to reflect the first three KSAOs. Burden proposed a reading comprehension exam in which the content would be a small sample of the procedures, laws, and regulations that are taught at the training academy. Applicants would read a section and then answer questions regarding the laws and regulations taught in that section. This type of test has been called a "miniature training and evaluation test." All the parties agreed that this job-related procedure would be a good way of assessing the first three KSAOs.

The job experts wanted to retain the interview. Burden and Santos agreed as long as the following conditions were met:

1. All interview questions would have to be job-related.
2. Critical incidents from the job analysis would be selected to assess the last five KSAOs.
3. Sample answers to each critical incident would be determined in advance. Interviewee responses would be rated on a five-point scale defined explicitly in advance.

EXHIBIT 2.8 *KSAOs Derived from the Task/Behavior Inventory*

1. Knowledge of federal law
2. Knowledge of procedures and regulations
3. Reading and verbal comprehension
4. Ability to perform effectively in dangerous situations
5. Ability to communicate effectively
6. Skill in interpersonal relations
7. Judgment ability
8. Ability to solve problems quickly and effectively

4. The same scoring method would be used for each applicant. All procedures would be used consistently for each applicant so that all applicants had the same chance of being selected.
5. All interviewers would be required to attend a training session to learn how to administer and assess the structured interview.

The supervisors agreed to these conditions. However, they did not want the interview to be completely structured. They felt that the interview should begin with a few questions regarding the applicant's past education and experience. Burden and Santos agreed to this with the stipulation that this information should not bias the candidate's assessment and scoring at the end of the interview.

When Burden and Santos returned to the agency, they were happy about what had transpired at the supervisory conference. The question that remained was the type of validation to be used on the newly developed selection procedures. Burden felt that they should validate the selection procedures with a criterion-related validity strategy. They would collect the scores for both the interview and the test and later compare them to either success in training or their performance appraisal at the end of the first year. Since Burden was familiar with these procedures, he felt that this was a preferred strategy over a content validity strategy. On the other hand, Santos felt that a predictive validity study was too costly and unnecessary. Since their newly developed procedures were job-related, a content validity approach was sufficient. Instead of arguing over which type of validation strategy to use, they decided to discuss the matter with Santos's supervisor and meet again later in the week.

QUESTIONS

1. Is there any evidence of adverse impact against any race, sex, or ethnic groups?
2. If the total selection process for a job has no adverse impact, should the individual components of the selection process be evaluated for adverse impact?
3. Which type of validation would you use? Why? What are the differences between content and criterion-related validity studies?
4. Evaluate the job analysis procedures used in this case. Is it necessary to do such a thorough analysis?
5. If you are doing a criterion-related validity study, should your criterion be success in training or on-the-job performance?

39 Case

The Use of Social Media for Employee Recruitment and Selection

Karen Johnston is a 55-year-old director of a small health planning agency in an urban area of the South. Her agency employs a total of 18 staff members, most of whom are female. As a graduate of the MBA program with a Healthcare concentration, she has been an active alumnus of that program at the local state university. She also serves as chairperson of the Community Advisory Board (CAB) for the program and has taken two student interns a year for her agency over the past eight years. The CAB advises the program faculty concerning curriculum, accreditation issues, internships, job placements, scholarships, etc.

Recently, Johnston was asked by the program's internship director to select one master's student intern for the upcoming fall semester and she agreed to do so. He then forwarded to her the resumes of three students for her consideration as he had done in the past. Previously, she had considered grade point average, previous work experience, and career goals in making her decision concerning who to interview and who to select for the internship.

This time she decided to also see if any of the internship candidates had posted profiles on social media Web sites such as Facebook, Twitter, or LinkedIn. To her surprise, all three (one male and two females) had posted profiles on at least one of these social media Web sites. Two of the three posted information regarding their student extracurricular activities, work activities, family, and friends. Karen found those to be helpful in helping her form a more complete picture of the internship applicant. However, the third profile posted on Facebook by one of the female applicants shocked her. She found semi-nude pictures, allusions to heavy drinking, and a comment that Lisa "was looking for a hot guy to bring out my wild side."

Johnston immediately called the internship coordinator and told him that she would like to interview the first two students and would select one for the internship. However, she told him that the third applicant should never have been allowed into the masters program and that he needed to have a long "heart-to-heart" talk with her if she was to have a future in the field of health services administration. She also suggested that this student might be counseled to seek employment in another field altogether. Then when the CAB met, Johnston described her experience to the faculty and executive board members. When the program director explained that faculty have little control over the personal lives of students, Johnston suggested that perhaps they need to counsel students concerning "professional behavior."

Questions

1. What lessons can you draw from this case regarding how students, employers, and faculty can use social media such as Facebook during the recruitment and selection process?
2. What policies, if any, should employers develop concerning the use of social media for various purposes, including employee recruitment and selection?

40 EXERCISE

Evaluating the Recruiting Function

I. OBJECTIVES

A. To make you aware of the necessity of evaluating the efficiency and effectiveness of various recruitment sources.

B. To provide you with practice analyzing data, drawing conclusions, and planning a strategy to remedy identified problems or deficiencies.

C. To make you aware of the linkages among staff turnover, recruitment sources, recruitment methods, and adequate staffing.

II. OUT-OF-CLASS PREPARATION TIME: 2 hours

III. IN-CLASS TIME SUGGESTED: 45 minutes

IV. PROCEDURES

Read the entire exercise, including the background on St. Vincent's Hospital. Then, using the data provided in Exhibit 2.9, do the calculations on Form 2.5. A yield ratio is the number of applicants necessary to fill vacancies with qualified people. It is the relationship of applicant inputs to outputs at various decision points. For example, the yield ratio for all recruitment sources in Exhibit 2.9 shows that 273 nurse applicants were generated over the three-year period from 2007 to 2009. Since only 221 were classified as potentially qualified, the yield ratio is 273/221 or 1.24 to 1. The yield ratio for "potentially qualified" among "walk-ins" is 1.26 (53 ÷ 42). The average cost per nurse hired among "walk-ins" is $119.23 ($1,550 ÷ 13). Students should form groups of two to four students each and calculate the yield ratios for each recruitment source at each stage of the recruitment process on Form 2.5. These data show that the hospital needs to start with more than five times as many applicants as it needs to fill job openings and more than 13 times as many applicants as it hopes to have as above-average performers.

Do the calculations for Form 2.5 on your own prior to class. Think about the implications of these data for future recruitment at the hospital. Then, look at Exhibit 2.10 in conjunction with the background description and think about the implications for the recruiting process. During the class period, form groups of three to five, which will act as a consulting team for the hospital. With your group, discuss and answer the questions at the end of this exercise. At the end of the class period, have a spokesperson for each group discuss the group's answers and rationale with the entire class.

BACKGROUND

St. Vincent's Hospital is a 260-bed hospital in a northeastern city affiliated with the Roman Catholic Church. The administrator is Sister Claire, a 56-year-old member of the Daughters of Charity religious order. During the last decade, the hospital operated with a nursing staff of approximately 450 registered nurses and experienced a nursing turnover rate of about 25 percent per year. The turnover rate was average for the city during this time period. However, it has accelerated to an average of 35 percent over the past three years.

These higher turnover rates have put additional pressure on the recruiting process to provide larger numbers of qualified candidates. However, Sam Barnett, director of human resources, has reported more difficulty locating qualified nurse candidates over the last three years. Barnett's office has prepared the recruitment data shown in Exhibit 2.9. The data show that 273 applicants (from all sources) had to be screened to produce 52 qualified candidates who accepted a job offer. One year later, 19 of these 52 had left the hospital. The last column shows the direct and indirect costs of recruitment by source, including clerical time, supervisor time, and direct costs, such as travel and postage. The human resource department has also conducted a telephone survey of all the nurses they could locate who did not accept a job offer from the hospital during the most recent three-year period. Reasons for such rejections are shown in Exhibit 2.10.

Sister Mary Louise, the 62-year-old director of nursing service, has conducted all off-site recruitment for many years. This includes attending both the local Nursing Job Fair and the State Nursing Association Annual Meeting. She has begun to feel burned out as a result of all her external recruiting and internal evaluation of candidates over the years.

At a recent meeting, she suggested that an outside group (your group) be brought in to analyze the recruiting process, identify problems and opportunities, and suggest improvements. Sister Mary Louise and Barnett readily agreed to an outside consultant because they are aware of current nursing shortages due to declining nursing school enrollments. St. Vincent's Hospital itself contributed to this enrollment decline by closing its own School of Nursing due to fewer applications and the high cost of operation.

EXHIBIT 2.9 *Data on Recruitment Sources for Registered Nurses at St. Vincent's Hospital, 2007–2009*

Recruitment Source	Number of Applicants	Potentially Qualified	Invitation for Interview	Qualified and Offered Job	Accepted Job	One-Year Survival	Above-Average Rating	Total Recruitment Costs
1. Internet applications	83	72	60	38	21	12	5	$1,145
2. Walk-ins	34	17	8	6	3	1	1	900
3. Employee referrals	13	12	7	5	4	3	2	400
4. Newspaper ads	24	16	8	4	2	1	0	750
5. Journal ads	19	18	10	8	4	2	2	450
6. Educational institutions								
Junior colleges	16	13	11	6	2	2	1	1,200
Hospital-based schools	8	8	3	2	1	0	0	800
University programs	24	24	16	14	10	8	7	1,300
7. Private employment agency	9	9	8	5	2	2	1	4,000
8. Public employment agency	8	4	2	1	1	0	0	600
9. Direct mail	15	14	4	3	1	0	0	450
10. Job fair	13	7	5	3	1	1	1	900
11. State Nursing Association meeting	7	7	4	3	0	0	0	1,150
Totals	273	221	146	98	52	33	20	$14,045

FORM 2.5 *Yield Ratios at Each Step in the Recruitment Process and Recruitment Cost per Nurse Hired, St. Vincent's Hospital, 2007–2009*

	Yield Rates						
Recruitment Sources	**Potentially Qualified**	**Accepted Interview**	**Offered Job**	**Accepted Job**	**One-Year Survival**	**Above-Average Rating**	**Average Cost Per Nurse Hired**
1. Internet applications							
2. Walk-ins							
3. Employee referrals							
4. Newspaper ads							
5. Journal ads							
6. Educational institutions							
Junior colleges							
Hospital-based schools							
University programs							
7. Private employment agency							
8. Public employment agency							
9. Direct mail							
10. Job fair							
11. State Nursing Association meeting							
Averages for all sources	1.24	1.87	2.79	5.25	8.27	13.65	

EXHIBIT 2.10 *Reasons for Nurse Rejection of a Job Offer from St. Vincent's Hospital, 2007–2009*

Reason	Number	Percent
Recruitment Processes		
Job attributes not communicated	2	4.3
Negative perception of recruiter	12	26.1
Negative perception of hospital	2	4.3
Lack of timely follow-up	13	28.3
Perceived lack of honesty in recruitment process	1	2.2
Negative information from recruiter	1	2.2
Job Attributes		
Location of hospital	3	6.5
Salary offer	2	4.3
Hours of work	2	4.3
Promotional opportunities	0	0.0
Fringe benefits	0	0.0
Working conditions	3	6.5
Perceived poor job "match"	5	10.9
Totals	46	100.0

Since recruitment of new nurses has begun to fall behind turnover of nurses employed at St. Vincent's Hospital, the vacancy rate has begun to increase. Five years ago, only 11 percent of staff nursing positions were unfilled. This percentage has now increased to 23 percent. One result has been an exhausting workload on the existing nursing staff. In addition to increased turnover, the symptoms of staff burnout (i.e., stress, conflict, absenteeism) are becoming more evident.

QUESTIONS

1. How would you evaluate the nurse recruiting strategy currently being used by St. Vincent's Hospital? Is the hospital using too few or too many recruiting sources? Why?
2. If you feel that the hospital is using too many recruitment sources, which ones would you eliminate and why?
3. What stage or stages in the recruitment process seem to be most amenable to improvements? What specific improvements would you suggest to decrease the yield ratios? Why?

41 EXERCISE

Selection Decisions

I. OBJECTIVES

A. To make you aware of the complex criteria often used to select candidates for administrative positions.

B. To help you develop skills in planning and implementing semi-structured interviews.

C. To give you practice in preparing for, participating in, or evaluating the selection interview.

II. OUT-OF-CLASS PREPARATION TIME: 2 hours

III. IN-CLASS TIME SUGGESTED: 45 minutes

IV. PROCEDURES

A. Read the entire exercise including the "Background," "Questions for the Semi-structured Interview," and the various forms. During the previous class period, the instructor should have selected eight students in the class to prepare for two in-class interviews in the following class period. The eight consists of four executive committee members, two applicants, and two observers (one for each interview). These eight will role play interviews of the two applicants or act as an observer for each interview.

B. Prior to class, the six interviewers or interviewees should prepare for their respective roles in the role playing exercise. Committee members should fill in the first two columns of Form 2.6 and the interviewer questions on Form 2.7 in pencil or on a separate sheet of paper. This will facilitate committee discussion, reduce the amount of class time needed for interview preparation, and save the forms themselves for the final list of criteria (Form 2.8) and interview questions (Form 2.7). Committee members should be prepared to play their roles (Form 2.7) as they would expect the described individuals to behave in real life. The observer for each group interview (two in total) read Form 2.8 in advance. Then, he or she should fill it out during the interview and be prepared to discuss it at the end of the class period.

The two applicants in each group should review their résumés in either Exhibit 2.11 or Exhibit 2.12 and be prepared to elaborate on any of the data in the résumé, as well as to provide supplementary information not on the résumé to the committee. An alternative to using two class members as job applicants is to use two individuals from outside the class.

C. During the class period, the four person interview committee should spend 10 to 15 minutes comparing notes and designing a final set of criteria and weighting system for Form 2.6 and interview questions for Form 2.7.

Neither the applicants nor the observers should be present during these discussions. When the committee is ready, the applicants should be called from outside the room one at a time. In the meantime, the applicants should be doing final preparations for their interviews, including consideration of how they will respond to hypothetical questions that may be asked.

Possible selection criteria the committee may want to consider are: previous experience as a hospital CEO, educational background, ability to "fit" into the organization in terms of personal views and goals, knowledge of Brookdale Hospital and its problems, ideas for solving the hospital's problems, interpersonal skills, communication skills, and administrative skills.

D. Each candidate is then interviewed for 10 to 15 minutes. After each interview, board members fill out the remainder of Form 2.6 including the rating of each candidate on each criterion, the total score for each, and any additional comments. The observer will take notes and make an evaluation on Form 2.8 during the interviews. At the conclusion of the two interviews, the committee will compare notes and make a decision concerning which candidate should be recommended for the position and why.

E. When the committee has finished the interview and assessment process, the instructor will ask each the committee and observers to report to the entire class in the following order: the committee decision and rationale, the performance of the two applicants, and each observer's report. Lessons learned concerning the selection interview process are then presented by both interviewers and interviewees. Depending on class size, this "wrap-up" phase should take 10 to 15 minutes.

BACKGROUND

Brookdale Hospital is a 420-bed proprietary (for-profit) hospital located in a large midwestern city. The hospital was originally founded by a group of local physicians in 1948. In 1982, they sold out to one of the national hospital chains and are now part of a large system of hospitals involving 49 hospitals with about 12,000 beds in 18 states (mostly in the Midwest). The corporation follows a policy of decentralization. Consequently, while corporate support services have been provided, the hospital has continued to operate with a great deal of autonomy.

Recently, the hospital has begun to experience declines in occupancy rates and increased annual deficits. John Rhodes has been the CEO for the past eight years. Two months ago, he suffered a stroke and, at the advice of his physician, has decided to retire at age 55. The board of trustees has appointed the associate administrator, Terry Bradford, as the acting administrator and CEO while a search for Rhodes's replacement is made. The executive committee of the board has advertised the position widely over the past six weeks in a variety of professional publications, including *The Wall Street Journal*.

As a result of the résumés generated through this recruitment process, the board has selected the two top candidates for the position: Terry Bradford and Chris Smith, an administrator of a small 60-bed hospital in a nearby city. Résumés for each are shown in Exhibits 2.11 and 2.12. The committee has also developed a job description for the position as shown in Exhibit 2.13.

The process for hiring a new CEO requires a formal vote by the entire board as well as concurrence by the president of the corporation. However, the latter two steps have always been formalities. The critical decision is the recommendation of the executive committee. This committee consists of the following four individuals: Sam Gordon, Amanda Simpson, Steve Bailey, and Jane Sears.

Gordon is a physician and the chief of the medical staff (salaried position), and has been with the hospital for 13 years. He is 58 years old and has a specialty in general surgery. He has been concerned about what he views as the eroding power of physicians' vis-à-vis administrators and outside regulators over the past few years. Consequently, he would like the

EXHIBIT 2.11 *Résumé 1*

TERRY A. BRADFORD
119 Brook Hollow Lane
Columbus, Ohio

Job Objective

To secure a position as chief executive officer for a large proprietary hospital in the Midwest.

Education

1982–1986: Oberlin College, Oberlin, Ohio
Major: Sociology
Degree: BA, June 1986, *cum laude*, GPA 3.52

1992–1993: Ohio State University, Columbus, Ohio
Major: Business Administration
Emphasis: Organization Behavior
Degree: MBA, June 1993, GPA 3.86
Member: Beta Gamma Sigma (national scholastic honorary in Business)

Other: After completing my MBA, I took two additional graduate courses in accounting and one additional course in finance at Ohio State University.

Employment History

November 2006–Present:	Acting Administrator, Brookdale Hospital, Columbus, Ohio
February 1995–November 2006:	Associate Administrator; Brookdale Hospital, Columbus, Ohio Duties: liaison between the CEO and the medical staff, nursing staff, and other major hospital departments; represents administrator at various functions; strategic planning and marketing; reviews financial and occupancy data.
June 1988–February 1995:	Assistant Administrator; Oakland Hospital, Oakland, Ohio Duties: worked with the Administrator and Associate Administrator on a variety of administrative functions in finance, personnel, marketing, and public relations.
August 1986–June 1988:	Personnel Assistant; Bayview Municipal Hospital, Bayview,Ohio Duties: designed personnel appraisal form, conducted selection interviews, designed and taught courses for supervisors, and designed advertisements for positions.

Personal

Date of Birth:	September 6, 1964
Height:	5'8"; Weight: 150 lbs.
Marital Status:	Divorced, no children
Hobbies:	Music, travel, and swimming

committee to recommend someone who can work well with physicians, understand their needs, and generally support their desires to provide high-quality patient care.

Simpson is president of the city council and was selected for both the board and the executive committee because of her political contacts. Her goals are to make sure the hospital survives, keeps its costs under control, and continues to provide some care for indigents. Since Brookdale is one of the major hospitals in the city serving her constituents, Simpson naturally is concerned that the corporation may shut its doors due to the deficits it has been experiencing. She feels the hospital has to be more innovative in developing and marketing new services to offset the declines in inpatient services.

EXHIBIT 2.12 *Résumé 2*

CHRIS A. SMITH

Home Address	**Office Address**
2057 Hickory Street	Administrator
Tiffin, Ohio	Morningside Hospital
	204 Jefferson Street
	Tiffin, Ohio

Personal: Married, two children

Educational Background:
BS—Heidelberg College, Tiffin, Ohio (1987)
MBA—Cleveland State University, Cleveland, Ohio (1992)

Experience:

Morningside Hospital, Tiffin, Ohio	November 1991–Present
Administrator	June 2006–Present
Associate Administrator	June 1998–June 2006
Assistant Administrator	November 1991–June 1998
Eastside Hospital Financial Manager, Tiffin, Ohio	June 1988–November 1991
McLains Department Store Financial Manager, Tiffin, Ohio	January 1987–June 1988

Member: Rotary Club and First Baptist Church

Interests: Snow skiing and politics

Bailey is president and CEO of Applied Electronics, a very successful company that he founded 18 years ago. He admits he still does not know much about health care, but has been a member of the board for 12 years due to his entrepreneurial talents and his business contacts. His view is that the hospital needs to become more entrepreneurial and businesslike, and focus on services that are profitable. He also believes that the hospital has not done enough to raise funds through private philanthropy.

Sears is the president of a local bank. She has an MBA from the Wharton School and has been in banking for 22 years. Her major concern is the deteriorating financial position of the hospital. In her view, the new CEO should have excellent financial management skills as well as an ability to work well with physicians. She views the previous CEO (Rhodes) as deficient in these areas.

The committee has invited both Bradford and Smith to interview for the position of CEO. The outline for the selection process is shown on Form 2.6 and the form for questions to be developed by the committee is on Form 2.7.

QUESTIONS FOR THE SEMI-STRUCTURED INTERVIEW

In its purest form, a structured interview occurs when the interviewers bring to the interview a list of predetermined questions to ask the interviewee. The advantage is that the interviewers have previously discussed and agreed upon the relevant criteria. During the interview, all interviewers focus on these criteria. Weighting of these criteria is often used as well. This systematic process usually results in higher levels of consistency among interviewers than is the case with unstructured interviews.

EXHIBIT 2.13 *Job Description: Chief Executive Officer, Brookdale Hospital*

Description of Work

General Statement of Duties: Supervises and coordinates administrative work of a complex nature involving the entire hospital and all its components; represents the hospital to outside stakeholders.

Supervision Required: Implements policies developed by the board of directors.

Supervision Exercised: Plans, organizes, motivates, coordinates, and directs a staff of administrative and clerical personnel. Total direct supervision involves over 15 individuals.

Example of Duties

1. Initiates and coordinates activities related to long-range planning and marketing of the hospital's services.
2. Develops and enforces policies and procedures related to administrative functions.
3. Coordinates major staff services, including budget, personnel, medical services, nursing services, dietetics, and housekeeping.
4. Develops and compiles administrative reports as required by the board or external regulatory agencies.
5. Performs related work as required.

Required Knowledge, Skills, and Abilities

Extensive and broad knowledge of complex management systems (internal and external) in a healthcare environment. Skill and ability in planning, marketing, personnel management, and financial management. Ability to relate to external stakeholders, including the board of directors.

Qualifications for Appointment

Education: Graduation from a college or university with major coursework in business administration, public administration, or health administration.

Experience: Ten years or more of progressively responsible experience in administration or management.

However, structured interviews do not allow the interviewee to discuss a topic of his or her choice or to provide additional information on areas that require further explanation. An unstructured interview emphasizes creating a supportive climate and helping the interviewees discuss values, goals, objectives, and career plans.

A compromise that retains the benefits of a structured interview while also creating the openness of the unstructured interview is the semi-structured interview. Here, the interviewers not only develop a set of structured questions to evaluate the candidate based on the agreed-upon criteria, but also ask open-ended questions, such as "What are your long-term career goals?" and "Why is that important to you?"

Develop a list of up to ten questions to ask the two applicants and decide which committee members should ask which questions. Be sure to consider the criteria identified on Form 2.6 as well as some open-ended questions designed to learn more about the applicant. Write these questions on Form 2.7.

FORM 2.6 *Criteria for Selecting a CEO and Ratings of Applicants Based on These Criteria*

Criteria: Major Dimension of the CEO Job (based on the job description/ personal characteristics desired	Weight of the Criteria (1–5)	Job Applicant Rating on the Criteria (1–10)		Total Score (Weight × Rating)		Comments About Each
		Bradford	Smith	Bradford	Smith	
1.						
2.						
3.						
4.						
5.						
6.						
7.						
8.						
9.						
10.						
Total Scores						

FORM 2.7 *Questions for Interview**

1.

2.

3.

4.

5.

6.

7.

8.

9.

10.

*Develop interview questions that are not biased or illegal, but which relate to the performance dimensions developed in Form 2.6.

FORM 2.8 *Observation Sheet*

1. How well did the committee establish rapport with each applicant?

2. How well did each of the candidates respond to the committee's questions? What improvements would you suggest? Why?

3. Approximately what percentage of the 15-minute interview time was spent listening to the applicant and what percentage consisted of committee questions and/or comments? How appropriate was this breakdown?

4. Did the committee overemphasize negative information, ask illegal questions, show bias based on irrelevant factors, or otherwise treat either applicant unfairly?

5. Did the committee probe unclear areas, or did it allow short answers that did not provide necessary information?

6. What is your overall assessment of the success of the committee in eliciting relevant information for making this selection decision? Why?

7. How well did the questions asked of the interviewees reflect the criteria established in Form 2.6?

42 EXERCISE

Selection Interview Role Play

I. OBJECTIVES

A. To help you develop skills in conducting selection interviews.

B. To provide you with practice in applying the basic principles of effective interviewing.

II. OUT-OF-CLASS PREPARATION TIME: 30–90 minutes, depending on role played (Students who play the applicant will need to prepare a résumé.)

III. IN-CLASS TIME SUGGESTED: 45 minutes

IV. PROCEDURES

The class should be divided into groups of three: an interviewer, applicant, and observer. Roles should be assigned ahead of time so you will have time to prepare your role. This is especially important for those of you who will play the role of interviewee since you are to use your own résumé and qualifications during the role play. The interviewer should prepare a set of interview questions. Read the scenario that follows and the role description provided by the instructor. Participants should assume that the interview is taking place in a campus placement office. The role play begins when the applicant arrives for the interview, and ends when both individuals have accomplished their objectives. At the end of the role play, the interviewer completes the interviewer's report (Form 2.9) and shares it with the applicant. Next, the observer provides feedback on his or her observations to the group (Form 2.10). The group then identifies and discusses the hardest part of the interview from both the interviewer's point of view and the applicant's perspective. If time permits, the entire class then discusses the reliability and validity of the interview as a method of selecting applicants for jobs.

SCENARIO

The director of college recruiting for Duro Insurance Company is presently recruiting college students for its administrative trainee program. The one-year training program involves a combination of on-the-job and formal classroom training. Upon successful completion of the training, a candidate is assigned a position as assistant department supervisor.

Duro Insurance Company ranks in the top 15 percent of life insurance companies nationally with in-force insurance in excess of $6 billion. Duro markets all forms of insurance, bonds, and pension products on an individual and group basis. More recently, the company added diversified financial services, including discount brokerage services, real estate financing, and mutual funds. The company is divided into six major divisions: Employee Benefits, Commercial Insurance, Individual Life, Automobile, Homeowners, and Diversified Financial Services and functionally into several major operating departments: Sales, Underwriting, Administrative, Loss Prevention, Actuarial, Claims, Legal, Financial and Investments, Advertising and Public Relations, Personnel, and Research and Policy Development. Duro has over 25,000 employees and more than 300 field offices throughout the country. Management at each field office consists of a manager, several department heads, and their assistants. The company has enjoyed a pattern of steady growth and expansion over the years.

Job Description for Administrative Trainee

1. Handle day-to-day administration of field office, including direct supervision of office clerks.
2. Plan and oversee the use of space, furniture, and equipment on a continuing basis and recommend changes as necessary.
3. Supervise computer processing operations for issuing and servicing insurance policies, including claims.
4. Implement and maintain accounting and collection procedures. The trainee works closely with the department head in learning these duties.

Job Qualifications

1. BS/BA with business management background (knowledge of accounting desired).
2. Ability to communicate effectively.
3. Ability to handle detail.
4. Ability to plan and direct activities of subordinate personnel.
5. Demonstrated leadership potential.
6. Knowledge of computers and software packages including Microsoft Office.

Additional Job Data

1. The trainee position reports directly to a department head.
2. Expected career progression is to assistant department supervisor (1–2 years) and, with continued development, to department head (4–5 years after supervisory assignment).
3. The position requires relocation.
4. The company offers competitive salaries and benefits, including a tuition repayment plan and in-house career planning and development.

FORM 2.9 *Interviewer's Report*

Applicant ______________________ Position ______________________

Date ______________________ Interviewer ______________________

Rate the applicant's background and behavior, taking into consideration the factors listed for each area. Circle a rating for each factor. Give an overall rating, also.

1. Presentation (appearance, manner, oral communication skills, interest, motivation):

   Poor 1 2 3 4 5 Excellent

2. Education (major, intellectual abilities, academic achievement, knowledge of field):

   Poor 1 2 3 4 5 Excellent

3. Work experience (related experience, skill and competence, job performance, interpersonal skills, leadership):

   Poor 1 2 3 4 5 Excellent

4. Summarize candidate's strengths:

5. Summarize candidate's weaknesses:

6. Overall evaluation and recommendation:

   Poor 1 2 3 4 5 Excellent

Recommendation: ( ) Invite for field visit ( ) Do not invite

Comments:

FORM 2.10 *Observation Sheet*

1. What was the quality of the interaction between the interviewer and applicant?

2. What type of interview did the interviewer use (structured, semi-structured, or nonstructured)? How well did it work?

3. Were the questions job-related?

4. What did the interviewer do to put the applicant at ease?

5. Did the interviewer listen? Did the interviewer spend too much time talking?

6. Did the interviewer follow up on questions not completely answered?

7. Did the interviewer gain enough information to make a decision about the applicant?

8. General observations.

43 EXERCISE

Which Selection Procedure Is Most Effective?

I. OBJECTIVES

A. To examine the strengths and weaknesses of four different methods for selecting new employees.

B. To enhance your oral communication skills.

II. OUT-OF-CLASS PREPARATION TIME: 30 minutes to prepare for the debate

III. IN-CLASS TIME SUGGESTED: 50–75 minutes

IV. PROCEDURES

Your instructor will divide the class into five groups at the end of class prior to conducting this exercise. There will be four debating groups consisting of three to five members each and one or more groups of "judges" that consist of the remaining class members. Debaters will be assigned one of four positions and told to prepare to argue in favor of that position. Judges will be told to read the textbook chapter pages that cover those positions. The issue to be debated is: Which approach to selecting new employees is relatively most effective? The positions are: 1) the structured interview; 2) the unstructured interview; 3) ability and personality tests; and 4) reviewing applications and résumés, and talking to or getting letters from listed references.

At the start of the next class, your instructor will announce that a four-way debate will be held. The judges' role in the debate is to "search for the truth." They are to listen to the different sides presented and then, after the debate is finished, to tell the class what they believe is the "correct" answer to the debate question, not who "won" the debate.

The debate consists of two rounds. The purpose of Round One (15–20 minutes) is for each team to learn the position of the other debating teams. Hence, each team has up to five minutes to explain their position as comprehensively as possible. At the completion of Round One, the debating teams are given up to ten minutes to prepare criticisms of each of the other three teams for Round Two. During this intermission, judges are to discuss what they have heard and begin to formulate their own position.

In Round Two (15–20 minutes), each debating team is given up to five minutes to criticize the position of each of the other teams. Unlike a traditional debate, teams are not allowed to rebut the criticisms made by others. They must simply listen to them. Round Two ends when Team Four has finished criticizing the position of the other three teams.

After the debate has ended, the judges have five minutes to discuss the issue among themselves and to arrive at a consensus, if possible. The judging team(s) then explains its decision to the debaters.

44 Exercise

Selecting from Imperfect Applicants

I. Objectives

A. To make you aware of the difficulties involved in selecting from a group of applicants who are not well qualified.

B. To give you practice in making selection decisions.

C. To familiarize you with possible selection criteria.

II. Out-of-Class Preparation Time: 10 minutes to read the exercise and determine which applicant should be hired

III. In-Class Time Suggested: 30–45 minutes

IV. Procedures

Either at the beginning of class or before, read the exercise and determine which of the three applicants should be hired. You must hire one of the three people, even though none are perfect candidates.

After each class member has individually determined which applicant should be hired, the instructor will divide the class into groups of three or four. Each group must then discuss each applicant and examine each person's strengths and weaknesses. Based on this analysis, applicants are to be ranked in terms of desirability. After all of the groups are finished with their analysis, a representative from each group will present the group's decision as to which applicant should be hired, the criteria used, and the reasoning behind the decision.

Situation

Buck Fleming operates a two-person saw mill in a small village in one of the northern states. The village has a population of about 60 during the winter months and about 800 during the summer months. It is located on a large lake, and has a general store, a bar, a volunteer fire department building, and a small post office. The nearest larger town is about 45 miles away and has a population of about 5,000.

After contracting with property owners, Fleming cuts trees on their property and takes the logs to his mill, saws them into boards, and then trucks them to buyers. If the trees are veneer quality, he does not cut them into boards himself but sells them to another mill. Fleming does not pay the property owner until after the logs have been sold, thereby minimizing his out-of-pocket expenses. Once logs arrive at his mill, they are run through a machine, aptly called a debarker, which removes the bark. Then, Fleming saws the logs into boards of various lengths and widths, moves then along a conveyor, and stacks them in piles to dry out. When the boards are dry, he loads them onto his truck and delivers them to buyers.

Fleming has had a difficult time hiring the one extra person he needs to run his operation. Most last only a short time and then quit. The job is quite dangerous, extremely dirty, and must be performed outside in the hot summer sun or in the cold, oftentimes snowy fall and spring. Little work gets done during the coldest winter months. Mosquitoes and black flies are another problem, particularly during May and June. Several years ago, an employee was working underneath a piece of heavy equipment when a log brace fell over, killing the man. Everyone in the area knew about this tragic accident, making it harder for Fleming to hire a new person.

Fleming wants to hire someone who could do all the jobs related to his operation, except running the saw that cuts the logs. He reserves this job for himself. He needs an employee who can drive a bulldozer to make a road to get to the trees, cut down trees either with a chain saw or a tree shearer, operate a skidder and a front-end loader, and drive a large logging truck. In addition, the person needs to be able to run the debarker, stack logs and boards, and help perform maintenance on all of the equipment. The employee will frequently come into contact with land owners when cutting trees on their property, so a good first impression is helpful, as well as a friendly personality. Fleming is willing to train someone to perform all of these operations if necessary, but would prefer someone who already has some of the needed skills. Fleming believes that the two most important selection criteria are the employee's ability to come to work on time every day and not to quit after a short time period.

The price of lumber increases during booms in the housing and remodeling business and decreases during a recession. Now, prices are low which makes it hard for Fleming to make a profit. As a result, he feels that he can only pay an employee $11.00 an hour with no benefits except those required by law. Fleming realizes that this is low, but it is the best he can offer until lumber prices rise. His most recent employee quit because he was offered a job that paid more, leaving Fleming in the position of needing a new helper now.

Fleming recently placed an advertisement in the local newspaper and received calls from three applicants. He then interviewed each and was not impressed with any of them. Nonetheless, he needs to hire one of them soon. The information on each applicant is given below. Some of this information he learned directly from the applicants, and some he obtained by talking with his friends who knew the applicants. In such a rural area, everyone knows almost everyone.

Chuck Maki

Chuck Maki is a polite, personable, nice-looking 22 year old who graduated from high school. He lives within one mile of the saw mill with his parents and knows the area and its people well, having lived here all of his life. Although Maki did not offer the information, Fleming knew that he had been in jail twice over the past three years for a total of about eight months. He was arrested for DUI and his license was suspended. While driving on a suspended license, Maki was arrested again. He has also been arrested for car theft and vandalism. When Fleming directly asked him about this, Maki replied that he knew he had a problem with liquor. In all instances he had gotten drunk and done "stupid things," but he has been sober for two weeks. Maki's driver's license is currently suspended but he hopes to get it back shortly. In the meantime, his parents will drive him to work or he can walk. Chuck has no prior logging experience, having worked as a bartender for a few years after graduating from high school. He is currently unemployed and is willing to start work immediately.

Bud Hoover

Bud Hoover is approximately 25 years old and has never finished high school. For the past month, he has lived in a trailer with three friends about 20 miles from the saw mill and is currently unemployed. He grew up in Kentucky and has worked in a variety of jobs, keeping most of them for less than six months. During the past three years, he had held five different jobs, all in different towns. He has had experience as a pizza delivery driver, a car washer, a tire changer, a dishwasher, and a yard maintenance employee. He has no knowledge of logging equipment, but says he likes working on trucks and other equipment. Hoover seems to be an incessant talker and is a heavy smoker. He has an older car for getting to work and can start work after he returns from a trip in two weeks.

Jim Bryce

Jim Bryce is in his mid-thirties and has worked in the construction trade since dropping out of high school. He was laid off from his job in Florida five months ago due to a lack of work and has not found a new job since. Several years ago he fell off of a barn roof and hurt himself badly. Then, a year later he cut his hand with a miter saw, needing further hospitalization. Jim accumulated so many medical bills that he needed to declare bankruptcy. He wears his hair long, has several tattoos, and needs dental work. He lives about 35 miles from the mill, temporarily staying with his uncle, and has an old truck that needs repair. Jim loves to work outdoors, and the cold and heat do not bother him. He has a good knowledge of construction but not of logging, logging equipment, or the area. He is available for work immediately.

45 INCIDENT

The Ethical Selection Dilemma at Integrity Motors

BACKGROUND

Integrity Motors has been retailing quality used cars and trucks for the past ten years. It is located in a large midwestern city, and has become the largest and most successful used car dealership in the region. Integrity Motors employs 11 full-time salespersons. Timmy Blackburn, the owner, wants to maintain a policy of having a lean, yet highly productive staff, which means that the employees have to be dependable, highly competent, and willing to work at a high level of productivity for long hours each day.

After ten years at Integrity Motors, the sales manager was resigning to start his own business. Blackburn felt he needed the same type of employee he had had in the position—someone who had considerable experience as a sales manager, was a good motivator, had good communication and management skills, was creative, and who would be committed to the dealership for many years. Although Blackburn felt it prudent to take the necessary time to carefully select a new sales manager, time was of the essence because the end of the year was approaching and the inventory needed to be drastically reduced.

Applications for the job started pouring in almost immediately. After a week, 45 applicants had expressed interest in the job, of which ten potentially suitable candidates were invited for interviews. A panel comprised of the office manager, Helen Smith; the service manager, Joe Washington; and Timmy Blackburn interviewed the ten applicants. Based on the interviews, it was clear that one candidate, Gladys Morrison, was outstanding compared to all other applicants. Morrison had recently moved to the area from a metropolitan city where she was a sales manager for 15 years. Everyone agreed that she was the perfect candidate. The next morning an offer would be extended to Morrison. Everyone left the meeting feeling satisfied that they had made an excellent choice.

A NEW DEVELOPMENT

The next morning when Blackburn arrived at the dealership he was met by Smith and Washington, who seemed troubled. Apparently, after the meeting the prior evening, Smith happened to meet an old friend at a convenience store. The friend told Smith she was four months pregnant and that, coincidentally, her new neighbor was also four months pregnant. To Smith's surprise, the pregnant neighbor was Gladys Morrison, the person to whom the dealership would extend a job offer the next morning. Smith said nothing to her friend about Morrison's employment inquiry or pending job offer, yet throughout the night, Smith pondered about the potential hire.

The next morning, as Smith shared this development with Blackburn and Washington before Gladys Morrison was contacted, all three discussed the potential consequences of hiring Morrison. Washington was astounded that Morrison had not informed them of her pregnancy. Blackburn quickly told him that legally she did not have to tell them, and furthermore, any employment decision could not be based on her pregnancy. Smith observed that though legally this was true, from a practical standpoint the dealership could not afford to be without a sales manager for an extended period of time. Blackburn, too, was concerned about her potential absence as well as her potential inability to work for long periods under intense pressure, especially when they needed to reduce inventory. Smith also reminded them that although Morrison was clearly the best applicant, there were at least nine other applicants who would be suitable sales managers.

QUESTIONS

1. What are the legal and ethical issues involved in this case? Was it ethical for Gladys Morrison to have applied for the position in the first place?
2. Should the owner hire Morrison or some other applicant? Should the information about the pregnancy be considered?
3. If Morrison is hired, how could Integrity Motors accommodate her pregnancy?

Contributed by James C. Wimbush, Indiana University

46 INCIDENT

The Exit Interviews and Employee Retention

William James has recently been hired as the director of human resources for an academic medical center located in the Northeast. While he was interviewing for the position, several administrators and physicians told him that employee morale, particularly among registered nurses, was extremely low. James later learned that the annual turnover rate of nurses at this facility has averaged 18.4 percent as compared to 11.6 percent in the metropolitan area over the past three years.

James was aware that all exiting employees are required to complete an exit interview questionnaire and interview prior to receiving their final paycheck. He then asked his assistant to pull the files for all exit interviews of departing nurses and prepare a summary of the major reasons for leaving and specific suggestions for how the facility could increase its retention of nurses.

When the results were compiled, James was disappointed. The utility of these data was very low. Most of the respondents indicated they were leaving for personal reasons, family responsibilities, or another job offer. Very few volunteered recommendations for how the facility could improve nurse retention even when asked directly on both the questionnaire and during the interview. The recommendation mentioned most frequently was better parking.

The prevailing opinion of individuals with whom James spoke was that departing employees are reluctant to discuss any sensitive issues or concerns for fear of alienating the interviewer or supervisor. He was told no one wanted to possibly jeopardize their recommendation to other employers due to anything they might say during the exit interview. Through his informal conversations with nurses and nurse supervisors, he knew there were many problems and concerns shared by many nurses including inadequate staffing, lack of respect and support from supervisors and top management, favoritism in salary increases and promotions, and high stress levels due to all of the above. Yet, he was unable to document these problems and others with the current exit interview data.

James is now attempting to determine the best methods of identifying employee problems and assessing employee reaction to the organization, its various components, and various human resource policies and programs. He is also interested in determining the factors which cause many of the long-tenured nurses to stay.

QUESTIONS

1. Discuss the nature and causes of the problem of nurse retention.
2. Should James attempt to improve the exit interview process? If so, how should this be done?
3. What other assessment alternatives should he consider using in addition to, or rather than, exit interviews in order to determine the underlying causes of turnover and enhance retention in the future?
4. How can James use the information generated about why nurses stay or leave to improve nurse retention?

47 INCIDENT

Nepotism

Though Ellen Arnold had been with the firm less than six weeks, she had already caused considerable problems for Jim Staples, Doris Nusbaum, and the architects. Staples was the office manager whose branch of a large architectural firm had 25 architects and 8 personal assistants. While he was in charge of the entire office, Nusbaum was in charge of the assistants who were not assigned to work for particular architects, but were assigned by Nusbaum to tasks on an as-needed basis.

Ellen Arnold had been brought to the office by her father, one of the firm's founders who worked at a different office. The father announced that he had hired his daughter to work for Nusbaum during this and future summer vacations from college. Unfortunately, Arnold had no skills whatsoever that related to the duties required. In addition, the office was fully staffed and did not need any additional help.

Nusbaum was irate when she learned that she was to find work for and supervise Arnold. She was particularly upset that Arnold was hired without the firm following the standard selection process and that Arnold was just "dumped on her doorstep." She told Staples, "Ellen has no knowledge of architecture whatsoever. I have no work for her. I don't want to have anything to do with her!"

On her first day of work, Arnold was shown her desk but was assigned no specific tasks. Within a few days, she introduced herself to all of the architects and started spending more and more time in their offices. Wanting to make a favorable impression on Arnold's father, the architects willingly talked with her at length. One of the young architects was particularly taken by her, and vice versa. She spent more time in his office than in any other office. Meanwhile, the other personal assistants were starting to complain about all of the attention that Arnold was receiving and that she was not doing her share of the administrative tasks. In addition, the architects were falling behind in their work. A vicious rumor was circulating that Arnold had a brother who also might be thrust upon the office. During all of this, Nusbaum refused to have anything to do with Arnold and reminded Staples that she was his problem.

QUESTIONS

1. What are the major problems in this case?
2. If you were Jim Staples, what steps would you take to solve the problems depicted in this case?
3. What are the advantages and disadvantages of having a "no nepotism" policy?

48 SKILL BUILDER

Evaluating Job Application Forms

I. OBJECTIVES

A. To familiarize you with the criteria for selecting questions to put on an application form.

B. To give you practice in evaluating the questions on an application blank.

II. TIME REQUIRED TO COMPLETE: 1 hour

III. INSTRUCTIONS

Review the application form that appears in Exhibit 2.14. This form is used by United Holy Radio Network for their administrative and clerical employees. You should thoroughly review the legal requirements for pre-employment inquiries and other relevant information on application forms found in your text. Use the guide below to evaluate the questions that appear on the application. Prepare a short write-up summarizing your findings and make specific recommendations for improving the questions.

QUESTIONS TO BE ASKED IN EVALUATING APPROPRIATENESS OF APPLICATION BLANK ITEMS

1. Is this question job-related?
2. Will answers to this question have an adverse impact in screening out members of protected groups (i.e., disqualify a significantly larger percentage of members of one particular group than of others)?
3. Is this question really needed to judge an applicant's qualifications and suitability for the job?
4. Does the question constitute an invasion of privacy?
5. Can the applicant's response to this question be verified?

EXHIBIT 2.14 *Job Application Form*

United Holy Radio Network Application for Employment

PHOTO

Name: ______________________________
(Last) (Middle initial) (First)

Street Address: ______________________________

____
(City) (State)

Sex: **Male** **Female** **Age:**______

Own home: Yes No How long?______ Rent: Yes No How long?______

Phone No. (___) ______________________________

Marital Status: Married Divorced Never Married Widowed (circle one)

If married indicate name of spouse: ______________________________

Of what country are you a citizen?: ______________________________

Indicate languages spoken fluently: ______________________________

List all physical disabilities:______________________________

Religion: ______________________________

Church membership: ______________________________

Name of Minister: ______________________________

How often do you attend church? ______________________________

List church activities:______________________________

Do you smoke?: Yes No Do you consume alcoholic beverages?: Yes No

Have you ever been arrested?: Yes No Indicate offenses: ______________

Military experience: ______________ Type of discharge: ______________

Education

High school name: ______________ Date of graduation: ______________

Business or technical school name: ______________ Degree: ______________

Attended: ______________ Date of graduation: ______________

Junior/community college name: ______________________ Degree: ______________

Attended: ______________________ Date of graduation: ______________

College name: ______________________ Degree: ______________

Attended: ______________________ Date of graduation: ______________

Work Experience

Name of employer: ____________ Job title: ____________ No. of years: ________

Reason for leaving: ______________________________

Name of employer: ____________ Job title: ____________ No. of years: ________

Reason for leaving: ______________________________

Name of employer: ____________ Job title: ____________ No. of years: ________

Reason for leaving: ______________________________

I certify that all the information which I have given in this application is true, accurate, and complete. I understand that any misstatement or omission of a material fact may be a cause for dismissal.

Date: ______________ Signature: ______________________

Source: Adapted from Robert D. Gatewood and Hubert S. Field, *Human Resource Selection* (New York: Dryden Press, 1987), p. 279.

49 SKILL BUILDER

Staffing for a Telecommuting Job

I. OBJECTIVES

A. To give you practice in revising a job description for a telecommuting job.

B. To enhance your understanding of how to prepare a staffing plan for a telecommuting job.

C. To familiarize you with some of the differences between staffing for telecommuting job environments versus staffing for traditional job (office) environments.

II. TIME REQUIRED TO COMPLETE: One to two hours

III. INSTRUCTIONS

A large pharmaceutical company located in the Northeast is one of the leading manufacturers of pharmaceuticals in the United States. Because of the intense competition in the industry and the heightened competition for highly skilled personnel, the company believes that quality-of-work-life (QWL) is a key factor for achieving a competitive advantage. In support of this belief, the company is considering the adoption of a telecommuting work arrangement for selected jobs.

The job of public relations specialist has been identified as an appropriate job for telecommuting because the job responsibilities are mostly information-related activities that require independent mental effort with no supervisory responsibilities. Exhibit 2.15 below contains the current job description for the public relations specialist, which reflects the primary job activities and qualifications for a full-time, in-office public relations specialist. There is currently only one job incumbent, and that person has resigned.

You have been asked to develop a plan for recruiting and hiring a replacement who will telecommute from home.

A. What method of job analysis do you recommend to determine the job requirements and job specifications for a telecommuting job? Is the method you recommend different from the method you would use if the job were performed in a traditional office environment?

B. What procedures do you recommend for recruiting and hiring a telecommuter? Are the procedures you recommend different from the procedures you would use if the job were performed in a traditional office environment?

C. What changes would you make to the job description in Exhibit 2.15 to reflect the telecommuting nature of the job?

D. What other recommendations would you make in order to ensure the successful implementation of a telecommuting work arrangement?

EXHIBIT 2.15 *Job Description*

Job Title: Public Relations Specialist

Department: Public Relations

Reports To: Director of Public Relations

General Summary: Serves as a writer on numerous firm publications; coordinates materials; writes, edits, and proofs articles, public relations publications, and advertising copy.

Essential Job Functions:

1. Writes, edits, and proofs public relations articles, newspaper copy, and human interest stories.
2. Writes advertising copy in conjunction with the marketing department.
3. Writes, edits, and coordinates printing and layout of company newsletter.
4. Meets with executives to determine public relations needs.
5. Meets with media officials and the public to publicize firm's accomplishments.
6. Attends informational meetings at the main office on an as-needed basis.
7. Gives presentations at meetings and other public events.
8. Performs other related duties as assigned by management.

Education and Experience Required: Degree in art/graphic design; demonstrated ability to use computer hardware/software; some experience in television or public speaking; considerable knowledge of journalism principles, English grammar and usage; demonstrated ability to write newspaper, news, and human interest articles, reports, brochures, and advertising copy; demonstrated ability to work and communicate effectively with others.

Contributed by Diana Deadrick, Old Dominion University

50 SKILL BUILDER

Test/Interview Validation

I. OBJECTIVES

A. To enhance your understanding of the test/interview validation process.

B. To give you experience in calculating the validity of a test.

C. To give you experience in preparing a scatter diagram (optional).

II. TIME REQUIRED TO COMPLETE: 1 hour

III. INSTRUCTIONS

Assume you are the human resources director for a large hotel. During the hiring process, all job applicants are required to undergo an extensive interview with you or with one of your assistants. Each applicant is scored on how well they perform during the interview from 1 (very poorly) to 100 (highly effective). Several months ago, a testing organization met with you and told you that your selection process might be improved if you gave every applicant a general intelligence test, in addition to the interview. They suggested that you buy tests from them for $40 each and conduct a pilot study. So, you asked the 30 employees you hired most recently to take the test. The Pilot Study table shows the test and interview scores for these 30 employees. It also shows the overall score each employee received on his or her performance evaluation conducted by his or her supervisor.

Your task is to review the following two tables and answer the questions below:

1. Examine the correlation coefficients shown in the Study Statistics table. Should the firm use the test to hire future employees or is the interview alone sufficient? Explain your answer.

2. The validity coefficient between the general intelligence test score and the performance evaluation score is shown in the table. Use the formula below to verify that the calculation is correct. To assist you in making the calculation, the following formula is provided:

$$R \text{ (validity coefficient)} = \frac{N\Sigma XY - \Sigma X \Sigma Y}{\sqrt{[N\Sigma X^2 - (\Sigma X)^2][N\Sigma Y^2 - (\Sigma Y)^2]}}$$

   where N = number of subjects.

3. At the option of your instructor, prepare a scatter diagram showing the interview scores (X-axis) and the performance evaluation scores (Y-axis).

Study Statistics

General Intelligence Test Data		Interview Data		Combined Data	
Numerator	44470	Numerator	129170	Numerator	86820
X's	32264	X's	98684	X's	47205
Y's	400565	Y's	400565	Y's	400565
Denominator	113683	Denominator	198819.9	Denominator	137509
Correlation	0.39118	Correlation	0.649683	Correlation	0.6314

Pilot Study Data

Employee	Intelligence Test	Interview Score	Average Combined Score	Performance Evaluation Score
1	75	80	77.5	172
2	77	71	74	141
3	67	61	64	128
4	65	59	62	173
6	73	58	65.5	155
7	63	52	57.5	126
8	71	78	74.5	151
8	71	63	67	181
9	79	88	83.5	176
10	77	63	70	136
11	88	89	88.5	178
12	74	73	73.5	151
13	69	80	74.5	173
14	72	76	74	148
15	71	83	77	185
16	66	77	71.5	138
17	61	74	67.5	133
18	74	89	81.5	181
19	64	80	72	188
20	73	62	67.5	140
21	78	77	77.5	177
22	67	71	69	173
23	81	94	87.5	185
24	75	81	78	175
25	66	74	70	138
26	70	62	66	133
27	77	82	79.5	181
28	75	83	79	173
29	81	85	83	188
30	76	69	72.5	128
SUMS	2176	2234	2205	4805

Contributed by Steve Maurer, Old Dominion University

PART

3

Developing Effectiveness in Human Resources: Training, Career Development, and Performance Appraisal

Orientation/Training/Career Development

51 CASE

Career Development at Electronic Applications

Electronic Applications Corporation is a major producer of silicon chips for the computer industry. It is located southeast of San Francisco in an area of high technology firms. Since its founding in 1972, the company has grown rapidly in terms of sales and profits, thus enhancing its stock price many times over. Human resource policies, however, have tended to lag behind company growth. Emphasis has been on reactive policies to meet the regulatory requirements of external stakeholders such as the federal government. In short, human resources have not been a high priority.

Recently, Harold Sweeney has been hired as director of human resources for the company. Sweeney had previously served as assistant personnel director for a large "blue-chip" corporation in southern California. He accepted his present position not only because of an increase in pay and responsibility, but also because of what he termed "the challenge of bringing this company from a 1970s human resources mentality to one more compatible with the realities of the 2000s."

Sweeney has been on the job for four months and has been assessing the situation to determine the more significant human resource problems. One problem seems to have been the high turnover among electrical engineers who work in research and development and are the core of the research function. Prior to the 2008–2010 financial crisis, the turnover rate averaged about 30 percent per year over the past three years. As a result of the recent financial crisis, however, unemployment in Silicon Valley has increased to 9.7 percent. Most technology companies are not hiring at all or are only hiring individuals on a highly selective basis. The result is that most employees have decided to stay put in the short term, but will be looking to take advantage of more attractive opportunities elsewhere when and if the economy improves. Sweeney was aware of these intentions and wanted to take steps now to minimize future employee turnover.

In assessing the cause of the problem, Sweeney checked area wage surveys and found Electronic Applications paid 5 to 8 percent above the market for various categories of electrical engineers. Since the company did not have a formal exit interview system, he could not check out other possible explanations through that mechanism. However, through informal conversations with a large number of individuals, including the engineers themselves, he learned that many of the engineers felt "dead-ended" in the technical aspects of engineering. In particular, the research and development department had lost some of the younger engineers who had been considered to be on the "fast track." Most had gone to competitors in the local area.

One particular research and development employee who impressed Sweeney was Helen Morgan. Morgan is 29 years old, has a BS degree in Electrical Engineering from California Institute of Technology, and is studying for her MBA at the University of Santa Clara at night. Helen had been employed for seven years at Electronic Applications, three in an entry-level engineering position and four as a section chief. The latter promotion was the highest position in research and development other than the position of director of research and development.

Morgan claimed that "the company doesn't really care about its good people." In her view, the present director, Harry James, does not want to allow his "better people" to move up in the organization. He is more interested in keeping them in his own department so he can meet his own departmental goals without having to orient and train new employees. Morgan also claimed she was told she "has a bright future with the company" by both James and the former personnel director. Her performance appraisals have been uniformly excellent. She went on to criticize the company for using an appraisal form with no sections for dealing with employee development. Morgan recommended that steps be taken to remedy each of the problems she identified. Among these steps were helping employees identify future development opportunities, rewards for supervisors who successfully mentor subordinates, planning to identify future job opportunities, better communication of job opportunities, identification of career paths and career ladders, greater efforts to help employees achieve work/family life balance, childcare assistance, and telecommuting opportunities.

Sweeney checked out the information Morgan had provided him and found it to be accurate. Moreover, he heard through the "grapevine" that she is in line for an excellent position with a nearby competitor. Clearly, he has an even greater challenge than he had anticipated. He realizes he has an immediate problem concerning high turnover of certain key employees. In addition, Sweeney also has a series of interconnected problems associated with career development. However, he is not quite sure what steps to take and in what order.

QUESTIONS

1. Describe the nature and causes of the problem faced by Harold Sweeney.
2. What additional questions should Sweeney ask or what additional information is needed before proceeding toward a solution to this problem? Why?
3. What are the individual and organizational benefits of a formalized career development system?
4. If Sweeney decides to develop a formalized career development system at Electronic Applications, what components or types of services should be offered? Why?
5. Should the career development activities be integrated with other human resource management activities? If yes, which ones? Why?
6. What criteria should Sweeney consider to evaluate good candidates for promotion? What criteria could be used to evaluate the performance of supervisors in development of their subordinates?

52 CASE

The Safety Training Program

Houghton Refrigeration Company builds refrigerators for large appliance companies. It employs about 300 people, mostly assembly-line workers, and is located in a small rural town in Ohio. The company typically builds, on a contract basis, chest freezers and small bar refrigerators. On occasion, however, it also builds standard size refrigerators. The president of the company is a former engineer, as are most of the other executives. These individuals are very knowledgeable about engineering, but have received little training in the basic principles of management.

During the summer months, volume at the factory increases significantly, and the company needs to hire about 40 new employees to handle the heavy workload. Most of these new employees are college students who attend a small private college located about 15 minutes from the plant. Some high school students are hired as well.

When a new employee is hired, the company asks him or her to complete an application and then to show up at the plant gate ready for work. Employees receive no orientation. The worker is shown to a work station and, after a minimum amount of on-the-job training, the new employee is expected to start performing a job. Most of the jobs are quite simple; hence, the training is typically completed within ten minutes. The first-line supervisor usually shows the employee how to do a job once, then watches while the employee does the job once, leaves, and comes back about 20 minutes later to see how the employee is progressing. Typical jobs at the plant include screwing 14 screws into the sides of a freezer, placing a piece of insulation into the freezer lid, and handing out supplies from the tool room.

The company has had excellent experience with college students over the years. Much of the success can be attributed to the older workers coming to the aid of the new employees when difficulties arise. Most new employees are able to perform their jobs reasonably well after their on-the-job training is completed. However, when unexpected difficulties arise, they are usually not prepared for them and need assistance from others.

The older workers have been especially helpful to students working in the "press room." However, Joe Gleason, the first-line supervisor there, finds it amusing to belittle the college students whenever they make any mistakes. He relishes showing a student once how to use a press to bend a small piece of metal, then exclaims, "You're a hot-shot college student; now let's see you do it." He then watches impatiently while the student invariably makes a mistake and then jokingly announces for all to hear, "That's wrong! How did you ever get into college anyway? Try it again, dummy."

One summer, the company experienced a rash of injuries to its employees. Although most of the injuries were minor, the company felt it imperative to conduct a series of short training programs on safe material-handling techniques. The president of the company realized that OSHA requires firms to maintain a safe and healthy work environment, and that it is important that employees know how to lift objects safely. The major issue was who should conduct the training. The human resource director was a 64-year-old former engineer who was about to retire and was a poor speaker. The only other employee in the human resource department was a new 19-year-old secretary who knew nothing about proper handling techniques. Out of desperation, the president finally decided to ask Bill Young, the first-line supervisor of the "lid-line" to conduct the training. Young recently attended a training program himself on safety and was active in the American Red Cross. He reluctantly agreed to conduct the training. It was to be done on a departmental basis with small groups of 10 to 15 employees attending each session.

At the first of these training sessions, Young nervously stood up in front of 14 employees, many of whom were college students, and read his presentation in a monotone voice. His entire speech lasted about one minute and consisted of the following text:

> *Statistics show that an average of 30 people injure their backs on the job each day in this state. None of us wants to become a statistic.*
>
> *The first thing that should be done before lifting an object is to look it over and decide whether you can handle it alone or if help is needed. Get help if there's any doubt as to whether the load is safely within your capacity.*
>
> *Next, look over the area where you're going to be carrying the object. Make sure it's clear of obstacles. You may have to do a little housekeeping before moving your load. After you have checked out the load and route you're going to travel, the following steps should be taken for your safety in lifting:*
>
> 1. *Get a good footing close to the load.*
> 2. *Place your feet 8 to 12 inches apart.*
> 3. *Bend your knees to grasp the load.*
> 4. *Bend your knees outward, straddling the load.*
> 5. *Get a firm grip.*
> 6. *Keep the load close to your body.*
> 7. *Lift gradually.*
>
> *Once you've lifted the load and moved it, you'll eventually have to set it down—so bend your legs again—and follow the lifting procedures in reverse. Make sure that your fingers clear the pinch points. And, finally, it's a good idea to set one corner down first.*

After Bill's speech ended, the employees immediately returned to work. By the end of the day, however, everyone in the plant had heard about the training fiasco, and all, except the president, were laughing about it.

Questions

1. Evaluate the company's on-the-job training program. Should it be changed?
2. Should the company install an employee orientation program for new factory workers, or is one not necessary?
3. What changes should be made in the company's safety training program?
4. What other ways might a firm emphasize safety and curtail accidents, other than training?

53 CASE

The Mentoring Problem at Walnut Insurance

Tom Morrison, president of Walnut Insurance, was sitting at his desk reading a letter he had just received and thinking about a recent meeting with his vice presidents. He knew he had to make a decision regarding whether to implement a new mentoring program, but he did not know what that decision should be at the moment.

Walnut Insurance has been selling liability insurance to firms in one particular industry for over 50 years. Its specialized niche in the insurance industry has made it highly successful. It employs about 2,400 individuals who work in 12 regional offices throughout the United States and at its Midwestern headquarters.

Walnut Insurance has six senior male vice presidents who report directly to Morrison. Over the years, these individuals have traveled between the various regional offices, working primarily with the insurance sales representatives. The VPs perform numerous functions when visiting the regional offices. They go out on overnight sales trips with the representatives to learn about customer problems, assist agents with policy questions, and provide training; they evaluate agents to determine who has the potential to be promoted; they pass on the firm's values and culture, which places heavy emphasis on honesty and satisfying customer needs; they assist agents in interpreting company policies; and they determine what new policies need to be developed.

Over the years, these VPs have performed one other valuable service to new employees—they have informally mentored some of them. Typically, each VP would pick out five or six promising agents and take them under his wing. He would get to know the agents well, point out strengths and weaknesses, and help them develop plans for achieving management positions. Over the years, this approach has worked quite well.

However, in the last two years the firm hired over 50 new agents and almost two-thirds of them were women. These individuals were college graduates who majored in a variety of disciplines. They were hired based on their sales skills, initiative, self-confidence, assertiveness, and physical appearance. Previously, almost all of the new hires were men. Morrison believed that the present informal mentoring system might result in women being excluded, so he thought that a formal system should be considered.

Thus, at one of the firm's regular retreats, Morrison broached the subject with his VPs. He commended them for their willingness to mentor agents voluntarily in the past, noted that many of the regional managers were a product of this mentoring, explained his concerns regarding the need for female agents to receive equal mentoring treatment, and asked them if they thought the process should be formalized by assigning specific agents to specific VPs.

Morrison's suggestion went over like a lead balloon—not a single person liked the idea in the least. In fact, they strongly opposed it and told Morrison as tactfully as they could. One VP explained that he was an elder in the church and had strong religious convictions. He did not want to travel with female employees on overnight sales calls because it might tarnish his image among his evangelical friends. He had no problem working with female employees in regional offices and had done so for many years. But, he did not want to travel with them.

Three other VPs were opposed to the idea because they were fearful of sexual harassment suits being filed against them. They knew that Title VII of the Civil Rights Act states that it is unlawful to harass a person because of that person's sex and that sexual harassment is defined as unwelcome sexual advances, requests for sexual favors, and other verbal or physical harassment of a sexual nature. The also knew that the law states that harassment is illegal when it is so frequent that it creates a hostile or offensive work environment or results in an adverse employment decision. They noted that a recent insurance trade publication article described numerous cases in which managers in several other insurance firms had been charged with harassment. The article explained that the law is unclear in many ways and how even if one is innocent of a charge, one's career can be ruined. The VPs demanded to know how and whether the firm would stand behind them if charged with sexual harassment.

One other VP objected to the idea because he wanted free choice in selecting employees to mentor. He argued that only the best agents are deserving of mentoring and that it would be a waste of time to mentor everyone. He asked, "Why should we mentor someone who does not have the potential to become a manager?" Another VP objected because he knew that his wife would not approve of any plan that would require that he work closely with young female agents, particularly at night in faraway locations.

After hearing all of these objections, Morrison asked the VPs to give further thought to the issue. He restated that mentoring was critical to the firm's success and that it was important that women not be left out of the process.

In the week that followed, Tom had not heard anything more regarding the issue from any VP. However, he had received a letter from one wife (see Exhibit 3.1) and it was clear what she thought of the idea. Nonetheless, the final decision was his to make.

EXHIBIT 3.1 *Letter from a VP's Wife*

January 23, 20xx
1105 Edgewater Dr.
Sometown, USA

Mr. Tom Morrison
President, Walnut Insurance Company

Dear Tom,

I am writing to you regarding the new mentoring proposal that is being considered. My husband told me about it at dinner last week and I have been worried about it ever since.

As you may know, my husband and I have been married for 28 years and have raised three lovely children. We are dedicated to each other and have strong family values. We try to act as good role models to our children and to others.

To be honest, I am very concerned about what effects the new mentoring program might have on our marriage. My husband is faithful to me and I trust him with other women under typical circumstances. However, the new program involves special circumstances and I do not trust the women he might need to mentor. Some of these women may be so ambitious that they will stop at nothing to get promoted. They would not hesitate to destroy a marriage or my husband's career if they thought it would help them get ahead.

I would appreciate it if you would find a different alternative. Surely, some other approach would accomplish your goals.

Sincerely yours,

Joyce Butler

Joyce Butler

QUESTIONS

1. If you were Tom Morrison, would you implement a formal mentoring program at Walnut Insurance? If so, how would you address the VP's concerns?
2. What alternatives to a formal mentoring program are available to Morrison?

54 CASE

Management Development: The I-MBA Request

Warren Vander, HR director, and Delane Beck, general manager at Nipigon Mining Products Corporation, were meeting to discuss an important request they had just received from Thomas Williams, a control engineer. Williams had a BS in Electrical Engineering from a well-known Western university and had been with the firm for eight years. He had read an advertisement in the local paper regarding a new I-MBA program offered by State University and wanted to know if the firm would pay the tuition. The two-year program would cost close to $50,000, is limited to 50 students, and requires that students take approximately 20 online classes and attend two one-week residency experiences. The advertisement stated that the program offers an integrated curriculum and focuses on leadership, strategic planning, marketing, management information systems, human resource administration, and production management. Since Williams's request was the first of its kind at the firm, any decision made would be precedent setting for employees who want to take classes offered through the Internet.

The meeting focused on a number of topics. First and foremost was the $50,000 price tag. Vander was somewhat shocked by the cost and wondered if there was not a cheaper alternative. He knew that many universities were now offering programs through the Internet and that they were not cheap, but he questioned why this program would cost so much. He wondered whether the firm should spend such a large sum on one person and whether Williams should be required to pay some, or most, of the cost. Vander noted that $50,000 would pay for a lot of classes for many employees at the nearby community college and that the firm could hire outside trainers to conduct a management development program at the company for that same amount. He reasoned that even if the firm needed to pay outsiders $2,000 per day, it could buy 25 days of management development training for up to 30 employees. He figured this might be more beneficial to the firm than spending a large sum on just one person.

Furthermore, Vander questioned whether the firm should spend such a large sum on Williams. He knew that Williams had been with the firm for eight years and had always received high performance ratings. He also knew that Williams held a critical position in the firm and was always on-call, meaning that if equipment failed at any time, the firm reserved the right to ask him to come to work above and beyond his normal work hours. This precluded Williams from taking regular classes at any university. While Williams was technically competent, he was also a "computer geek." He lacked strong interpersonal skills and tended to be arrogant and defensive. Vander also wondered whether Williams would remain with the company once he finished his degree. He worried that Williams would finish the program and then, with a new credential in hand, leave for a better opportunity elsewhere. By the same token, Vander was concerned with how Williams might react if the firm did not grant his request. Would he quit the firm and join one that would pay for an Internet-based program?

Beck was skeptical regarding the quality of the program and whether it was as rigorous and as educationally sound as a traditional one. She knew that the State University's College of Business had an excellent reputation, but this program was new and untested. She wondered if the program would be fraught with problems given that the faculty would be offering it for the first time. She also wondered if the program would sufficiently improve Williams's weak interpersonal skills to make him capable of being promoted to plant manager, to vice president of manufacturing, or to an even higher position. Beck noted that if Williams completed this program, he would have face-to-face contact with other students for just the two one-week residencies. She questioned whether this would be sufficient to improve his interpersonal skills. On the other hand, she reasoned that spending $50,000 to improve Williams's overall management skills might be worth it to the firm if he was capable of assuming ever-increasing responsibilities, even if the program did not vastly improve his interpersonal skills.

After discussing Williams's request for some time, Beck and Vander concluded that the firm had sufficient funds to pay for employees to complete I-MBA programs out of its training and development budget. They felt that under the right conditions, it might be beneficial for the firm to do so, given that it did not presently have any formalized management development programs. However, in order to be consistent, they would need to develop a comprehensive policy that would spell out criteria for determining whether the firm should grant I-learning requests. What they did not know was what those criteria should be and whether Williams's request should be granted in light of these criteria. They also did not know if there would be a better alternative for developing management skills.

QUESTIONS

1. What other management development approaches, other than the I-MBA program, could Nipigon Mining Products Corporation use to improve managerial skills?
2. What criteria should the firm use to determine if it will pay for employees to enroll in any degree program offered on the Internet, including an I-MBA program?
3. Should the firm grant Thomas Williams's request?

55 Exercise

Design and Evaluation of Training Programs

I. Objectives

A. To help you determine which training methods are most appropriate for achieving particular objectives.

B. To show you the linkages between training objectives, training methods, and training evaluation.

C. To help you learn how to identify and write training objectives.

D. To build skill in the evaluation of training programs.

II. Out-of-Class Preparation Time: 1 hour

III. In-Class Time Suggested: 45 minutes

IV. Procedures

Prior to the class meeting in which this exercise will be discussed, read the entire exercise and use a pencil to complete Forms 3.1 and 3.2. Or you may use a separate sheet of paper. At the beginning of the class period, the instructor should divide the class into discussion groups of three to five students. Each group should begin by completing Form 3.1. If you are unfamiliar with any of the training methods listed, consult your textbook or ask your instructor.

Look at each training objective/outcome and then determine which training methods would be most appropriate for achieving each of the four training objectives on Form 3.1. Since each group member comes into the class period with his or her own ideas on which training method is most appropriate for achieving which objectives, there may be a need for some discussion and negotiation before a group consensus can emerge.

Put an "x" beside the method that seems most appropriate for achieving each objective or outcome. For example, if you believe that classroom instruction would be a good method of facilitating knowledge acquisition on the part of a training program participant, put an "x" in that space. Then, put an "x" wherever any particular training method seems appropriate for achieving particular training objectives or outcomes. For each of the four objectives or outcomes, you should have at least two, but no more than four, training methods that are identified as most appropriate.

Now, look at the data in Exhibit 3.2. These data are taken from a training needs analysis of executives and middle managers at Corporation X. The percent opposite each training need indicates the percentage of executives and middle managers citing each of the four top-rated training needs.

This company has had no previous formal training programs for its employees, and the newly hired director of employee development has asked your group to answer the following questions:

1. What training objectives and training needs do you select as the highest priority for future training (see Exhibit 3.2)?
2. What training methods should be used to meet this need and the related training objectives (see Form 3.1)?

FORM 3.1 *The Effectiveness of Alternative Training Methods for Achieving Various Training Objectives/Outcomes*

	TRAINING OBJECTIVES					
Training Method	**Knowledge Acquisition**	**Attitude Change**	**Problem-Solving Skills**	**Interpersonal Skills**	**Participant Acceptance**	**Knowledge Retention**
Information Processing: Lecture (with questions)						
Conference (discussion)						
Sensitivity training						
Laboratory training						
Observation Closed-circuit TV						
Programmed instruction						
Correspondence courses						
Videos						
Reading lists						
Simulation: Cases						
Incidents						
Role playing						
Business games						
In-Basket exercises						
On-the-Job: Job rotation						
Committee assignments						
On-the-job coaching						
Feedback from performance appraisal						
Apprenticeships						

EXHIBIT 3.2 *Results of a Training Needs Assessment*

Survey of Executives and Middle Managers Top Four Areas of Executive and Middle Management Training

	Percentage citing need
Performance appraisal techniques	44
Strategic planning	38
Employee motivation	32
Marketing	27

FORM 3.2 *The Relationship between Training Objectives and Training Methods*
Occupational Group: Executives and Middle Managers Training Need:
____________________ (Choose one of the needs identified in Exhibit 3.2.)

Training Objectives	Training Methods	Evaluation Methods
1.	1.	1.
2.	2.	2.
3.	3.	3.

3. What training evaluation method should be used to evaluate each training method or program?

Before answering the questions and completing Form 3.2, review the information in Form 3.1 and Exhibit 3.2. Select the priority training need for executive and middle managers for the coming year. Write that priority training need on Form 3.2.

Now, develop specific objectives for the training program or programs you are recommending. You may have up to three objectives and three training programs or methods. These will be listed on Form 3.2 as well. If your group selected strategic planning as one of the programs, then possible objectives might be increased knowledge about the process of strategic planning or successful development of a strategic plan for the corporation or the executive's department. Likewise, an objective for a performance appraisal program might be the design of an appropriate performance appraisal form and process for the individual middle manager's particular situation.

The final step is to determine the most appropriate method of evaluating the particular training program or programs. The four major methods of evaluation in order of their degree of complexity and difficulty are as follows:

1. Participant reaction—usually determined by a questionnaire immediately at the conclusion of the training program.
2. Learning—assessment of knowledge about or attitudes toward a particular subject, both before and after a training experience.

3. Behavioral change—changes in on-the-job behavior or performance as measured by performance appraisals, subordinate's perceptions, supervisor's perceptions, and/or individual productivity data.
4. Organizational effectiveness—decreases in departmental or organizational costs, turnover, absenteeism, and grievances, and increases in departmental or organizational sales, income, or productivity as compared to a control group of those not attending training.

QUESTIONS

1. Once you had determined the training need and training objectives, how did you determine which training method would be most appropriate?
2. Identify one or two training evaluation methods you recommended on Form 3.2. Why did you choose this evaluation method and what problems might you encounter in using it in a valid way?
3. What are the most effective training or educational methods to facilitate your own learning? Why?

56 EXERCISE
On-the-Job Training

I. OBJECTIVES

A. To provide you with practice in conducting on-the-job training.

B. To make you aware of the problems a supervisor may encounter when training employees.

II. OUT-OF-CLASS PREPARATION TIME: One to two hours

III. IN-CLASS TIME SUGGESTED: 45 minutes

IV. PROCEDURES

An important task for most supervisors is to instruct new employees on the methods and procedures necessary to perform various job tasks. Initially, the employee may be totally unfamiliar with a particular task. This places an additional burden on the manager to make his or her instructions as clear and precise as possible. In this exercise, you will be asked to train one or more members of the class on how to perform a task. After the training is complete, it will be critiqued.

Preparation for the training can be done individually or in groups of three to five members, at the instructor's option. If groups are used, the instructor will divide up the class during the class period prior to the one in which this exercise will be conducted. Each group will then meet outside of class to prepare for the training. Each individual or group should begin by selecting a task to teach one or more class members. For example, one of the following could be picked:

- How to lift heavy objects safely.
- How to fold a napkin like those in fancy restaurants.
- How to tie a special knot used by tree surgeons, Merchant Marine or Navy personnel.
- How to fix a dripping faucet.
- How to use a volt-ohm meter such as an electrician might use.
- How to use a Blackberry or other communication device.
- How to use a complex calculator.
- How to apply for a job online.
- How to set up a blog.

In selecting a task, pick one that is performed in industry, one that most class members do not already know how to perform, and one that is sufficiently complicated that trainees cannot perform instantly. Remember, you will have to provide all of the materials necessary to perform the task.

Finally, you must choose the best approach for conducting the training (lecture, demonstrations, and so on) and the steps that will be followed when conducting the training. If you are working in groups, a spokesperson (the one who will actually conduct the training for the group) should also be selected.

At the start of class, the instructor will select four or more groups/individuals to actually conduct on-the-job training. Depending upon the task, the instructor will also select one or more students to serve as trainees. At this point, the trainers will, one at a time, conduct training. This will be followed by a critique of each training session by all class members. Toward the end of class, those groups/individuals who did not actually conduct training during class will briefly explain how they would have conducted their training.

57 INCIDENT

The Orientation Problem

Carol Burgess is a letter carrier and a part-time trainer of letter carriers for the U.S. Postal Service in a major city on the west coast. She trains all new letter carriers in her service area, which encompasses the northern half of her state. Over the past five years she has trained 318 new letter carriers. Typically, the training is offered prior to the new letter carrier's entry onto the job, although sometimes it occurs shortly thereafter.

The training program typically encompasses both the orientation of new employees to the U.S. Postal Service and the development of specific skills needed by the new letter carrier. The latter involves practice in casing mail (i.e., sorting) to appropriate locations of a case in preparation for delivery, reading maps, determining appropriate sequencing of delivery, and customer relations. The total training program takes three full days (one day of orientation and two days of skills training).

The orientation part of the training program encompasses both an orientation packet and a discussion of various Postal Service policies and procedures. The orientation packet typically includes information about employee benefits, holidays, copies of certain standard forms (i.e., IRS withholding forms), outline of emergency and accident procedures, key terms used in the U.S. Postal Service, copies of the health and life insurance options, and telephone numbers and locations of the personnel department and other important offices. In addition, an explanation of the U.S. Postal Service operation and purpose is provided. This explanation includes the training to be received, the letter carrier's duties and responsibilities, job standards and expected production levels, Postal Service rules and regulations, and the chain of command for reporting purposes are also provided. Burgess concludes her orientation with an offer of help and encouragement for the future.

The assumption built into the orientation is that it will be supplemented at the job site by the direct supervisor who will provide all the necessary information about the particular facility, the personnel at the facility, the area covered by the route or routes to which the new employee will be assigned, and the additional written information such as the employee handbook and the union contract. According to Postal Service policy, each new letter carrier should get three days of on-the-job training, of which one is paid for by the training division and two are charged to the supervisor's production. Burgess learned from subsequent conversations with her former trainees over the past five years that the orientation provided by the direct supervisor varied from practically nothing to fairly extensive. In some stations, the supervisor greeted the new employee, introduced the person to one other employee, and explained their own expectations regarding attendance, personal conduct, and productivity. Then, the employee was given an assignment and allowed to "sink or swim." Several supervisors were known in the Postal Service to be "SOBs." While 83 percent of new hires have survived their probationary 90-day period over the past three years, less than 20 percent survived in certain stations.

Last night Burgess received a telephone call from Edith Jones, one of her former trainees who finished training ten weeks ago. Jones is a single parent with two school-age children who had left her job as a secretary and taken the letter carrier job in order to make more money. Jones was in tears as she described her experience at her station. Her supervisor had given her no written materials, introduced her to only one other employee, and has shifted her from route to route over the ten weeks she has worked at the facility. No help or support of any kind has been offered, but the supervisor has continually berated her for the number of hours she has taken to case and deliver routes. She had tried to study maps during her days off in order to learn the various areas covered by various routes, but this only helped a little.

Each route had to be delivered in a particular order and it took time to learn the sequence. The other letter carriers were all stressed and working overtime themselves. Consequently, they ignored her and offered no assistance. Jones told Burgess that she was on the verge of quitting. Burgess told her to "hang in there because it does get easier with time."

As a result of all the complaints she had received from former trainees (some of whom survived the 90-day probationary period), Burgess decided to recommend to the area postmaster a program to train supervisors as to how to orient new letter carriers. However, she was not sure what specific items the supervisors should include in their new employee orientation and how to train them.

QUESTIONS

1. Describe the nature and causes of the U.S. Postal Service orientation problem in this case.
2. What types of orientation for new employees should direct supervisors provide at the work site?
3. What training methods should be used to train the supervisors, assuming approval of the proposal?
4. What written materials should the supervisor provide for new letter carriers in light of what Carol Burgess already provides?
5. In addition to the written materials discussed in the previous question, what else should the supervisor do to orient new letter carriers?

58 Skill Builder

Identifying Training Needs through Task Analysis

I. Objectives

A. To introduce you to the process and purposes of assessing training needs.

B. To give you practice in determining training needs for a job.

II. Time Required to Complete: 2 to 3 hours

III. Instructions

There are generally three analyses used to determine an organization's training needs: 1) organization analysis, 2) task or operations analysis, and 3) person analysis. This assignment allows you to perform a task analysis for a particular job by interviewing and observing a job holder. A task analysis involves systematic collection of data about a specific job. Its purpose is to determine what an employee should be taught to perform the job at the desired level. It generally includes a description of the major tasks of the job, standards of performance, how the tasks are to be performed to meet the standards, and the skills, knowledge, and abilities necessary. You will conduct the task analysis by following the steps described below:

Step 1: Select a job to analyze. You may choose a job currently held by a relative, friend, fellow student, etc. (If you completed "Exercise 30: Writing Job Descriptions" in Part 2, you may use that job.) Ask the job holder if you may interview him or her about the position and/or also observe him or her performing the job.

Step 2: Obtain a job description for the job you selected or prepare one by interviewing the job holder. The job description should describe in general terms the worker's major duties and responsibilities. For example, a job description for an accounts receivable clerk might include the following duties and responsibilities:

a. Invoice shipments to customers on a monthly basis.

b. Prepare journal vouchers at the end of the month to record cash receipts and sales by product lines.

When preparing the job description, be sure to include those things that are critical to performing the job satisfactorily, no matter how infrequently or briefly they occur, and the knowledge, skills, and abilities needed.

Step 3: This step involves identifying the tasks associated with performing each of the major duties of the job. You are to identify the overt, observable behaviors that are involved in performing the job. Arrange (if possible) to observe the worker performing his or her job and develop a list of the tasks involved. A task listing includes behavioral statements of how the job is to be performed. Using the example for the accounts receivable clerk, the tasks associated with invoicing customers might include:

a. Pull and review invoice master.

b. Extend and update invoice master.

c. Add correct discount and freight charges.

d. Make necessary amount of copies on copy machine.

When you complete this step, you should have a report that includes the title of the job, the major duties (responsibilities) of the job, the tasks associated with each duty/responsibility, and the knowledge and skills required of job incumbents.

Step 4: Once you have completed Steps 1–3, answer the following questions and include them in your report:

a. What training would benefit a person performing the job? If you had to design a training program for the job, what content areas would be needed, based on your analysis?
b. What training method would be best (on-the-job training, seminars, apprenticeships, vestibule, etc.)? Why?

Performance Appraisal

59 CASE *The Self-Appraisal Problem*

Leroy Washington, human resource director at Engel Products, was faced with a problem that he had not experienced before and was uncertain how to proceed. The problem was related to the firm's self-evaluation appraisal process. This process requires supervisors to evaluate themselves by completing two forms. The first form, Responsibilities and Goal Accomplishments Self Evaluation Report (see Exhibit 3.3), requires that supervisors write down their primary job duties/responsibilities along with the objectives that they had agreed to accomplish during the past year. They are to evaluate themselves from 1 (Outstanding) to 4 (Unsatisfactory). They also need to write an overall performance summary. The second form, Career Development Self Evaluation Report (see Exhibit 3.4), is used for training and development purposes and asks supervisors to indicate their strengths, evaluate themselves in terms of ten criteria, and develop plans for improving their skills and knowledge. It also asks supervisors to explain their career interests by specifying what jobs they aspire to hold in the future. For each objective, they are required to specify the criteria they will use to judge whether the objective was met and a date by which the objective will be accomplished.

Washington's major problem was that one of the sales staff supervisors had not completed her self-evaluation on time. The firm had a policy that all supervisors were to be evaluated annually by their immediate manager. The policy stipulated that each supervisor was to complete a self-evaluation and turn it into his/her immediate manager by a specific date. Prior to seeing this self-evaluation, the manager would also complete an evaluation on the supervisor. The two would then meet, trade evaluations, compare the two documents, and discuss differences. The completed evaluations were then turned in to the HR director for review.

Unfortunately, Carol McCalmont had not turned in her evaluation by the deadline. Washington told McCalmont's manager, Janet Weber, that the deadline had passed and asked Weber to remind McCalmont to quickly turn in the self-evaluation. One week later, the self-evaluation had not been completed; McCalmont stated she was still working on it and would turn it in soon. Another week went by, and McCalmont still had not submitted the self-evaluation, so Washington told Weber to let McCalmont know that she would not receive a scheduled raise until the report was completed.

Two more weeks passed and nothing happened. Then, Washington received a file that contained a performance review for McCalmont, written by Weber. However, the file did not include McCalmont's required self-evaluation. Washington immediately called Weber to find out why McCalmont had not completed the report and why Weber had submitted her evaluation in the absence of a self-evaluation. Weber responded that she could only guess as to why McCalmont had not completed the report: the self-appraisal process was too time-consuming, and she did not want to admit that her performance was unsatisfactory in some areas. Weber added that she did not want to hold up McCalmont's raise any longer and that is

EXHIBIT 3.3 *Responsibilities and Goal Accomplishments Self-Evaluation Report*

Instructions: List below your major job responsibilities and the objectives you set for yourself to accomplish during the past year. Then, rate yourself on each of these items as follows:

1—Outstanding—Your performance far exceeds this job requirement. You far exceeded this goal.

2—Commendable—Your performance exceeds this job requirement. You exceeded this goal.

3—Competent—Your performance met this job requirement. You met this goal.

4—Unsatisfactory—Your performance did not meet this job requirement. You did not meet this goal.

Job Responsibilities	*Rating*
1.	
2.	
3.	
4.	

List other job responsibilities and ratings on a separate page.

Goal Accomplishments (List Goals)	*Rating*
1.	
2.	
3.	
4.	

List other goals and ratings on a separate page.

PERFORMANCE SUMMARY (Using the space below write a summary of your job performance for the past year. Attach additional sheets if necessary.)

EXHIBIT 3.4 *Career Development Self-Evaluation Report*

PART A—STRENGTHS. Describe below your specific technical, interpersonal, managerial, and other job-related strengths.

PART B—DEVELOPMENTAL NEEDS. Indicate below the technical, interpersonal, managerial, or other job-related weaknesses you perceive in yourself.

PART C—IMPROVEMENT PLANS. State below what steps you plan to take to improve your weaknesses, including any training/education you would like the firm to offer to you.

PART D—SKILL EVALUATION. Evaluate yourself in terms of the ten skills listed below.

SKILL	**Unsatisfactory**	**Competent**	**Commendable**	**Outstanding**
1. Work quality	4	3	2	1
2. Technical skills	4	3	2	1
3. Productivity	4	3	2	1
4. Adaptability	4	3	2	1
5. Interpersonal skills	4	3	2	1
6. Planning skills	4	3	2	1
7. Initiative	4	3	2	1
8. Decision making	4	3	2	1
9. Analytical skills	4	3	2	1
10. Profit orientation	4	3	2	1

PART E—FUTURE JOB. Indicate what job or jobs you would like to hold in the future.

why she completed and submitted her evaluation. She believed that a small raise was warranted and that McCalmont's failure to complete a self-evaluation should not disqualify her from receiving the raise.

QUESTIONS

1. What action should Leroy Washington take in response to Carol McCalmont's and Janet Weber's actions? Should McCalmont be granted a raise even though she had not completed her self-evaluation?
2. Evaluate Engel Product's self-appraisal system. Should it be changed to make it more effective? Is it too time-consuming?
3. Should the firm eliminate the self-appraisal portion of its appraisal system?

60 CASE

Mills Paper Company: Performance Management or Age Discrimination?

Lance Amato, CFO for Mills Paper Company, sat at his desk dreading the upcoming meeting with John Carpenter, a general accountant with the company. He was going to notify Carpenter of his termination from the company. Although it was going to be a difficult meeting, Amato felt the company had no choice and had done everything possible to assist Carpenter in meeting the performance expectations that had been set for him. As he sat waiting for the meeting to begin, Amato reviewed Carpenter's performance record and history at Mills.

Carpenter had been hired by Mills Paper Company two years earlier. At the time, he was 56 years old and had come to Mills with considerable experience. When hired, Carpenter signed a written performance agreement, a patent and confidentiality agreement, and a standard ethics letter. Mills used a management by objectives performance appraisal system for its managerial staff. The expectations and objectives of positions were put into a performance agreement annually. Within one week of employment, Carpenter and his supervisor at the time, Henry Castagnera, had agreed upon the objectives and performance metrics for Carpenter's position. Carpenter signed the MBO agreement.

Carpenter's tenure at Mills Paper was marred by a number of poor performance appraisals and demotions. In the first quarter after he started work, Carpenter received a poor performance rating from his direct supervisor. At the time, several managers, including the president of Mills, expressed their disappointment and concern about Carpenter's performance as division controller (see Exhibit 3.5). However, the files indicated that despite the poor performance rating, Carpenter received a seven percent salary increase the first year of his employment.

Due to the reorganization of the company shortly thereafter, Carpenter was assigned to a different division and supervisor. His new supervisor, Bob Crane, had prepared a set of objectives for Carpenter. During a mid-year review, Crane rated his performance as "needs improvement." The review he submitted contained substantive comments to support the rating (see Exhibit 3.6). As part of the improvement plan Crane developed for Carpenter, it was agreed that his performance would be reviewed again in three months. Crane had noted the following in Carpenter's personnel file at that time, "There has not been positive action in order to improve, and in some areas we have even lost ground."

EXHIBIT 3.5 *Comments from John Carpenter's Performance Appraisal*

- Information furnished not consistently accurate
- Poor supervision of direct reports
- Accounting information not submitted on time
- Managers not satisfied with the financial guidance provided
- Paucity of key financial information available concerning manufacturing operations
- Slow response to requests for information

EXHIBIT 3.6 *Excerpts from Performance Appraisal Conducted by Bob Crane*

- Lack of solid response and follow through on specific requests for assistance
- Organization concerning financial aspects of strategy preparation and budgeting was not good
- No solid proposals given on how to improve the effectiveness of the accounting department
- Managers not satisfied with responses and state they were "wishy-washy"
- Very little improvement around routine reporting
- No initiative in putting together a better financial forecasting form

Crane made further suggestions for Carpenter's improvement that included meeting with general managers at Mills to help him understand their needs. He also charged Carpenter with developing and issuing a new forecasting form for use in the division. When Carpenter did not meet performance expectations, he was demoted by Crane to financial analyst with a change in title, reduced grade and responsibilities, but remained at the same pay. Once again, Carpenter was told his performance needed to improve.

Subsequent papers in the file showed Carpenter's performance did not improve or ever reach the level expected of someone with his background and skill. In a last ditch effort to manage Carpenter, Amato had given him the option of being demoted to a general accountant or being terminated for inability to perform his job. Carpenter chose to accept the second demotion with decrease in salary from $65,000 to $61,000. A set of performance objectives were developed for Carpenter in his new position. However, after two months it was clear that Carpenter was not able to meet the minimal targets that had been set for him. His financial reports continued to be of poor quality and were inaccurate. Finally, the decision was made to terminate Carpenter. As Amato reviewed Carpenter's file and the performance reviews, Amato wondered why they had not dismissed him earlier.

Amato looked up when he heard a knock on his door. It was Carpenter. After a rather formal greeting, he told Carpenter he was terminated for poor performance and would receive 21-weeks severance pay, payment for unused vacation time, and could also use the company's outplacement services. Carpenter reacted first with shock and then anger. He slammed the door as he left Amato's office. Two months later, Mills Paper Company was notified that Carpenter had filed a complaint with the local EEOC Office alleging age discrimination, unfair performance appraisal, and negligent and intentional infliction of emotional distress.

QUESTIONS

1. Evaluate Mills Paper Company's management of John Carpenter's performance. What are the strengths and weaknesses of their approach to performance appraisals (i.e., management by objectives)?
2. Do you agree or disagree with Lance Amato's observation that Carpenter should have been terminated earlier?
3. Review Exhibit 3.7, which lists employment laws relevant to performance appraisals. Do you think that Carpenter prevail in his charges against Mills? Why or why not? What are the elements of a legally defensible performance appraisal system?

EXHIBIT 3.7 *Legislation Relevant to Performance Appraisals*

LAW	PURPOSE	IMPLICATIONS FOR PERFORMANCE APPRAISALS
Title VII of Civil Rights Act of 1964	Outlaws discrimination based on race, color, sex, religion, or national origin.	Protection against performance appraisal policies and procedures and outcomes that are discriminatory; appraisal criteria must be job related and consistently applied.
Civil Rights Act of 1991 (CRA 1991)	Allows jury trials, compensatory and punitive damages in discrimination cases; alters burden of proof and other technical aspects of some cases.	Reduces plaintiff's burden of proving that particular practices of employer (e.g., performance appraisals, selection systems) caused discrimination; performance appraisal procedures should be well-documented; proper training should be provided to evaluators; consistent application of performance standards; there should be an appeal process for employees.
Equal Pay Act of 1963	Prohibits gender-based differences in pay for equal work, subject to limited exceptions.	Performance appraisal ratings results can be used to invoke and justify exceptions in performance bonuses (e.g., merit-based pay distinctions); men and women with similar performance ratings should receive similar bonuses.
Age Discrimination in Employment Act (ADEA) 1967	It is unlawful to discriminate against a person because of his/her age (40 or over) with respect to any term, condition or privilege of employment, including hiring, firing, promotion, performance evaluation, layoff, compensation, benefits, job assignments and training. The law applies to private employers, state, federal, and local governments as well as employment agencies and labor unions.	Provides protection against use of performance appraisal procedures and results to perpetrate age-based discrimination; evaluators should avoid stereotyping based on age and only use job-related performance criteria.
Americans with Disabilities Act (ADA) 1991	Prohibits employment discrimination based on disability.	Limits appraisal criteria to essential job functions and requires reasonable accommodation as to how performance is appraised.
At-will Employment	A doctrine of American law that defines an employment relationship in which any party can break the relationship with no liability, provided there was no express contract for a definite term governing the relationship and there is no collective bargaining agreement. Several states now recognize implied contracts that may be "implied" in human resource policies in employee handbooks or promises that were made at the time of employment.	Performance appraisal criteria and results must be job-related or based on the contract agreements (if there is a contract); termination cannot be based on unlawful discrimination; a company should follow its termination procedures as specified in company policies and handbooks.

61 EXERCISE

EvalSim—A Performance Evaluation Exercise

I. **OBJECTIVES**

A. To familiarize you with some of the problems related to the use of performance appraisals and to provide alternative approaches for solving these problems.

B. To give you practice in making decisions and writing memos to employees regarding performance appraisal issues.

II. **OUT-OF-CLASS PREPARATION TIME:** 20 minutes to read exercise plus one hour to complete e-mail Items, either individually or with group members, and write responses

III. **IN-CLASS TIME SUGGESTED:** 45 minutes to discuss all e-mail Items

IV. **PROCEDURES**

This exercise can be done individually or in groups of three to five members, at the instructor's option. You are to begin by reading all of the material presented in this exercise. Assume that you are responsible for developing and maintaining the O'Leary Organization's performance appraisal system. You are to assume further that the items that follow were waiting in your e-mail when you arrived at work after a three-week vacation. First, you (or your team) are (is) to respond in writing to each employee who sent you an e-mail. Second, explain on a separate sheet of paper what additional actions you would take with reference to each item. For example, if you believe that you should gather additional information before making a final decision on an item, explain what information you would want. Or, if you believe that additional memos or discussions with someone in the company are needed, explain this. You (or your team) should bring both the memos and the "Additional Action" sheets to class. Be prepared to present and defend these materials during the class discussion.

SITUATION

The O'Leary Organization is a medium-sized organization with headquarters in the Midwest. You may assume that the organization is a manufacturing company, a hospital, an insurance company, a university, or virtually any other medium-sized organization with which you are familiar.

The training and development section consists of you or your team. In addition to conducting training, you have full responsibility for the organization's performance evaluation system. The O'Leary Organization's present performance appraisal system, which you are to assume you or your team designed, requires that all employees be evaluated by their supervisor on a periodic basis. All employees are evaluated at the end of a 90-day period (the initial employment period) and on a yearly basis thereafter. The performance appraisal form used by the organization is shown in Exhibit 3.8. Supervisors are required to complete this form for each of their employees at the appropriate time, discuss the evaluation with the employee, ask the employee to sign the form at the end of the evaluation interview, and return the completed form to the human resource department.

EXHIBIT 3.8 *The O'Leary Organization Performance Appraisal Form*

NAME ______ IDENTIFICATION NUMBER ______

TITLE ______ DEPARTMENT ______

TODAY'S DATE ______ APPRAISAL PERIOD ______ Annual

FROM___ TO___ 90 day

Part I Performance Rating

	1	2	3	4	5
Ability					
Attendance					
Attitude					
Appearance					
Conduct					
Initiative					
Work with Group					
Promotability					
Quantity of Work					
Quality of Work					
Overall Level of Performance					

1—Unsatisfactory 2—Below Average 3—Satisfactory 4—Good 5—Excellent

Part 2 Additional Questions: Answer the following on a separate sheet of paper.

1. List your major goals for the next year.
2. Describe additional training that you believe you need to achieve those goals.
3. State what you believe are your major strengths and weaknesses.
4. Do you have any additional comments or suggestions for improving your job performance or work environment?

Prepared by ______ Title ______

COMMENTS BY REVIEWED EMPLOYEE:

Employee's Signature ______ Date ______

(Employee signature does not indicate agreement, merely acknowledgment of this report.)

E-Mail Items

Item 1

To: HR Department
From: Tom Morrison, Accounting Department
RE: 90-Day Employee Evaluation

I just received my 90-day employee evaluation and received mostly 3s on it. My boss explained his evaluation to me by saying that I was making good progress on the job. He added that if I continue to show improvement, I will receive 4s and 5s like the more experienced employees do. Why am I being evaluated against older, more experienced workers? That doesn't seem right. I believe that considering my limited experience, I deserve "excellent" evaluations.

Item 2

To: HR Department
From: Paul Lands, Computer Center
RE: Performance Evaluation

Joe Meena and I started together at the O'Leary Organization two years ago. We are both in the Computer Center doing the same job, only he works one shift, and I work another. Two weeks ago, when we compared our performance evaluations, I discovered that he received all 5s whereas I received mostly 4s. The thing that irks me is that he and I both know we are doing an equally good job. His boss is just more lenient in his evaluation than is my boss. I don't think this whole system is fair, particularly since he may get promoted (based on his performance evaluation) before I do. Can't something be done about this?

Item 3

To: HR Department
From: Jill Best, Manager
RE: Performance Appraisal Form Question

I am a relatively new manager and am filling out the Performance Appraisal Form for the first time on one of my employees. I am not clear what some of the terms on the form mean. Specifically, I don't know what is meant by the term "conduct" or by the term "attitude." Would you please explain them to me?

Item 4

To: HR Department
From: Sue Peters, Supervisor
RE: Administering Employee Evaluations

I have recently received from your office a request to conduct evaluations this month on three of my employees. As you probably know, I was promoted to this supervisory position just one week ago as a result of the former supervisor's termination. I don't feel that I can presently conduct a fair evaluation of these employees. Do you want me to do them anyway?

Item 5

To: HR Department
From: Karen Blackwell, Supervisor
RE: Evaluation of Heather Morrison

This morning I conducted an evaluation interview with Heather Morrison. Although I had given her a 4 on initiative last year, I gave her a 2 in that category this year. When I told her this, she became very angry and said the evaluation should have been at least a 3 and probably a 4 again. I attempted to explain my evaluation to her, but she wouldn't listen. Instead, she continued to argue with me, but could not give me any concrete examples that would allow me to improve her rating on this category. If a situation like this comes up again, how should I handle it?

Item 6

To: HR Department
From: Howard Adams, Supervisor
RE: Necessity of Signing Evaluation Forms

Recently I conducted a performance evaluation interview with Harold Wallace. At the end of the interview, when I asked him to sign the appraisal form at the bottom, he refused. I asked him if the evaluation was accurate, and he said yes. I also explained to him that signing the form only represented an acknowledgment that he had been evaluated. He replied that he had nothing to gain from signing the form, and, therefore, why sign it? I don't know what I should do. Harold is somewhat of a problem and is often quite stubborn.

Item 7

To: HR Department
From: Margaret Windell, Purchasing
RE: Annual Performance Review

I have a rather troublesome question to ask you. I would ask it of my boss but she is currently in the hospital. For the last 23 years I have received an overall performance review, and my evaluations have all shown that I am an excellent employee. I am six years from retirement and, frankly, I have reached the point where performance evaluations aren't of any consequence to me. I know I am doing a good job. I know I won't get promoted or transferred, and I am at the top of my pay grade. So why should I continue to be evaluated formally?

Item 8

To: HR Department
From: Sarah Wade, Maintenance Engineer
RE: Employee Appraisal Form

When I was over in the HR Department yesterday looking at my file, I saw the appraisal form that was completed on me one month ago. I was shocked to see the following statement written on it under "Remarks": "Sarah has a very poor work attitude and doesn't appear willing to change it." My boss, Marilyn Turner, had also changed my evaluation on "attitude" from 4 to a 2. I am positive the negative statement was not on the evaluation form when I signed it. Needless to say, I want you to do something about this!

Item 9

To: HR Department
From: Chris Green, Supervisor
RE: Performance Evaluation of Bill Young

Next week, I must conduct a performance evaluation interview with Bill Young who works by himself in the evenings. While I was completing the evaluation form on him, I realized that it was impossible for me to evaluate him on one of the evaluation categories, "Work with Group." What should I do? I am afraid if I leave it blank it will affect his "Overall Level of Performance" score and hence, his chances of promotion.

Item 10

To: HR Department
From: Jeff Skala, Finance Department
RE: Confidentiality of Performance Evaluation

As you know, over the past year I have been experiencing a series of personal problems, all of which have adversely affected my job performance. These problems reflected themselves on my recent performance evaluation as my "marks" slipped from mostly 4s to mostly 2s. I can't disagree with my evaluation, but I don't think it was right for my boss, Helen Jackson, to tell two of my co-workers that she had given me a 1 on "Quality of Work." It seems to me that this type of information should be confidential since it is none of their business.

62 EXERCISE

Performance Appraisal Interview Role Play

I. OBJECTIVES

A. To allow you practice in conducting a performance appraisal interview.

B. To compare and contrast different approaches to the performance appraisal interview.

C. To help you develop sensitivity toward communication problems in performance appraisal interviews.

II. OUT-OF-CLASS PREPARATION TIME: 20–30 minutes

III. IN-CLASS TIME SUGGESTED: 45 minutes

IV. PROCEDURES

A. Read the exercise before coming to class.

B. Four students should be selected to participate in two different performance appraisal interviews (A and B). Two will play the role of the employee and two will play the role of the supervisor. Role assignments should be made in the prior class period or before class begins. The instructor will provide role sheets.

C. The persons playing the role of the employee should read "Employee's Role."

D. The person playing the role of supervisor A should read the "Supervisor Role A," and the person playing the role of supervisor B should read the "Supervisor Role B."

E. During the class period in which the role plays will occur, all role play participants should be taken outside of the classroom and given time to prepare their respective roles. All other members of the class are to observe the two different sets of interviews and record their observations on separate sheets of paper.

F. Supervisor A conducts a 10–15 minute appraisal interview with one of the employees in the front of the class. The other role play pair remains in the hall outside the classroom until their turn.

G. After the first role play is completed, the second role play pair enters the classroom and conducts its appraisal interview. The first role play team joins the rest of the class to observe the interview.

H. The entire class discusses both interviews.

SITUATION

Tri-City Health Services is a large non-profit center providing basic outpatient health services and health education programs to low-income families in the Southwest. The center employs over 40 physicians and nurses and more than 200 other workers in various staff positions. Pat Smith has been working as a junior assistant in the fund raising and grants department for the past two years and has worked on the children's health care program. Smith has done well in performing her job—all performance objectives have been met or surpassed for the year. However, this year she has been reprimanded on more than one occasion for spending too much time on the Internet. On one occasion Smith was supposed to be at a meeting, only to be found busy adding to her Facebook page. Company reports show that Smith's Internet usage is the highest of all staff in the department.

Each year on the anniversary date of the employee's hire, his or her supervisor must conduct a performance appraisal interview. Chris Jackson, the supervisor of Pat Smith, has completed the performance evaluation form shown in Exhibit 3.9 and is ready to discuss the evaluation with Smith.

Instructions for Observers

Your task is to evaluate two different sets of performance interviews. As you observe the interviews, consider the following:

1. How did the supervisor begin the interview? Was the purpose of the interview clearly stated?
2. What type of interview approach did the supervisor use? Who did most of the talking: the employee or the supervisor?
3. Did the supervisor learn how the employee feels about the job or about his or her performance?
4. Did both parties gain a clear understanding of the problem and its solution?
5. Were any specific action plans made to resolve the problem(s)?
6. Are there any ways in which the supervisor could improve the interview? How?
7. Which interview was most effective? Why?

EXHIBIT 3.9 *Performance Evaluation Form*

I. Rating Categories

Performance Dimensions	Performance Level	Points (Maximum = 5)
Quality of Work (The degree to which the employee's work is free of flaws)	*Excellent*	5
Quantity of Work (The total amount of acceptable work completed within time and resources available)	*Excellent*	5
Attendance (Includes absences and tardiness)	*Poor*	1
Cooperation (The degree to which the employee cooperates with and is respected by co-workers)	*Average*	3
Initiative and Self-Reliance (The degree to which the employee is independent and self-directed)	*Excellent*	5
Work Timeliness (The degree to which the employee exhibits skill in planning and scheduling activities; uses work time efficiently)	*Below Average*	2
Responsibility (The degree to which the employee is willing to accept responsibility for details in work)	*Above Average*	4
Total Points		25

II. Objectives and Goals

A. Did the employee set any specific work-related goals this performance period?
Yes (X) No ( )

B. If yes, what were they?
To complete and implement a fund-raising program by April 1.
To obtain a 15 percent increase in federal grants by April 1.

C. To what extent were they met?
Employee met or exceeded both objectives. The fund-raising effort was very successful (over $25,000 was raised) and federal grants have been increased by 18 percent this year.

Overall evaluation of goal achievement? *Excellent*

III. Overall Evaluation of Employee Performance (support evaluation with comments)

The employee has done a fine job on performance objectives but continues to have a problem with tardiness. Based on this, the overall rating for the year is average (25 out of 35 points). I do not recommend the employee for a promotion at this time.

IV. Performance and Career Development

Instructions: This section should be discussed and completed during the appraisal interview with the employee.

1. What action could the employee take in the coming year to improve his/her performance?
2. What specific support is needed by the employee to improve his/her performance?

3. What kind of work or job does the employee want to be doing in the next two years? Five years?
4. What training and development would the employee benefit from in the coming year? Be specific.

V. Performance Goals for Coming Year

Instructions: The supervisor and employee must complete the table below and list the employee's goals and key performance indicators for the coming year:

Key Performance Area	Goals	Key Measures

Supervisor Signature Date Employee Signature Date

63 EXERCISE

Which Performance Appraisal Format Is Most Effective?

I. OBJECTIVES

A. To examine the strengths and weaknesses of four different methods for appraising employees.

B. To enhance your oral communication skills.

II. OUT-OF-CLASS PREPARATION TIME: 30 minutes to prepare for the debate

III. IN-CLASS TIME SUGGESTED: 50–75 minutes

IV. PROCEDURES

Your instructor will divide the class into five groups in the class prior to conducting this exercise. There will be four debating groups consisting of three to five members each and one or more groups of judges that consist of the remaining class members. Debaters will be assigned one of four positions and told to prepare to argue in favor of that position. Judges will be told to read the textbook chapter pages that cover those positions. The issue to be debated is: Which approach to appraising employees is the most effective? The positions are: 1) trait appraisal instruments such as the graphic rating scale; 2) behavioral appraisal instruments such as the behaviorally anchored rating scale; 3) a ranking or forced distribution system; and 4) outcome appraisal instruments such as management by objectives.

At the start of the next class, your instructor will announce that a four-way debate will be held. The judges' role in the debate is to "search for the truth." They are to listen to all four sides presented and then, after the debate is over, tell the class what they believe is the correct answer to the debate question, not who won the debate.

The debate consists of two rounds. The purpose of Round One (15–20 minutes) is for each team to learn the position of the other debating teams. Hence, each team has up to five minutes to explain their position as comprehensively as possible. At the completion of Round One, the debating teams are given up to ten minutes to prepare criticisms of each of the other three teams for Round Two. During this intermission, judges are to discuss what they have heard and begin to formulate their own position.

In Round Two (15–20 minutes), each debating team is given up to five minutes to criticize the position of each of the other teams. Unlike a traditional debate, teams are not allowed to rebut the criticisms made by others. They must simply listen to them. Round Two ends when Team Four has finished criticizing the position of the other three teams.

After the debate has ended, the judges have five minutes to discuss the case with each other and arrive at a consensus, if possible. The judging team(s) then explains its decision to the debaters.

64 Exercise

Ethical Performance Appraisal Issues

I. Objectives

A. To make you aware that many performance appraisal decisions involve ethical issues.

B. To familiarize you with some of the many ethical performance appraisal issues.

C. To familiarize you with various criteria that can be used to determine if an action is ethical.

D. To make you aware of some of the reasons why a manager may be tempted to act unethically when evaluating subordinates.

II. Out-of-Class Preparation Time: 15 minutes to read each of the situations presented and answer Question 1 below

III. In-Class Time Suggested: 20–40 minutes

IV. Procedures

At the start of class, the instructor will divide the class into teams of three to five students. Your group should discuss each of the situations below and answer the following questions in the space provided:

1. Is the manager in the case acting in an ethical manner? Yes or No? (Answer Y or N under the letter "E" below.)
2. Would your group act in the same manner as the manager? Yes or No? (Answer Y or N under the letter "G" below.)

After all groups have answered the questions above, the instructor will ask one or more of them to present their answers.

In trying to answer the first question, your group may want to consider some or all of the questions listed below that could be used to judge whether an act is ethical. You may also want to consider other criteria/questions provided by your instructor or suggested in the textbook.

A. Does the action involve intentional deception?

B. Does the action purposely benefit one party at the expense of another?

C. Is the action fair and just to all concerned?

D. Would you or the manager feel comfortable if the action were made public, or must it remain a secret?

E. Would you need to justify the action by telling yourself that you can get away with it or that you will not need to live with the decision's consequences? Would you recommend the action to others?

F. Will the action build goodwill and better relationships?

INSTRUCTIONS: Read each of the following scenarios and answer questions 1 and 2 above in the space provided with either a "Y" for Yes or an "N" for No.

SCENARIO

E	G		
___	___	1.	A supervisor has an employee who is an outspoken homosexual. The supervisor does not like homosexuals. As a result, the supervisor purposely rates him lower than deserved on his performance appraisal form.
___	___	2.	A firm has recently been charged with discriminating against minorities. The firm denies the charges but asks all supervisors to make sure they do not discriminate. In order to avoid any possible discrimination charge, a manager rates one poor performing minority employee higher than deserved on the performance appraisal form.
___	___	3.	A manager has a male subordinate who is married with three children. This employee is a known womanizer and has been spotted by several employees socializing with women other than his wife, including prostitutes. The supervisor does not believe this is appropriate and rates the employee lower than deserved on the performance appraisal form.
___	___	4.	A female employee who recently had a baby negotiated a change from full-time to part-time status with the HR department. Her supervisor, also a working mother, resents the fact that she is able to spend more time at home with her child. The supervisor rates her lower than deserved on the performance appraisal form in an attempt to force her to switch back to full-time status or to quit.
___	___	5.	A firm has a 360-degree performance appraisal system that includes asking all subordinates to rate and evaluate their boss. A manager wants to be promoted so he gives all employees higher performance evaluations than they deserve in hopes that they, in turn, will rate him higher.
___	___	6.	A manager realizes that an employee's attendance is so poor that she is likely to get terminated within the next few months. So, in order to build a more solid case against the employee and further justify the inevitable termination, the manager rates the subordinate lower than deserved on the performance appraisal form.
___	___	7.	A manager wants to get promoted in order to get a substantial raise. He believes that he will be judged, in part, in terms of how effective he has been at developing high-performing subordinates as evidenced by his subordinates' performance appraisal scores. In order to enhance his promotion chances, he rates his employees higher than deserved.
___	___	8.	A manager wants to give one particularly hard-working, reliable subordinate a big raise in order to keep her from accepting a job elsewhere. The manager does not want to have to replace this employee and train a new one. However, there is limited raise money available, and it is based on merit. So, he rates another employee lower than deserved, thereby reducing this person's raise, in order to be able to give the other a larger raise.
___	___	9.	A manager wants to get rid of a disliked subordinate, so she rates the employee lower than deserved in hopes that the employee will quit.
___	___	10.	A manager wants to help a subordinate who has become a friend to get a promotion, so she gives her a higher evaluation than deserved.

PART

4

Implementing Compensation and Security: Compensation, Incentives, Benefits, and Safety and Health

65 CASE

The Overpaid Bank Tellers

State Bank is located in a southwestern town of about 50,000 people. It is one of four banks in the area and has the reputation of being the most progressive. Russell Duncan has been the president of the bank for 15 years. Before coming to State Bank, he worked for a large Detroit bank for ten years. Duncan has implemented a number of changes that have earned him a great deal of respect and admiration from bank employees and townspeople alike. For example, in response to a growing number of Spanish-speaking people in the area, he hired Latinos and placed them in critical bank positions. He organized and staffed the city's only agricultural loan center to meet the needs of the area's farmers. In addition, he established the state's first "uniline" system for handling customers waiting in line for a teller.

Perhaps more than anything else, Duncan is known for establishing progressive human resource practices. He strongly believes that the bank's employees are its most important asset and continually searches for ways to increase both employee satisfaction and productivity. He feels that all employees should strive to continually improve their skills and abilities and, hence, he cross-trains employees and sends many of them to courses and conferences sponsored by banking groups such as the American Institute of Banking.

With regard to employee compensation, Duncan firmly believes that employees should be paid according to their contribution to organizational success. Ten years ago, he implemented a results-based pay system under which employees could earn raises from 0 to 8 percent each year, depending on their job performance. Raises are typically determined by the bank's HR committee during February and are granted to employees on March 1 of each year. Six years ago, in addition to granting employees merit raises, the bank also began giving cost-of-living raises. Duncan had been originally opposed to this idea but could determine no alternative.

One February, another bank in town conducted a wage survey to determine the average compensation of bank employees in the city. The management of State Bank received a copy of the wage survey and was surprised to learn that its 23 tellers, as a group, were being paid an average of $22 per week more than were tellers at other banks. The survey also showed that employees holding other positions in the bank (e.g., branch managers, loan officers, and file clerks) were being paid wages similar to those paid by other banks (see Exhibit 4.1).

After receiving the report, the HR committee of the bank met to determine what should be done regarding the tellers' raises. The committee knew that none of the tellers had been told how much their raises would be, but that they were all expecting both merit and cost-of-living raises. They also realized that, if other employees learned that the tellers were being overpaid, friction could develop and morale might suffer. The committee knew that it was costing the bank over $26,000 annually to pay the tellers. Finally, they knew that as a group the bank's tellers were highly competent, and they did not want to lose any of them.

EXHIBIT 4.1 *Wage Survey Results: Comparative Salaries of Local Bank Officers*

Position	Bank 1	Bank 2	Bank 3	State Bank
Commercial Loan Officer	$78,600	$79,500	$77,900	$78,400
Consumer Loan Officer	59,200	54,700	55,760	59,000
Mortgage Loan Officer	57,100	55,900	59,500	57,200
Branch Manager	57,700	59,400	58,800	58,400
Assistant Branch Manager	40,800	40,400	40,600	40,300
New Accounts Officer	33,900	33,800	33,700	33,800
Officer Trainee	33,200	33,000	33,400	33,300

Average Weekly Earnings of Local Bank Tellers

	Bank 1	Bank 2	Bank 3	State Bank
Tellers	$482	$479	$485	$504

QUESTIONS

1. If you were on the HR committee of State Bank, what decisions would you suggest regarding raises for the tellers?
2. How much faith should the HR committee place in the accuracy of the wage survey?
3. Critique State Bank's policy of giving merit raises that range from 0 to 8 percent, depending on job performance.
4. Critique the bank's policy of giving cost-of-living raises. Do you think that they should be eliminated?

66 CASE

Rewarding Volunteers

BACKGROUND

Northern University is a large university in a small college town in the Northwest. After several years of political pressure, internal conflicts, and negotiations, the university applied for, and was granted, an FCC license for a new public radio affiliate. The general goals of the station were to provide quality noncommercial alternative broadcasting with an emphasis on local and national news, jazz, and classical music. The station would have no paid commercials but would broadcast public service announcements and cultural events.

A short-term objective was to assemble and train a volunteer staff (mostly students and faculty) until funds could be provided for an all-professional staff of experienced board operators and program announcers. Exhibit 4.2 shows the organization structure of the radio station. The general manager, chief engineer, news director, administrative assistant, and program director were all full-time paid positions. All of the other positions were either part-time employees, part-time work-study students, or unpaid part-time volunteers. The latter were mostly university faculty and their spouses.

The students volunteered to get training and experience, which they hoped would propel them into careers in the media. Faculty volunteered either for the new experience or because they liked playing particular types of music. The others volunteered to help the station and to meet new people. Volunteers were trained and used as both announcers and in "behind the scenes" positions such as board operators. Many of the board operators were told they could become announcers in the future.

EXHIBIT 4.2 *Organizational Structure of the Station*

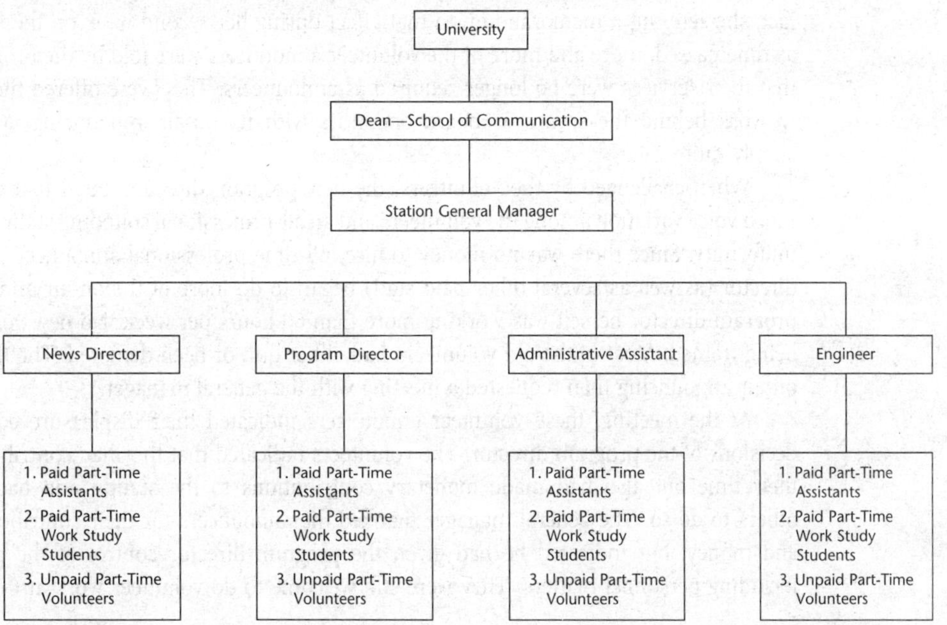

The program director's responsibilities included developing the on-air program schedule, which consisted of National Public Radio (NPR) standards such as "Morning Edition" and "All Things Considered" as well as jazz in the mornings and classical music in the afternoons. He also developed the volunteer training program (including both equipment operation and on-air announcing) and scheduled and supervised the volunteers and work-study students. The program director also did some on-air announcing and worked as the internal liaison, coordinating the various departments. He reported directly to the station general manager, who was responsible for all aspects of internal station management as well as developing and sustaining relationships with external constituencies.

PROBLEMS

The person hired initially as program director had a leadership style that did not fit well in a volunteer-oriented organization. Specifically, he was task-oriented and had few skills in managing others. This leadership style contributed to conflicts within the organization, and the program director left the organization by mutual consent after nine months on the job. The position of program director remained unfilled for nine months.

During that time period, the general manager and the administrative assistant split the work ordinarily done by the program director, including the recruitment, selection, training, and scheduling of the volunteers. However, none of these activities were ever institutionalized in terms of written policies and procedures. For example, there were no written job descriptions for volunteers explaining duties and responsibilities for particular positions. Nor was there any formal feedback system for evaluating volunteer performance and/or receiving volunteer input. Voluntary recruitment and opportunities for volunteer training were also reduced during this period.

After nine months a new program director was hired. She had previous experience as a program director at another public radio station and came highly recommended. Her initial statement was one of amazement at the high quality of announcing among the volunteers. In fact, she sent out a memorandum to that effect during her second week on the job. However, as time passed, more and more of the volunteer announcers were told by the program director that their services were no longer required as announcers. They were offered the opportunity to work behind the scenes as board operators with no on-air announcing. Most chose to simply quit.

When challenged by the volunteers, the new program director stated that there was too much voice variation among the volunteers and an all-professional sounding station needs more uniformity. Since there was no money to hire full-time professional announcers, the program director (as well as several other paid staff) began to do more of the on-air announcing. The program director herself was working more than 60 hours per week. No new volunteers were being trained. Most of the old volunteers had either quit or been demoted. The five still doing on-air announcing then requested a meeting with the general manager.

At the meeting, these volunteer announcers indicated their displeasure concerning the decisions of the program director. The volunteers indicated that they had contributed not only their time but also had made monetary contributions to the station and had encouraged others to do so. The general manager thanked the announcers for their contributions of time and money, but indicated he had given the program director control of the programming including personnel matters. They were still welcome to do volunteer work at the station and could continue announcing "for the time being." The volunteers were not happy with this response and promptly submitted their resignations.

The general manager now had a bigger problem on his hands. The paid staff were already spread too thin and stretched to the limit even before the latest volunteer resignations. The station was committed to 20 hours of programming each day. NPR daily programs and prerecorded tapes could not fill the entire programming gap since they also required staff time to produce. The station clearly was in a crisis situation.

QUESTIONS

1. Describe the fundamental problem in this case together with its causes.
2. What specific mistakes were made by (a) the general manager and (b) the program director?
3. Did you ever do unpaid volunteer work? What were your purposes/goals and to what degree did you achieve them?
4. What types of rewards are most appropriate for volunteers? To what degree were these provided to volunteers at the radio station?
5. What steps should the station general manager take now?

67 CASE

Evaluating Nontraditional Incentive Systems: Howe 2 Ski Stores

Howe 2 Ski Stores is a chain of three ski and snowboarding shops located in the suburbs of a large eastern city. Maria Howe, a ski enthusiast and business school major, started the company ten years ago after her college graduation with financial backing from her family and several friends. From its inception, Howe 2 Ski Stores was intended to provide state-of-the-art equipment and clothing for skiers at all skill levels, from beginner to champion. It was to be staffed by employees who were themselves advanced skiers and could provide expert advice on the choice of clothing and equipment, and it was intended to have a quick response time that would permit the last-minute purchase of equipment and clothing prior to a ski trip.

Howe originally drew from a pool of skiing friends and fellow students to staff the stores and still prefers to hire part-time employees with skiing expertise who might leave in a year over more stable, full-time employees with less expertise and interest in the sport. Whether administrative staff, cashiers, clerks, or molders (employees who fit bindings to skis), employees were encouraged to keep up with the latest skiing equipment and trends, attend ski vendor shows, try out demo equipment, and give feedback on the store's inventory in order to help provide the highest quality, state-of-the-art equipment and advice for the customer.

Suggestion boxes were placed in the store and Howe herself regularly collected, read, and acted upon the suggestions made by the clerks and customers. She developed special advertising campaigns to build an image for the nearby slopes in order to increase the market. As the business grew, Howe even added a line of rental equipment in order to lower the costs and encourage people to try the sport.

Although profits grew irregularly due to weather effects and the faddish nature of the sport, Howe's efforts paid off in the long term, and within four years business had grown sufficiently to permit the opening of a second Howe 2 Ski Store in another suburb about ten miles from the first. In order to increase sales, about six years ago, Howe took a chance on the growing snowboarding market and the East Coast location and added a line of equipment for this sport. Snowboarding had caught on especially among Generation X and 75 percent of people who snowboard are under age 25. The move turned out to be a very good one. The snowboarding market increased by more than 300 percent in four years and continues to experience a slower but stable pattern of growth as snowboarding became a Winter Olympic sport in 1999. The snowboard market had also spawned a whole line of complementary accessories and apparel. Young snowboarders preferred a "hip hop" look of hooded flannel shirts and baggy pants. This market has enabled Howe to smooth out the number of sales occurring throughout the year.

Three years ago, Howe was able to open a third store, located within a 15-mile radius from the other two. Although managers have been hired to run each of the stores and the total number of employees has grown to 65, Howe's basic strategy has remained the same—high quality, state-of-the-art products, a knowledgeable staff, and quick response time. Profits from the stores have continued to grow, although at a slower rate. Competition from other ski stores has also increased noticeably within the last two years.

The threat of increased competition has been exacerbated by signs that employee productivity has begun to slide. Last year, there were eight occasions where expensive ski orders were not delivered in time for the customers' ski vacations. Although Howe used a variety of maneuvers to retain the customers' patronage (such as paying for the customers to rent equipment of equivalent quality, express-shipping the equipment to the customer as soon as it was delivered, and lowering the price of the equipment), the costs of these late orders were high. She realizes that word of these kinds of incidents could significantly damage the store's reputation for exceptional service. Furthermore, at least 15 percent of all ski orders were more than two days late, even though customers did not miss a trip or vacation as a result.

In an attempt to respond to these difficulties, Howe instituted a merit performance system for the molders (employees who fit the binding to skis). Although productivity seemed to increase for awhile, waves of discontent happened all over the stores. The molders felt that their merit ratings were inaccurate because the store managers could not observe them much of the time. Further, they argued that their performance would have been much higher had not other employees interrupted them with questions about appropriate bindings or failed to clearly identify the appropriate equipment on the sales tickets.

Other employees also complained because they were not given the opportunity for merit pay. The buyers, who visit ski shows, examine catalogs, and talk with sales representatives in order to decide on the inventory, argued that their work was essential for high sales figures and quality equipment. Sales clerks claimed that their in-depth familiarity with an extensive inventory and their sales skills were essential to increasing sales. They also noted their important role in negotiating a delivery date that the molders could meet. Similar arguments were made by the people in the credit office who arranged for short-term financing if necessary and the cashiers who verified costs and checked credit card approvals. Even the stockers noted that the store would be in a bad way if they did not locate the correct equipment in a warehouse full of inventory and deliver it in a timely manner to the molders.

Howe had to concede that the employees were correct on many of these points, so she suspended the merit plan at the end of the ski season and promised to reevaluate its fairness. Even more convincing were several indications that productivity problems were not limited to molder employees. Complaints about customer service increased 20 percent during the year. Several customers noted that they were allowed to stand, merchandise in hand, waiting for a clerk to help them, while clerks engaged in deep conversations among themselves. Younger college student employees were often found listening to music on their iPods. Although Howe mentioned these concerns to employees in the stores when she visited and asked the store managers to discuss them in staff meetings, the complaints from customers continued.

A record number of "as is" skis were sold at the end of the season sale because they were damaged in the warehouse, the store, or by the molders. The closing inventory revealed that 20 percent of the rental equipment had been lost or seriously damaged without resulting charges to the renters because records were poorly maintained. Regular checks of the suggestion boxes in the store revealed fewer and fewer comments. Employees just did not seem to notice these problems, or worse, did not seem to care.

Howe was very bothered by all these factors and felt they could not be attributed to the growth of the business alone. She knew it would be impossible to maintain her competitive position with these events occurring in her stores. At a recent Small Business Forum meeting, Howe heard the guest speaker, a university professor, suggest that employers consider a group of non-traditional incentive plans in order to increase employee motivation and involvement and reduce the costs of operating. For example, some companies were using time-off schemes, gainsharing, bonuses tied to new product knowledge, and contests and prizes. Howe decided to investigate these topics further to see whether they might be appropriate for her stores.

QUESTIONS

1. Given the background information about Howe 2 Ski Stores, discuss the feasibility of implementing lump sum bonuses, pay for knowledge, profit sharing, and gainsharing plans. What plan or plans would you recommend that Howe look at most closely and why?
2. Assuming that Howe decides that a gainsharing plan is feasible, what could be done to increase the likelihood of success?
3. What negative effects are likely to result from even the successful implementation of a gainsharing plan?

Contributed by M. Susan Taylor, University of Maryland and J. Kline Harrison, Wake Forest University

68 EXERCISE

Executive Bonuses and Incentives

I. OBJECTIVES

A. To help you understand the complexities involved in designing an executive compensation system that will reward performance in areas which are sustainable and result in long-term organizational success.

B. To demonstrate the necessity to balance financial and non-financial criteria for executive compensation in both the short term and long term.

II. OUT-OF-CLASS PREPARATION TIME: 1 hour

III. IN-CLASS TIME SUGGESTED: 1 hour

IV. PROCEDURES

1. Read the entire exercise including the Background information below before class. After reading the Background information in the case, review information in your text or on the Internet on the topics of "Executive Bonuses" and "Executive Incentives."
2. Then, form groups of three to five students in class and answer the questions on Form 4.1 regarding a possible new design for an executive compensation system at Internet Applications. Once these questions have been discussed by the group and a group consensus (or majority opinion) on each has been reached, write your answers on Form 4.1.
3. The groups should then complete Form 4.2, which is partially completed for you but leaves space for additional short-term and long-term criteria for executive compensation. As you consider your plan, be sure to evaluate incentives that (if goals are accomplished) will make the company and its products sustainable over the long term. Add additional criteria as you see fit. Then, indicate for each criterion you retain what percent of total compensation should be based on each and how each should be divided among short-term bonuses and long-term stock options.
4. After completing Forms 4.1 and 4.2, the group should inform the instructor. When all groups have finished steps two and three, each group should have a spokesperson orally summarize their recommendations, the rationale for them, and their potential downsides for the entire class.

BACKGROUND

Internet Applications is a medium-sized computer software company that has grown rapidly since its inception 20 years ago in a large Texas city. While the company has had its "ups and downs" over the 20-year period, it has grown to be one of the top 1,000 U.S. companies in terms of total revenues. The company is currently doing well financially with revenue and earnings growth per share each up approximately 10 percent over the past year. However, its stock price is still approximately 50 percent below its previous peak price of 48 dollars per share achieved 10 years earlier.

The board of directors consists of some local public officials as well as industry experts and financiers, many of whom are CEOs of other companies in Texas. The current CEO, Donald Tisdale, was appointed to the position three years ago. Recently, the board was shocked to see their company and the CEO highlighted in the annual *BusinessWeek* survey, which listed executives who did the least to earn their pay in the last year. Among the factors sighted was the lagging stock price, earnings that were still below those achieved four years earlier before the "financial crisis," and a board that continued to increase the CEO's total annual compensation despite the lagging earnings and stock price. As a result, the CEO's total compensation was approximately 580x that of the average employee in the company.

The board has based its short-term and long-term CEO compensation on the earnings of other CEOs in the metropolitan area and in the industry. They have also relied on an executive compensation consultant who indicated the CEO's total compensation was well within industry norms. As a result, the board was insulted by the *BusinessWeek* article and felt inclined to write a defense of their pay practices. However, one member suggested they seek some additional information before responding in a formal way.

The board asked their human resource vice president, Henrietta Peach, to make a recommendation concerning this issue. She suggested the director of compensation, Ellen Bennett, should conduct a study of executive compensation and make recommendations to the board. Bennett agreed and has asked your instructor to assist in her research and future recommendations. Your instructor has asked each team in the class for their analysis and recommendations as noted in Forms 4.1 and 4.2 in this case.

Your instructor has also shared with you the following information that he and Bennett have discovered in their research:

- Executive compensation consists of five components with mean percentages in U.S. corporations as follows:

    1. Big salary (35%)
    2. Short-term incentives or bonuses (24%)
    3. Long-term incentives or stock plans (31%)
    4. Benefits (5%)
    5. Perquisites (5%)

- Greater use of both short-term and long-term executive bonuses and stock incentives among top and middle managers is associated with higher subsequent levels of profitability.

- There is a high level of current pressure from the Securities and Exchange Commission (SEC) as well as some large pension programs (TIAA-CREF and CALPERS) to better link pay and performance among executives. Toward that end, they have proposed guidelines for executive compensation. These pension funds have described executive compensations in many of the companies in which they hold stock as "Heads I win, tails we flip again." As a result, they believe that excessive executive compensation dilutes stockholder equity and the returns of those who hold stock in the company. The problem is that in these companies executive pay is higher each year regardless of profitability, stock price, or meeting the needs of employees or customers.

- The late Peter Drucker, 20 years ago, indicated that executive pay was "off the charts" at that time. He recommended that the CEO total compensation should be no more than 20x the pay of the average rank and file employee.

- Current practices for determining executive compensation use competitive benchmarking by a compensation committee within the board of directors that utilizes comparisons with similar companies in terms of size, sales, industry, geographic region, etc. They also tend to use executive compensation consultants who have been recommended by other companies. Some critics have claimed that these consultants may have a conflict of interest in that boards tend to hire and re-hire those who "rubber stamp" their particular compensation preferences.

- CEO compensation among U.S. corporations is approximately 400x that of the average worker in these companies. This ratio is much higher than the same ratio in other developed countries. In fact, U.S. top executives are the highest paid in the world. This has created a "trust gap," or a frame of mind, among employees that leads them to mistrust senior management intentions, doubt their competence, and resent their self-congratulatory pay. This issue has become salient when the same companies simultaneously engage in large-scale layoffs and downsizing. Research indicates that companies with higher pay differentials between executives and rank and file employees have lower levels of employee and customer satisfaction and declining market shares.

- Short-term incentives are usually given annually and may take the form of either cash or stock. Annual bonuses may also be based on achievement of specific objectives. Long-term incentives usually take the form of stock options used to link stockholder and executive incentives.

- Today the goal is to provide executive incentives that address the concerns of stockholders, employees, and customers. Companies that address all three stakeholders in their executive compensation tend to perform better in financial terms over the long run.

- Balanced score cards have been developed to provide a more comprehensive evaluation of the organization's performance, taking into account not only stock price and financial returns but also employee satisfaction, customer satisfaction, market share, measures of product or service quality, innovation and product leadership, and low levels of employee turnover. The alleged benefits of balanced score cards are that they allow executives to focus on not only short-term financial results but also on factors which build future economic and non-economic success.

FORM 4.1 *Questions Regarding Executive Compensation Plans*

1. What short-term (bonuses) and long-term (stock incentive plans) ideas for executive incentives do you suggest? Why?

   Bonuses:

   Stock Incentives:

2. What percentage of total executive compensation should be in the bonus category and what percent should be in the stock incentive category? Why?

   Short-Term Bonuses:

   Long-Term Stock Incentives:

   Why?:

3. How would you address the interest of stockholder, customers, and employees in your executive compensation plan?

   Stockholders:

   Employees:

Customers:

____

____

____

4. Do you approve of the following executive compensation reforms that have been suggested by critics and in Congress? (Yes or No)

- Require stockholder approval for all executive pay packages. _____
- Require a standard ratio between CEO total compensation and that of the average employee in the company. _____
- Require compensation committees of the board of directors to be composed of "public members" (non-CEOs). _____
- Require compensation committees to justify their pay recommendations in terms of some combination of increased employee satisfaction, customer satisfaction, product innovation, and market share. _____

FORM 4.2 *Recommended Criteria and Metrics for Proposed Executive Compensation Plan*

Percentage of Compensation
Total (Incentives) (Bonuses)
(Company Stock)

Stockholders:

- Earnings Growth per Share
- Stock Price Increase per Share
- Cash Flow per Share
- Growth and Market Share

____

____

____

Employees:

- Employee Retention
- Employee Satisfaction
- Percent of Employees Receiving Training
- and Development

____

____

____

Customers:

- Measured Quality of Products
- Product Innovation
- Customer Satisfaction

____

____

____

Benchmark Ratio of CEO Total Compensation to Average Employee Pay ________: 1

69 EXERCISE

Allocating Merit Raises

I. OBJECTIVES

A. To make you aware of the difficulties involved in making merit raise decisions.

B. To familiarize you with possible criteria a manager can use in making merit raise decisions.

II. OUT-OF-CLASS PREPARATION TIME: 10–20 minutes to read exercise and decide each professor's merit raise

III. IN-CLASS TIME SUGGESTED: 30–40 minutes

IV. PROCEDURES

Either at the beginning of or before coming to class, you should read the exercise and determine merit raises for each professor.

To start the exercise, the instructor will divide the class into groups of three to five students. Each group should develop a fair procedure that will be used to determine merit raises and then decide the dollar raise to be given to each professor. After each group finishes, one member will write the raise amounts on the board or overhead for all class members to see. Then, once all groups have disclosed their raises, a spokesperson for each group will explain the procedure used to determine their raises.

SITUATION

Small State University is located in the eastern part of the United States and has an enrollment of about 8,000 students. The College of Business has 40 full-time and more than 30 part-time faculty members. The college is divided into five departments: Management, Marketing, Finance and Accounting, Decision Sciences, and Information Technology. Faculty members in the Management Department are evaluated each year based on three primary criteria: 1) teaching, 2) research, and 3) service. Teaching performance is based on student course evaluations over a two-year period. Service to the university, college, profession, and community is also based on accomplishments over a two-year period. Research is based on the number of journal articles published over a three-year period. Teaching and research are considered more important than service to the university. In judging faculty performance, the department chair evaluates each professor in terms of four standards: Far Exceeds Standards, Exceeds Standards, Meets Standards, and Fails to Meet Standards. The results of this year's evaluations are shown in Exhibit 4.3.

Due to financial problems and cutbacks this year, Small State University has agreed to give raises totaling just $6,300 to the Management Department. Your task as department chair is to divide the $6,300 among the faculty members. Keep in mind that these raises will likely set a precedent for the future and that the professors will view the raises as a signal for what behavior and achievements are valued.

A profile of each of the professors is provided below.

Professor Houseman: 55 years old; 25 years with the university; teaches Principles of Management sections; teaches over 400 students per year; has written over 40 articles and given over 30 presentations since joining the college; wants a good raise to catch up with others.

EXHIBIT 4.3 *Department Chairs' Rating of Job Performance*

Professor	Current Salary	Teaching	Research	Service
Houseman	$92,000	Exceeds	Exceeds	Meets
Jones	$116,000	Exceeds	Far Exceeds	Exceeds
Ricks	$135,000	Meets	Meets	Far Exceeds
Matthews	$97,000	New Hire	New Hire	New Hire
Karas	$100,000	Far Exceeds	Exceeds	Meets
Franks	$90,000	Meets	Fails to Meet	Exceeds

Professor Jones: 49 years old; 10 years with the university; teaches Human Resource Management and Organizational Behavior; stepped down as department chair three years ago; teaches about 200 students a year; has written over 30 articles and two books since joining the college; recently received an $80,000 grant for the college from a local foundation, and wants a good raise as a reward for obtaining the grant.

Professor Ricks: 61 years old; 6 years with university; teaches Labor Relations and Organizational Development; stepped down as dean of the College of Business two years ago and took a $20,000 pay cut; teaches about 180 students per year; has written only two articles in the last six years due to administrative duties; very active in the community and serves on several charity boards; wants a good raise to make up for loss of $20,000.

Professor Matthews: 28 years old; new hire—only four months with the university; teaches Employee Relations and Compensation Management; just graduated with a PhD; will teach about 110 students this year. To be competitive in the job market, the college paid Professor Matthews $97,000 plus provided a reduced teaching load for two years and a $6,000 per year summer stipend; none of the other faculty received this when they were first hired or subsequently; had two minor publications while a doctoral student but none since joining the college; wants a good raise to pay student loans and furnish a new residence.

Professor Karas: 32 years old; 4 years with university; teaches International Business and Honors sections of Management Principles; teaches about 150 students per year; won Teacher of the Year Award this year; published 12 articles in last four years; has been interviewing for a new job at other universities and may leave if a good raise is not forthcoming.

Professor Franks: 64 years old; 18 years with university; teaches Principles of Management and Human Resource Management; teaches about 150 students per year; principal advisor for management-major students; has not written any articles during the last four years; plans on retiring within two–three years, and wants a good raise to enhance pension plan.

70 EXERCISE

WageSim—A Compensation Administration Exercise

I. OBJECTIVES

A. To familiarize you with some of the problems involved in building and maintaining a compensation system.

B. To provide you with alternative approaches for solving some typical compensation-related problems.

C. To give you practice in writing memos to employees regarding compensation issues.

D. To familiarize you with job evaluation procedures.

II. OUT-OF-CLASS PREPARATION TIME: 20 minutes to read exercise plus one hour to respond to the E-mail Items (either individually or in a group)

III. IN-CLASS TIME SUGGESTED: 45 minutes to discuss all E-mail Items

IV. PROCEDURES

This exercise can be done individually or in groups of three to five members, at the instructor's option. You are to begin by reading all of the material presented in this exercise. Assume that you are responsible for developing and maintaining the Mack Organization's wage and salary system. Assume further that the person who previously had these responsibilities has just quit and left you all of the E-mail Items that follow. First, you (or your team) are (is) to respond in writing to each employee who sent an e-mail. Second, explain on a separate sheet of paper what additional actions you would take with reference to each item. For example, if you believe that you should gather additional information before making a final decision on an item, explain what information you would need. Or, if you believe that additional memos or discussions with someone in the company are needed, explain this. You (or your team) should bring both the memos and the Additional Action sheets to class. Be prepared to present and defend these materials during the class discussion.

SITUATION

The Mack Organization is a large organization headquartered in the midwestern United States. It has offices located throughout the country and employs over 700 individuals. You may assume the organization is a chemical company, a manufacturing company, a bank, a insurance firm, or any large organization with which you are familiar.

The Mack Organization's human resource department includes a compensation administration section that consists of two individuals, one of whom is you (or your team). The company has several different wage structures, including one for executives and one for clerical personnel. For compensation purposes, all clerical employees are divided into five job classifications. The organization's current wage structure for clerical personnel is shown in Exhibit 4.4.

HOW SALARIES ARE DETERMINED

Employee salaries directly relate to the work they do and how well they do it. Two major factors work together to establish the salaries payable for various jobs—job evaluation and salary ranges.

EXHIBIT 4.4 *Mack Organization's Wage Structure for Clerical Personnel*

Job Title	Salary	Number of Employees
Office Services Aide	$25,259 minimum $33,262 maximum	40
Office Services Assistant	$26,588 minimum $35,337 maximum	30
Administrative Assistant	$30,041 minimum $39,604 maximum	20
Senior Assistant	$34,628 minimum $45,083 maximum	40
Executive Assistant	$43,364 minimum $54,794 maximum	20

JOB EVALUATION

Job evaluation is a method of measuring the relative worth of each job in the organization compared to all the other jobs, based on an objective analysis of the duties and responsibilities of the position. The Mack Organization job evaluation is as follows: A description that defines the function of the job and lists the major duties performed is written for each job. Each description is then evaluated by a standing committee of employees from various areas of the organization who have a broad knowledge of the jobs that exist throughout the organization. Their evaluation is based on "yardsticks," including knowledge required, freedom of action, accountability, contacts with employees and customers, physical effort required, unusual working conditions, research responsibilities, and supervision or management responsibilities. Based on these yardsticks, the job is assigned a point value. By listing all positions according to their point value, the relative worth of each position is established.

GRADE LEVELS AND SALARY RANGES

Based on the total points received in a job evaluation, jobs are assigned to a grade level. Each grade has an entry or minimum salary and a maximum salary payable for the jobs in that grade; the amounts between the entry and maximum salary comprise the salary range for the grade.

Usually employees begin at the bottom of each salary grade. Employees are considered for a merit increase after six months of satisfactory service. After this, they may receive an annual merit increase upon completion of satisfactory service. There are a total of six possible merit increases. Cost-of-living increases are granted periodically by the organization to all employees.

E-mail Items

Item 1

To: Wage & Salary Division
From: Mary Wallace—Vice President
Re: Request for pay increase/promotion

This is to formally request your endorsement of my intent to promote Susan Anthony, an administrative assistant in my office, to the position of senior assistant. I realize a requirement for senior assistant is proficiency in Adobe InDesign (a desktop publishing program) and that Ms. Anthony is not yet proficient.

However, aside from this, Ms. Anthony possesses the necessary skills to perform all tasks in this office. Ms. Anthony has been with this office for five years and is a loyal and dedicated employee. I wholeheartedly encourage your endorsement of this recommendation and pay increase. A vacant senior assistant position is available in this office. Please advise as soon as possible.

Item 2

To: Wage and Salary Section
From: Kelly Actor
Re: Request for pay increase

I have been with this company for ten years. My present position with this company is senior assistant, at the maximum pay level. The Wispette Company has offered me a position that would give me a 9% increase in salary for similar duties. Since I do enjoy my work, I hate to leave. However, my financial obligations to my family leave me with no choice. My husband recently has been disabled, with no hope of employment for three years. As I mentioned, I have enjoyed my ten years with this company. My supervisor and I get along well. I have not missed any work during the ten years except for the two-week vacation during the summer. If you will match the Wispette Company's offer, I would prefer to stay with your company. I understand there is no opening for an executive assistant, which would be a comparable position. I need an answer soon.

Item 3

To: Wage and Salary Section
From: Jane Swenk, Supervisor
Re: Long-term employee wage dispute

M.O. Scott, an administrative assistant, expressed concern that her daughter, also an administrative assistant, was making an equal amount of money. M.O. has been employed for 28 years, her daughter for five. Merit raises are given yearly only for the first five years, and M.O. has not gotten one in 23 years. I don't think this policy is fair. M.O. should get something for her longer service. Please respond so I can explain the situation to her.

Item 4

To: Compensation Administration
From: HR Director
Re: Payroll budget for next month

Please prepare a payroll budget for next month for clerical employees. Make whatever assumptions you feel are necessary in doing your calculation. Just let me know what the assumptions are. Many thanks.

Item 5

To: Wage and Salary Section
From: Bob Franklin, Administrative Aide
Re: Pay inequity question

I was recently hired as an administrative assistant and received the minimum pay for this position. Why do some office service aides make more than I do? My duties and responsibilities are much greater than theirs.

Item 6

To: Compensation Section
From: Betty Dyer, Supervisor
Re: Pay for Tammy Tuff

Tammy Tuff is an excellent administrative assistant in my office. She does an outstanding job with all assignments and performs beyond standards for an administrative assistant in everything she does. She completes her assignments in half the time of other aides and voluntarily assumes extra duties after finishing her assignments. In addition to her outstanding performance, Ms. Tuff has improved morale in the office since she started nine months ago. She always has a smile on her face and brightens the day for co-workers with her pleasant disposition. Best of all, she makes others feel important, and this has carried over to their work. Everyone seems to take pride in their work; consequently, performance and productivity are up. Due to Tammy's influence, the turnover rate is zero, leaving her with no promotion potential in this office. Based on Tammy's excellent performance, skills that exceed the requirements of the job, and attitude that has improved morale, I feel that Tammy deserves to be paid as a senior assistant even though she is not one and there is no senior assistant vacancy.

Item 7

To: Wage & Salary
From: Chris Markley, Supervisor
Re: Pay question

I am relatively new to the position of senior assistant and was told that pay for my job is based on points. I thought it was based on job duties and performance. What do points have to do with it?

Item 8

To: W & S
From: McNamara, Department Manager
Re: Employee problem

Mary White, an office services aide, left two hours early yesterday, without permission, to attend a civil rights rally. Should she be paid for this time?

Item 9

To: Wage & Salary Section
From: Sue L. Ross, Supervisor
Re: Pay for Julie Tate

Julie Tate, senior assistant, has been temporarily assigned some of the duties of an executive assistant position. The position is temporarily vacant due to the executive secretary being gone for four weeks. Julie has been told by me that she may be assigned higher-level duties on occasion, but she is not satisfied. She insists that she deserves financial compensation for absorbing some duties of an executive assistant. None of the additional duties is too difficult for Julie to handle, and she actually does an excellent job on all assignments when she stops complaining about her unfair treatment. I am recommending that Julie be paid at the rate of an executive assistant position so that I can assign her higher-level duties whenever my executive assistant is on vacation or sick leave. This way Julie will not complain about the grade level of her work, and the flow of work in the office will proceed smoothly without disruption. Please respond to this recommendation.

Item 10

To: Wage and Salary Section
From: Doris Pope, Department Head
Re: Frances Brown, Administrative Aide

The administrative assistant in my department, Frances Brown, has decided she would like to work at home four days a week and in the office one day. Given her job duties, this will pose no problem for this office. However, I am not sure how this will affect her pay. Will it increase her pay or decrease it? Please advise.

Thanks.

---

71 EXERCISE

Ethical and Practical Compensation Dilemmas

I. OBJECTIVES

A. To familiarize you with a variety of different compensation dilemmas and possible solutions to them.

B. To make you aware that some compensation decisions involve ethical issues.

C. To familiarize you with various criteria that can be used to distinguish between ethical and unethical behavior.

II. OUT-OF-CLASS PREPARATION TIME: 5 minutes to read all or some of the Ethical Compensation Dilemmas below, as assigned by your instructor

III. IN-CLASS TIME SUGGESTED: 20–75 minutes, depending on how many of the Dilemmas below are assigned by your instructor

IV. PROCEDURES

At the start of class, you will be divided into groups of three to five and assigned one or more of the following ten Compensation Dilemmas to analyze. Your group should answer the questions asked at the end of each Dilemma and be prepared to present your decisions. While answering these questions, your group may want to address the questions below. They are designed to help you determine if an issue involves ethical considerations.

1. Does the action involve intentional deception?
2. Does the action purposely benefit one party at the expense of another?
3. Is the action fair and just to all concerned? The Golden Rule not only dictates that we "do unto others as we would have them do unto us" but also commands that we treat others as we might wish to be treated.
4. Would the manager feel comfortable if the action were made public or must it remain a secret?
5. Are managers justifying the action by telling themselves that they can get away with it or that they will not need to live with the decision's consequences?
6. Would the decision maker recommend the action to other managers or firms?
7. Will the action build goodwill and better relationships?

In answering the questions, you also may also want to consider three different schools of thought regarding ethical decision making. The Utilitarian Approach argues that decision outcomes should result in the greatest good for the greatest number of people. The Moral Rights Approach holds that decisions should be consistent with fundamental rights and privileges as set forth in the Bill of Rights or some other document such as the United Nations' Declaration of Human Rights. The Justice Approach stresses that decisions should be equitable and follow the distributive justice and fairness principle. Some argue that the ideal decision occurs when it is supported by the ethical standards of all three ethical approaches.

After all groups have finished their analysis (ten minutes or less) of each Compensation Dilemma, the instructor will call on one or more groups to answer the questions presented. This will be followed by a class discussion of each Dilemma.

COMPENSATION DILEMMAS

1. Based on an evaluation of the knowledge, skills, and abilities needed to do each job, a company has determined that two jobs (Job A and Job B) are equal. However, when the firm studies the labor market, it finds that applicants for Job A are plentiful whereas those for Job B are very scarce. Should the firm offer less pay to those who apply for Job A, or should the pay be equal?
2. Assume that the supply of electrical technicians is low so a firm hires a group of them at $18 per hour. Two years later, due to a recession, the supply of technicians is high so the market rate for them is now $15 per hour. Should the firm pay new hires $18 or $15? Should it lower the pay of existing technicians to $15?
3. Jim is given an extremely large raise because of his superb work record one year. As a result, he is currently earning $50,000 whereas others at the firm holding the same job are earning $45,000. Everyone expects Jim to continue to excel and enhance the entire unit's productivity. Unfortunately, Jim's performance drops off after the first year and is now just average. What should be done about his pay? Should it be reduced to reflect his current performance?
4. One year, Ethan's performance is truly spectacular (just as good as Jim's had been in the previous case). However, the company has no raise money available that year so no one, including Ethan, receives a merit raise. Is this appropriate?
5. Mary and Sue both work in the same department. Mary believes that Sue is being paid considerably more than she is. In fact, both employees are being paid about the same amount. Mary wants a pay raise and complains to her boss and the compensation manager. What should the compensation manager say, assuming the firm follows the policy of not revealing the pay of individual employees? Should Mary be told the amount of Sue's pay? Or, should Mary only be told that there is a "misunderstanding" and that her belief is incorrect? Or, should some other approach be taken?
6. When Mary was hired, she was told verbally that she would receive a raise when she finished her college degree and yet another raise when she was given additional responsibility. She accepted the job offer based on this understanding. However, during the next two years, the firm experienced slow sales and had to ask all factory employees to accept a 12 percent pay decrease. But Mary, who does not work in the factory, has finished college and has accepted more responsibility. Should she receive a raise?
7. Two firms in the chemical solvent industry decide to merge. Employees in the testing department of Firm A have enjoyed high pay for many years. However, Firm A is purchased by Firm B, which has a history of paying low wages. As a result, employees in Firm A's testing department earn on average $2.00 more per hour than those at Firm B. Upon completion of the merger, what wage levels should prevail? Should wages be cut for those who worked for Firm A? Or, should wages be increased for those in Firm B?
8. Sue is a 55-year-old employee of Company A. Her children are out of college and her parents have both died. Company A offers a child care program to all employees along with an elder care program. However, Sue, like many other employees, has no need for these services, neither now or in the future. Should the company retain these programs? Should alternative benefits for employees who have no use for such services be offered?

9. Helen works as an accountant for a firm in the textile industry. During non-working hours, she does extensive volunteer work for the American Red Cross, Meals on Wheels, and the American Heart Association. Helen's employer wants to maintain a favorable image in the community, so it wants every employee to donate money to the United Way. Should the employer pressure Helen to donate money? Keep in mind that if Helen does not donate money, other employees may not either, which could result in an unfavorable image in the community for the employer. On the other hand, Helen already donates time, which has a monetary value, and she may feel that it is unfair to be asked to donate even more.
10. Frank works 25 hours per week for a mail order firm in the packaging department. He receives no benefits other than those required by law. Frank does the same type of work as three other employees, all of whom work full time. These employees qualify for pensions, medical care, long-term disability, child care, etc. Is this a good business practice? Assume that Frank would like to work full time, really wants to receive benefits, and feels harmed because of his shortfall. On the other hand, the firm is not legally required to pay Frank benefits, Frank only works part time, and it would be expensive to pay benefits to all part-time employees, including Frank.

72 EXERCISE

Pay Inversion: Is It Practical and Ethical?

OVERVIEW

This exercise contains three different—but related—scenarios regarding pay inversion. Pay inversion is defined as "the hiring of new employees at a higher compensation level than that of current employees who have better skills and performance records." These scenarios examine the ethical and practical aspects of inversion from three different decision maker's perspectives.

I. OBJECTIVES

A. To familiarize students with the concept of pay inversion.

B. To examine different ethical approaches and how they may apply to pay inversion.

C. To examine the issue of whether an action is ethical irrespective of whether one is the beneficiary of an action, the victim of it, or a decision maker.

D. To familiarize students with the potential costs and benefits to a firm of inverting pay.

E. To examine alternatives to pay inversion.

II. OUT-OF-CLASS PREPARATION TIME: none, unless the instructor asks the class to read the exercise before class

III. IN-CLASS TIME SUGGESTED: 30 minutes

IV. PROCEDURES

To begin the exercise, the instructor will divide the class into groups of three to five students and ask each to select a spokesperson. Each group is to read Scenario I and answer the questions at the end. When all student groups have finished answering the scenario questions, the instructor will call on a representative from one or more groups to present the group's answers. The class will discuss the answers, and this same process will be followed for Scenarios II and III. The class will then develop conclusions based on the entire exercise.

In examining each of the scenarios, you will be asked to consider ethical aspects of pay inversion. In doing so, you may want to consider the following ethical philosophies:

1. Legalistic Approach. This approach argues that if an action is legal, then it is ethical.
2. Ethical Egoism. This approach contends that to be ethical, an action must be in the best interests of the decision maker. It argues that when making this determination, the decision maker need not take into consideration the effects the decision may have on others.
3. Utilitarianism. This approach argues that an action is ethical if it helps the most stakeholders and harms the least. This approach argues that decision makers need to do a cost/benefit analysis when making their decisions.
4. Distributive Justice. This approach contends that an action is ethical if it is fair. It argues that equals should be treated equally and unequals should be treated unequally.
5. Kant's Ethical Imperative Approach. This approach argues that an action is ethical if it shows respect for people. To be respectful, one needs to treat people only as they have freely consented to be treated beforehand.
6. Other Approaches (optional). As assigned by the instructor.

EXERCISE SCENARIOS

Scenario I—You have just graduated with a major that is in high demand. For example, you have an MS in biotechnology and are knowledgeable about mapping the human genome. You have been offered a very attractive job with a medium-sized firm. Your starting salary is at the current market wage for your major. A best friend who works for the same firm has told you that your starting salary is $3,000 more than experienced employees earn because your major is in high demand. They were hired by the firm before the current high demand for your type of skills materialized. Your friend tells you that your co-workers are very productive and skilled and they will train and mentor you. Assuming that this is your best job offer, would you accept it? Would it be ethical for you to do so?

Scenario II—You accepted the job and have been with the firm for three years. You have received excellent annual evaluations and significant merit raises. In fact, your supervisor said you will likely be promoted within the next few years. Recently, the firm's business has improved dramatically, and your department needs to hire a new employee. Given the shortage of applicants, the current average market wage has increased, and your boss offered a new graduate from your alma mater $3,000 more than you are receiving. Given your superior skills, you will be asked to train and mentor the new hire. Do you agree that the firm should pay the market rate? Would it be ethical for the firm to do so?

Scenario III—Based on your skills, performance, and years with the firm, you have recently been promoted to manager and given a significant pay raise. Because business continues to improve, you must hire one additional person. You return to your alma mater. Unfortunately, the supply of applicants is still small, and the demand is still large, so the market average starting salary is $3,000 more than the salary of any of the more highly qualified employees you supervise. Would you offer that amount to a new employee? Would it be ethical for you to do so? What are the costs and benefits to the firm of paying the higher salary? Are there any alternatives to paying higher salaries?

Contributed by Myron Glassman, Old Dominion University

73 INCIDENT

Merit Increases

Dr. Carl Jones is chairperson of the Department of Management in the College of Business Administration at a large state university in the East. He has been a member of the department for 14 years and a full professor for five years. Last summer he was asked to assume the chair after a screening committee conducted interviews and reviewed his resume and the resumes of three other candidates.

Dr. Jones was very excited about the new challenges and has begun several innovative projects to enhance faculty research and consulting. The teaching function in the department has always been first-rate while research has been somewhat weaker. Dr. Jones has continued to be very productive as a scholar, publishing three articles, two book chapters, and one proceedings article over the past year. He also made considerable progress on a management text of which he was a co-author. Finally, he remained active in his professional association, the Academy of Management, where he served as chair of one of the professional divisions.

The university's policy is that all salary increases are based only on merit. Dr. Jones had developed a very sophisticated performance appraisal system for his faculty to help him quantify salary recommendations. His point system considers and weighs different items in the areas of teaching, research, and service. Teaching and research are weighted 40 percent each and service is weighted 20 percent. For the coming academic year, his recommended salary increases averaged four percent and ranged from one to seven percent. Dr. Jones felt he had good documentation for all his recommendations.

Dr. Jones submitted his recommendations to Dean Edmund Smith and was pleased when all these recommendations were accepted. He then proceeded to schedule appointments to meet with each faculty member to discuss his recommendation, the reasons for the recommendation, and goals for the coming year. While a few of the faculty receiving lower increases indicated dissatisfaction with his weighting system, particularly the emphasis on research, these meetings generally went well.

Dr. Jones then submitted his own annual report detailing his accomplishments as chair as well as his more personal accomplishments. From his perspective, he felt he deserved at least a 6 percent increase since his department had made major strides in a number of areas while the other departments had been standing still. Moreover, none of the other chairs were professionally active on the national level and none had published in the past year. His teaching evaluations were also in the top 15 percent of faculty in the college.

Dean Smith sent out letters to all the department chairs in August. Dr. Jones was shocked to learn that his salary increase was just 4 percent. Information he received through the "grapevine" was that all the chairs had received the 4 percent increase. He also learned from one of the other chairs that the dean always gave the chairs equal percentage increases each year. Contrary to the official university policy, there were no distinctions based on merit. Dr. Jones was visibly upset about what he considered to be a major inequity. He then called the dean's secretary to schedule an appointment to discuss the situation with Dean Smith.

QUESTIONS

1. Describe the nature and causes of the compensation problem described in this incident.
2. Are "merit" salary increases always based on "merit"? Why or why not?

3. Why has Dean Smith had a policy of equal percentage salary increases for all department chairs despite the stated university policy? Are all the chairs equally meritorious?
4. How do you think Dean Smith's "merit" increases will affect Dr. Jones and his performance as department chair and faculty member? Why? What can Dean Smith do to motivate him if a large differential pay increase based on performance is out of the question?
5. What are the long-range benefits of a true "merit" program? What are the problems associated with the lack of such a "merit" system for department chairs?

74 SKILL BUILDER

You Be the Judge: Is This Job Exempt?

I. OBJECTIVES

A. To help you understand the application of the Fair Labor Standards Act (FLSA).

B. To help you understand how the law is applied in determining whether jobs are exempt or non-exempt under FLSA.

II. OUT-OF-CLASS PREPARATION TIME: 60 minutes

III. IN-CLASS TIME SUGGESTED: 45 minutes

IV. PROCEDURES

A. Read the exercise and review the Fair Labor Standards Act excerpt pertaining to exempt status (see Exhibit 4.5).

B. The class should be divided into groups of four students.

C. Each group should read each of the incidents that follow and answer these questions:

1. Analyze each case with respect to the tests that must be considered for determination of exempt status of executive, professional, or administrative jobs.
2. If you were the judge, how would you rule? Is the job exempt or non-exempt? Why or why not?

Case 1 Harry Phipps, Senior Professional Sales Representative

Harry Phipps was employed by K & K Pharmaceutical Company as a senior professional sales representative. Phipps' position required him to travel across doctors' offices and hospitals where he promoted the benefit of K & K's drug, Provita, to the prescribing doctors. K & K used this method in the hope that when doctors realized the benefit of Provita, they would prescribe the drug for their patients.

By law, Phipps could not sell the drug directly to doctors. The company provided Phipps with a list of target doctors, and he was expected to complete ten visits per day, and each doctor had to be visited at least once a quarter. K & K left the itinerary and method of achieving the targets up to Phipps. However, they did provide Phipps with a budget for the visits. He was also given pre-approved visual aids and had received training in basic "marketing" skills, a core message about the product, and how to gauge doctor interest in the product. Each representative was expected to develop a plan for how to handle his or her territory. Phipps had to complete post-visit reports and refer back to them in planning the next visit. Being successful in the job required some creativity since doctors were extremely busy each day with their patients. Phipps cultivated relationships with their staff and used this as a means to gain access to the doctors.

Phipps earned $66,000 annually but was not paid for overtime. He also had the use of a company car. K & K could award a bonus based on the number of actual prescriptions issued in Phipps' territory. After the completion of two months on the job, Phipps added up the time he spent in completing his work and found he was working more than 8 hours a day. He approached K & K and requested to be paid for overtime. The HR manager indicated that Phipps did not qualify for overtime because the job of senior professional sales representative is exempt under the Fair Labor Standards Act and that overtime is only available to

EXHIBIT 4.5 *FLSA Wage and Hour Exemptions for Executive, Professional, Administrative, and Outside Sales People Personnel*

Exemptions

The FLSA requires that most employees in the United States be paid at least the federal minimum wage for all hours worked and overtime pay at time and one-half the regular rate of pay for all hours worked over 40 hours in a work week. However, Section 13(a) (1) of the FLSA provides an exemption from both minimum wage and overtime pay for employees employed as bona fide executive, administrative, professional, and outside sales employees. Section 13(a) (1) and Section 13(a) (17) also exempt certain computer employees. To qualify for exemption, employees generally must meet certain tests regarding their job duties and be paid on a salary basis at not less than $455 per week. Job titles do not determine exempt status. In order for an exemption to apply, an employee's specific job duties and salary must meet all the requirements of the Department's regulations. An employee will qualify for exemption if he or she meets all of the pertinent tests relating to duties, responsibilities, and salary as stipulated in the applicable section of Regulations, 29 C.R.F. Part 541.

Executive Exemption

To qualify for the executive employee exemption, all of the following tests must be met:

- The employee must be compensated on a salary basis (as defined in the regulations) at a rate not less than $455 per week (or $380 per week, if employed in American Samoa by an employer other than the Federal Government), exclusive of board, lodging, or other facilities; and
- The employee's primary duty must be managing the enterprise, or managing a customarily recognized department or subdivision of the enterprise;
- The employee must customarily and regularly direct the work of at least two or more other full-time employees or their equivalent; and
- The employee must have the authority to hire or fire other employees, or the employee's suggestions and recommendations as to the hiring, firing, advancement, promotion, or any other change of status of other employees must be given particular weight.

Administrative Exemption

To qualify for the administrative employee exemption, all of the following tests must be met:

- The employee must be compensated on a salary or fee basis (as defined in the regulations) at a rate not less than $455 (or $380 per week, if employed in American Samoa by an employer other than the Federal Government), exclusive of board, lodging, or other facilities; and
- The employee's primary duty must be the performance of office or non-manual work directly related to the management or general business operations of the employer or the employer's customers; and
- The employee's primary duty includes the exercise of discretion and independent judgment with respect to matters of significance.

Professional Exemption

To qualify for the professional employee exemption, all of the following tests must be met:

- The employee must be compensated on a salary or fee basis (as defined in the regulations) at a rate not less than $455 per week (or $380 per week, if employed in American Samoa by an employer other than the Federal Government), exclusive of board, lodging, or other facilities; and
- The employee's primary duty must be the performance of work requiring advanced knowledge in a field of science or learning customarily acquired by prolong course of specialized intellectual instruction; or
- Require invention, imagination, originality, or talent in a recognized field of artistic or creative endeavor.

Outside Salespeople

The regulations under the FLSA exempt outside salespeople from both the overtime and minimum wage provisions. To be exempt, the following requirements must be met:

1) The employee's primary duty is:
   a. Making sales within the meaning of Section 3(k)[1] of the Act, or
   b. Obtaining orders or contracts for services or for the use of facilities for which consideration will be paid by the client or customer; and

2) She/he is customarily and regularly engaged way form the employer's place or places of business in performing such primary duty.

(a) The term primary duty is defined at Section 541.700. In determining the primary duty of an outside sales employee, work performed incidental to and in conjunction with the employee's own outside sales or solicitations, including incidental deliveries and collections, shall be regarded as exempt outside sales work. Other work that furthers the employee's sales efforts also shall be regarded as exempt work including, for example, writing sales reports, updating or revising the employee's sales or display catalogue, planning itineraries, and attending sales conferences.

(b) The requirements of Subpart G (salary requirements) of this part do not apply to the outside sales employees described in this section.

---

[1] *Section 3(k) of the FLSA defines sale as including "any sale, exchange, contract to sell, consignment for sale, shipment for sale, or other disposition."*

Source: U.S. Department of Labor, Employment Standards Administration, Wage & Hour Division, Exemption for Executive, Administrative, Professional, Computer & Outside Sales Employees Under the Fair Labor Standards Act (FLSA). www.dol.gov./dol/allcfr/ESA/ Title_29/Part_541/29CFR541.100.htm

---

non-exempt employees. Additionally, the HR manager pointed out that although a supervisor accompanied Phipps during his doctor visits on a few days each quarter, he was unsupervised 95 percent of the time. Phipps did not agree with this and argued that he had little discretion in doing his job because he had to follow company guidelines and was given a list of targeted doctors. Furthermore, since he did not work at the company's offices, he was technically an outside salesman. Phipps subsequently filed a class action suit on behalf of himself and the other senior professional sales representatives at K & K, arguing that their jobs were non-exempt.

Case 2 Cheryl Wiley, Auto Damage Adjuster

Cheryl Wiley was promoted from auto damage appraiser to auto damage adjuster after being employed with Auto Insurance for three years. In her former position as auto damage appraiser, she worked at one of Auto Insurance's drive-in locations inspecting damaged cars that remain in drivable condition. She performed this job under close supervision and all of her work had to be approved by the supervisor. The job was considered non-exempt and Wiley received overtime pay whenever she exceeded her required work hours.

In her new position as auto damage adjuster, Wiley had responsibility for "assessing, negotiating, and settling automobile damage claims." She spent a majority of her time appraising damaged vehicles and estimating repair costs, but also negotiating and settling claims with body shops over repair costs and with claimants over total loss vehicles. An auto damage adjuster had to determine how much Auto Insurance should pay to restore a vehicle to its pre-damage condition using the most economical parts available unless safety was a consideration. In assessing each vehicle, the adjuster used a software program to perform the analysis. While the software assisted with providing information on the cheapest parts and prices, the adjuster also had to make decisions not dictated by the software. For example, the adjuster had to figure out if there was pre-existing damage, interview claimants, negotiate with shops over repair times, and ensure claims were not fraudulent. All adjustors had set dollar limits on their negotiating authority. Wiley was a level 1 adjuster and had settlement authority up to $10,000. However, she could recommend settlements in excess of her authority, but they had to be approved by her supervisor. Auto damage adjusters report to supervisors who report to auto damage managers who in turn report to auto damage directors.

In the case of total loss vehicles, Wiley had to decide whether it was economically feasible to repair a vehicle or to pay the owner its value. These decisions were more time consuming because they involved thousands of dollars in additional liability for Auto Insurance. However, Auto Insurance had set standards for determining when to declare a vehicle a total loss. In her job as auto damage adjuster, Wiley handled on average more than 1,000 claims per year, totaling $2.5 million. About 20 percent of the yearly claims involved total loss vehicles. Wiley also worked under some supervision in the field one or two days a week at one of the drive-in locations. Wiley earned $41,000 per year in her new position but regularly worked in excess of 40 hours per week. When she asked about being paid for overtime, she was told that unlike her prior job, the auto damage adjuster position was non-exempt. Wiley did not agree and filed a lawsuit against Auto Insurance alleging she is entitled to overtime pay because her job is primarily administrative, using well-defined guidelines and policies.

Case 3 John Krauss and National Bank

John Krauss was employed by National Bank for two years as an underwriter. As an underwriter, Krauss evaluated whether to issue loans to individual loan applicants by referring to a set of guidelines, known as the Credit Guide, provided to him by the bank. The Guide specified how underwriters should determine loan applicant characteristics such as qualifying income and credit history. It also instructed underwriters to compare such data with criteria set out in the Guide. The Guide contained standards for what qualified a loan applicant for a particular loan product. National Bank also provided supplemental guidelines and product guidelines with information specific to individual loan products. Krauss was expected to evaluate the applications using the Credit Guide and approving the loan if it met the standards set. As such, he had no interactions with applicants since this was a back-office operation. Underwriters were evaluated not by whether the approved loans were paid back, but by measuring each underwriter's productivity in terms of average of total actions per day and assessing whether the underwriters' decisions met National's Credit Guide standards.

National Bank sometimes used incentive schemes based on number of decisions made to increase underwriter performance. Underwriters at National Bank earned a salary of $42,000 per year. To keep up with the number of applications he had to evaluate, Krauss regularly worked overtime. When he inquired about being paid for overtime, Krauss was told the underwriter position was exempt from the Fair Labor Standards Act. Krauss did not agree and felt that he was basically an administrative employee who performed work that was well-defined by the company. Subsequently, Krauss filed a lawsuit requesting that he be paid overtime for the hours he had worked in excess of the required forty for the past two years.

75 SKILL BUILDER

Developing a Wage Structure

I. OBJECTIVES

A. To familiarize you with how data obtained when using the point system approach to job evaluation can be used to develop a wage structure.

B. To give you practice in developing a wage structure.

II. TIME REQUIRED TO COMPLETE: 1 hour or less

III. INSTRUCTIONS

Examine the pay data below.

Pay Grade	Job Evaluation Points	Top of Grade	Position
1	100–200	$36,000	Control Operator I
2	201–300	$39,000	Control Operator II
3	301–400	$47,500	Control Operator III
4	401–500	$53,800	Control Operator IV

Exhibit 4.6 shows a partially completed pay structure for control operator positions. Your first task is to complete the chart for pay grades 2, 3, and 4. Construct pay steps for each of the remaining pay grades based on the following guidelines for "time in service" in each pay grade.

Pay Step Data

Entry wage: 65.5 percent of top for each pay grade

Step 1: After 1 year within the pay grade 70 percent of top

Step 2: After 3 years within the pay grade 75 percent of top

Step 3: After 5 years within the pay grade 82 percent of top

Step 4: After 8 years within the pay grade 90 percent of top

Top of grade: After 10 years within the pay grade

In addition, listed below are the names of employees in each pay grade and their current salaries. Your second task is to plot each one on Exhibit 4.7 and to determine which of the current salaries fall outside the appropriate pay grade.

Control Operator I:

Charles Hamilton—6 years' services—paid $30,218

Mary Richardson—10 years' service—paid $32,250

Control Operator II:

Jerry Smith—2 years' service—paid $29,250

Theresa Jones—5 years' service—paid $31,600

Control Operator III:

Alicia Wadsworth—5 years' service—paid $38,950

Connie Johnston—7 years' service—paid $40,380

Velda Prescott—1 years' service—paid $33,250

Control Operator IV:

Gloria Lopez—3 years' service—paid $40,350

Rosemary Jensen—5 years' service—paid $44,120

EXHIBIT 4.6 *Pay Structure for Office Staff Positions*

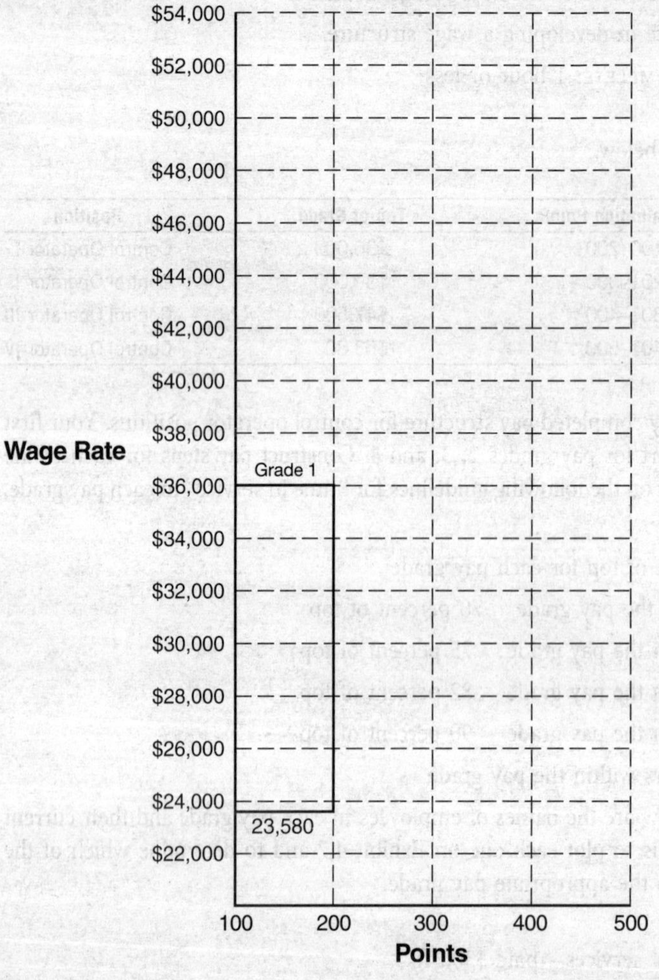

76 Case

Managing Nonmonetary Compensation

Andrew Nelson supervised the respiratory therapy department at Dunesbury Medical Center in Owatonna and Waseca, Minnesota, towns of 16,000 and 2,000, respectively. Though he worked mainly at the local hospitals, he was employed by Breathing Care Associates (BCA), which was affiliated with St. Luke's Hospital in Rochester, Minnesota.

Nelson graduated from the Mayo Clinic Respiratory Therapy Program and earned a BS in Biology from a Minnesota state college. Before accepting this supervisory position three years ago, he had been a staff therapist at Mount Olympus Medical Center in Milwaukee, Wisconsin. A highly respected professional, Nelson tried to keep up with current developments in his field. He was well-liked by staff and patients and had a good sense of humor. If there was one thing Nelson lacked, it was formal management training. He now wished he had taken some business courses during college.

Nelson did not belong to a labor union. His parents had owned a trucking business and had dealt with teamsters. Stories about their shenanigans soured Nelson on union membership. However, therapists at St. Luke's Hospital who were employed by BCA were represented by a bargaining unit.

Nelson's supervisor, Matt Barnes, used to call or visit the Dunesbury Medical Center at Owatonna regularly to see how things were going or to bring supplies. Lately, Barnes's visits were less frequent. Months could go by before Nelson saw him.

Since 1963, Dunesbury Medical Center had operated another facility in Waseca, about 12 miles west of Owatonna. In 2009, Dunesbury's board of directors decided to close the Waseca facility on June 30th for economic reasons.

Exhibit 4.7 shows an organizational chart for the respiratory therapy department at Dunesbury Medical Center in January 2009.

Beginning January 3, 2009, Barb Johnson took a six-week paid maternity leave permitted under BCA's temporary disability program. At the end of January, Ramona Black had surgery and took a six-week medical leave. That left only Nelson, Pam Picha, and Lynn Owens to staff the two facilities.

Nelson was under pressure from BCA to cut labor costs. For about a month, he worked six days per week. The length of his workday varied from 8 to 12 hours or more. On the days Nelson worked, he also was on call. If a patient had breathing difficulties, Nelson was called to the hospital after normal working hours. Sometimes he would not get called in for several days. On other nights, he might get called in two or three times. If a doctor wanted a patient to be on an artificial breathing machine, called a respirator, Nelson had to provide staff at the hospital 24 hours a day.

Since he was an exempt employee, Nelson received no overtime pay. Originally he was not paid for on-call hours either. Then, he successfully negotiated with BCA to get $10.00 per hour on-call pay. In January and February 2009 combined, Nelson worked more than 140 hours beyond his normal scheduled work week. His salary was about $65,000.

In March, Pam Picha resigned to move to Texas. Lynn Owens gave two weeks' notice on April 2; she had accepted a position in a Minneapolis hospital. While Nelson attended a Minnesota Association of Respiratory Therapists' Convention in mid-April, Ramona Black quit without giving notice. Nelson left the conference early to fill in at the Owatonna facility.

EXHIBIT 4.7 *Dunesbury Medical Center Organizational Chart*

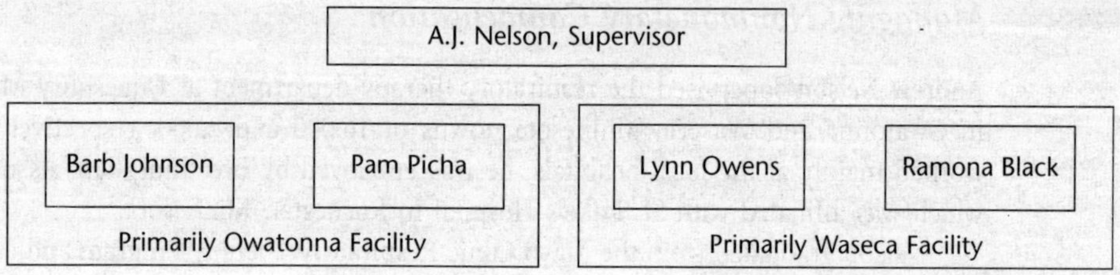

He began to feel he needed some time off from work as he was getting burned out with all of the overtime hours. Nelson's earned time account, which could be used for sick leave, vacation, holidays, and so on, had almost reached the 400-hour maximum. On April 21, Nelson asked Barnes if he could take a vacation from May 20–26. His wife had to attend a business meeting in New Orleans, and this would be a good chance for the family to spend a few extra days together sightseeing.

Upon receiving no reply from Barnes, Nelson sent him a note with the weekly payroll report of May 5 asking what decision had been made on his vacation request. In the meantime, Barb Johnson found out that Nelson was planning to take time off. She refused to work seven days in a row, which would have been necessary to provide adequate staffing in Nelson's absence. The previous summer, Nelson had worked seven days in a row so that she could take a vacation.

Finally, on May 12, Barnes called Nelson. "Good morning, Drew. Say about this vacation request. . .. I really can't let you take off right now. I can't force Barb to work seven days in a row. Besides, if she did, I'd have to pay her overtime." Nelson swallowed hard, but before he could reply, Matt ended their conversation.

BCA's policy on earned time accrual and use is presented in Exhibit 4.8.

QUESTIONS

1. What are Andrew Nelson's alternatives?
2. What do you think Nelson should do? Justify your answer.
3. Does the hospital administration have any obligation to help alleviate Nelson's situation?

EXHIBIT 4.8 *BCA's Policy on Earned Time Accrual and Use*

Earned Time

Personal time off from the workplace is important in maintaining good health. Breathing Care Associates is introducing an innovative program for earned paid time off. The program is called Earned Time, and has been nicknamed "ET."

Earned Time combines traditional programs of paid vacation time, paid legal and personal holiday time, and paid sick time into one "bank" of paid benefit time off. For each hour you work—up to 80 per pay period—an amount of Earned Time is deposited into your personal Earned Time (ET) Account. Then, as you decide you want to schedule time off, the hours accumulated in your personal ET Account are yours to use.

You begin to earn time with your first hour of work at Breathing Care Associates. And for each hour you work—up to 80 per pay period—Earned Time continues to accrue. The amount of Earned Time you accrue depends on your length of continuous service at Breathing Care Associates, your exemption status (non-exempt or exempt), and the number of hours you work.

These are also the usual components for determining accrual rates for paid holiday, sick, and vacation time. With this new program, however, you have the flexibility to schedule time off for whatever purpose you choose.

Maximum Accumulation Amounts

The emphasis of Earned Time is to offer you scheduled time away from work for whatever purpose you choose. Full-time employees are strongly encouraged to take 15 days off each year. Because unused Earned Time can be forwarded from year to year, it is possible to reach your Account Maximum if you do not use enough Earned Time each year.

Your personal ET Account has a maximum accumulation amount of two times your annual accrual rate. When you near your account maximum, it is your responsibility to schedule Earned Time off. If the account maximum is reached, no ET will accrue beyond it.

Example of Maximum Accumulation Amounts

Years of Service	Annual Accrual	Maximum ET Accumulation
2–4	200 hours (25 days)	400 hours (50 days)
10	248 hours (31 days)	496 hours (62 days)

Scheduling ET

ET is available as you accrue it. However, requests for paid time off must be approved by your supervisor, who will consider staffing arrangements and departmental operations before granting your request. Schedule ET with your supervisor as far in advance as possible. Often, at least a two-week notice is required for a scheduled absence.

Contributed by Margaret Foegen Karsten, The University of Wisconsin, Platteville

Benefits

77 CASE

Controlling Employee Benefit Costs

John DeCarlo is President and CEO of Quality Auto Parts, an automotive parts equipment manufacturer and supplier in the Southwest. The company was started by DeCarlo and his father in 1988 and now employs 812 people at four different sites. Revenues and profits increased steadily from 1988 until 2001. Both revenues and profits were down in 2001 and 2002 and after recovering from 2003 to 2006, they were again down from 2007 to the present. As a result of declining auto sales, auto parts were also hit hard during the recent recession. In order to contain costs, the company has begun to examine its employee health benefits.

THE PROBLEM

DeCarlo recently met with his vice president for finance (David Schramm) and his vice president for human resources (Harriet Windham) to determine how costs could be cut so the company could price its products more competitively relative to foreign competitors. At this meeting, he learned that employee benefit costs had increased at approximately twice the rate of increase for wages alone (8 percent versus 2 percent yearly average increases) from 2000–2010. In particular, the total employee health insurance costs increased from $4,680 per employee per year in 2000 to $9,869 in 2010. DeCarlo expressed frustration at these increases and asked what could be done.

Windham and Schramm invited DeCarlo to a meeting of healthcare providers, insurers, and employers, sponsored by the area Chamber of Commerce and scheduled for the following week. The topic of the meeting is the implications of the healthcare reform legislation passed by Congress and signed by the President in spring of 2010. Most employers did not know the details of the legislation, and there was much uncertainty regarding the legal status of some of the provisions in the legislation. At this meeting, they learned that some of the provisions might be repealed in the future. However, they also learned that taxes on such benefits would be increased, thus making such benefits more expensive to employers. This legislation made it more imperative that Quality Auto Parts and other companies offering health insurance benefits find a way of controlling the costs of such benefits. If not controlled, some forecasters have predicted that health benefit costs will be equal to the total profits of all U.S. corporations by the year 2016.

They also learned more about the nature and causes of this problem. Many of the speakers at the conference cited large catastrophic-illness claims, increased use of mental health and substance abuse services, increased use of medical services, high-technology medicine, cost-shifting from government programs (Medicare and Medicaid) to private insurance, high physician fees, the AIDS crisis, the demographics of employees in the auto industry (i.e., a higher percentage of older employees), and recent premium increases by both traditional and managed care plans attempting to recoup recent losses. One speaker noted:

"If businesses in the private sector don't make a profit, they are not going to exist. The continuing escalation of healthcare costs is threatening the very survival of some companies, particularly small companies. Smaller businesses increasingly bear the brunt of the spiraling costs because they have no one else to whom they can shift their costs."

Several possible solutions were discussed although there was no consensus regarding their effectiveness or applicability to particular situations. Among the cost containment suggestions were self-insurance, utilization review, managed care (i.e., health maintenance organizations and preferred provider organizations), wellness programs, flexible benefits, cost-sharing (i.e., higher deductibles and co-insurance), pre-admission certification for surgery, financial incentives for outpatient services, use of retail clinics, development of employer health clinics, mail order prescription drug programs, health savings accounts, use of variable co-payments for different types of divisions, implementation of a disease management program, and audits of employee dependence to assess eligibility. Many speakers emphasized that the health reform legislation is not likely to contain employer costs but rather to increase such costs. When Congress has intervened in the past, it has usually made the cost problem worse as a result of mandates that raise costs for both insurance companies and employers.

THE CHALLENGE

DeCarlo came away from the conference with a greater appreciation of the complexity of the problem of increasing employee health insurance costs and a greater determination to do something about it. However, he wasn't sure about his next steps. He viewed his company as a "preferred employer" because it had always paid above the market wage rates and its benefits were always more liberal than those of other U.S. companies and particularly those of foreign competitors. DeCarlo did not want to do anything to jeopardize his company's advantage in attracting and retaining high-quality personnel. At the same time, he realized that if no changes were made, his health insurance premiums may be greater than his total projected company earnings by the year 2016.

Quality Auto Parts' present health insurance plan (Blue Cross-Blue Shield) is a traditional indemnity insurance plan. All employees have one plan, which makes no effort to control the health-care services provided. Employees select their own physicians, and the insurance company pays reimbursement for whatever services are provided at whatever price the particular provider charges. Neither physicians nor employees have a financial incentive to economize in the use of services or to seek out low-cost providers. Physician reimbursement is based upon the number of procedures they perform and the physician reimbursement rate for each procedure.

DeCarlo decided to establish an employee health benefits committee that would report to him in one month with recommendations for containing health benefit costs while minimizing adverse employee reaction. Membership on the committee consisted of Windham, Schramm, and two other employees. You have been asked to serve as an employee member of this committee. The committee has recommended that DeCarlo consider four general options for the future: 1) stay with the current traditional indemnity policy with an average cost of $10,465 per year; 2) offer an HMO option in addition to the current plan; 3) establish a special self-insurance fund and negotiate preferred provider arrangements (PPOs) with local providers (i.e., discounted prices in exchange for the directing of these employees to these providers); or 4) the combination of catastrophic health insurance plan for major medical expenses coupled with a Health Savings Account (HSA) for smaller, more routine healthcare expenses.

The committee members are split on the four options. The other employee wishes to continue with the current plan, Schramm wants to adopt the self-insurance option, and Windham wants to offer the HMO option. DeCarlo, the CEO, has previously expressed interest in the catastrophic plan coupled with an HSA. All four are looking to you to make a recommendation and help them reach a consensus.

QUESTIONS

1. Describe the nature and causes of the employee health insurance cost problem in this case.
2. What information should the employee health benefits committee gather before making any recommendations? Why?
3. Given the desire of most employees to protect themselves from high healthcare costs, is there any way for Quality Auto Parts to continue to attract the best employees while containing health benefit costs? Why or why not?
4. On the basis of what you know about Quality Auto Parts, which of the four specific proposals would you be likely to recommend? Can the company adopt some combination of the three options? What do you recommend and why?

78 CASE

Domestic Partner Benefits

Baptist Hospital is a 360-bed facility in a large facility in the southeastern United States. Recently, the human resource management director, Joan Collins, has noted a higher than average employee turnover among nurses and other clinical professionals such as occupational therapist, physical therapist, and laboratory technologist. She is concerned that Baptist Hospital is losing good employees to other hospitals in the metropolitan region that offer more liberal domestic partner benefits. In fact, the hospital does not recognize such partners and provides no health benefits to them.

Most large companies in the region do offer such domestic partner benefits. For their purposes, they typically define a "domestic partner" as a person over 18 who shares living quarters with another adult in an exclusive committed relationship in which the partners are responsible for each other's common welfare. A standard definition typically includes requirements concerning a minimum age, a requirement that the couples live together, financial interdependence, a committed relationship, and a non-blood relative. Before such benefits can be provided, these companies typically require a signed and notarized affidavit specifying these requirements must be signed by both domestic partners and witnessed by a notary.

Collins has also done some research that indicates that those companies providing domestic partner benefits experience lower health benefit costs. The reason is that many unmarried heterosexual partners or homosexual partners do not have children and therefore such unions utilize fewer health services. Her research also showed that as a result of ongoing lawsuits in this area, many more employers may be forced to offer domestic partner benefits in the future.

While Collins is convinced that such a change in health benefits would be advantageous to the company, particularly in terms of recruiting and retaining employees, she is concerned that the hospital's culture is socially conservative. Consequently, she feels that the CEO, the executive team, and the board of directors may be less enthusiastic about implementing such a change than she is. Collins is therefore uncertain as to how to proceed and has asked your instructor for advice. Your instructor has presented the case to the class but has changed the name of the institution so that students will not know the identity of the facility.

QUESTIONS

1. Would you recommend that Joan Collins bring this issue before the CEO and the board of directors and recommend implementation? Why or why not?
2. If you believe that Collins should recommend implementation of domestic partner health benefits, what are the potential benefits to Baptist Hospital, and how would she document these?
3. What are the potential disadvantages to the hospital, and what steps should she recommend to address these potential disadvantages?

4. Do you see any differences between heterosexual domestic partners and gay domestic partners in terms of the health benefits that should be provided? If so, how would you differentiate the two and why?
5. Are you aware of any companies that provide domestic partner health benefits and, if so, how effective have these programs been in attracting and retaining employees?
6. Is there any relevant research on the topic of domestic benefits and, if so, what does this research show?

79 EXERCISE

Flexible Benefit Plan Choices

I. OBJECTIVES

A. To familiarize you with how flexible benefit plans work.

B. To give you an understanding of some of the benefits offered in a flexible benefit plan.

C. To give you experience in selecting benefits.

D. To give you an understanding of the criteria individuals use in selecting benefits.

II. OUT-OF-CLASS PREPARATION TIME: 10 minutes to read the exercise and select benefits

III. IN-CLASS TIME SUGGESTED: 30–40 minutes

IV. PROCEDURES

Assume that you recently graduated from college and are just starting a new job at a large firm. You will be receiving a starting net pay (net of all taxes and mandatory deductions) of $30,000. Your task is to read the Benefit Policy described below and determine which benefits you would select. Keep in mind that any money you spend on additional benefits will reduce the $30,000 per year you can spend on other things such as housing, entertainment, and travel. After each student in the class has selected the benefits he or she would choose, the instructor will divide the class into groups of three to five. Then, each student will explain his/her selections to the rest of the group along with the rationale behind the decisions. After each student is finished, your group needs to prepare a list of criteria (reasons you would or would not want a benefit) that were used in making the benefit selections. These criteria will then be written on an overhead or blackboard for class discussion.

BENEFITS POLICY

Your company offers full-time employees the opportunity to participate in a broad range of programs to meet specific needs. Employees are responsible for selecting the benefits that best meet their needs.

PRE-TAX HEALTHCARE PREMIUM PAYMENTS

The firm offers employees a medical care program that includes doctor's visits, hospital services, emergency room visits, and diagnostic laboratory tests. Our program allows employees to pay a portion of their health insurance premiums through payroll deduction to receive a tax break by having the premiums deducted from their paychecks before taxes are calculated. New employees must opt into pre-tax within 31 days of employment to receive the benefit. The firm pays the remainder of your healthcare fees. However, if you choose this benefit, you will need to pay $65 per month for an employee-only policy, $137 per month for an employee plus one more family member policy, and $185 per month for total family coverage.

FLEXIBLE REIMBURSEMENT ACCOUNTS

Section 125 of the Internal Revenue Service's (IRS) Code allows employees to choose certain pre-tax benefits as an alternative to taxable monetary compensation. These include a medical and a dependent care reimbursement account.

MEDICAL REIMBURSEMENT ACCOUNT

This account allows an employee to set aside pre-tax dollars to pay for medical, dental, and vision care, or other eligible expenses not covered by the health plan. There is a $5,000 per plan year maximum and $10 is the minimum contribution per pay period. The employee must have maintained eligibility to participate in the healthcare plan described above for six or more continuous months to participate in the Medical Reimbursement Account.

Dependent Care Reimbursement Account

This account allows you to set aside pre-tax dollars to pay for eligible dependent care expenses such as child care. You are eligible to enroll within 31 days of employment. Maximum amount during a plan year is:

$2,500–married and filing tax returns separately from spouse.

$5,000–single, or married and filing jointly.

$10 is the minimum contribution per pay period.

Retirement

You will be automatically enrolled in our firm's retirement plan after 1,000 hours of service. Upon retirement or termination of service, you will receive 2 percent of your annual compensation for each year of service. Your pension is vested if you have three years of service with the firm. See your Benefits Office for more details.

Employee Stock Purchase Plan

You are allowed to purchase common stock in this firm at a 15 percent discount off the fair market value through payroll deduction. Contributions are deducted on an after-tax basis. See the Benefits Office for details.

Life Insurance

Full-time employees of our firm have life insurance provided, effective the first day of employment, as a condition of employment. It provides two kinds of insurance—life and accidental death and dismemberment. The amount of insurance coverage is equal to the employee's annual salary rounded to the next highest thousand, and then doubled. An amount equal to four times the employee's salary is payable in the event of accidental death. Coverage is also provided for accidental blinding or dismemberment. Premiums are paid by the firm.

Optional Life Insurance

Additional optional life insurance is available and is administered by a large life insurance firm. It is available for employees and their spouses and dependents. Premiums are paid by the employee through payroll deduction. To receive up to $200,000 coverage without proving good health, you must request within 60 days of employment. Your cost will depend upon your age:

Monthly Rate per $10,000 Coverage

Under 25	25–29	30–34	35–39	40–44	45–49
$0.40	$0.50	$0.70	$0.80	$1.30	$2.20

Price quotes are also available for those over 50. Check with the Benefits Office.

Optional Long-Term Care Insurance

Long-term care insurance is offered to full-time employees, their spouses, parents, and parents-in-law. Employees enrolling within 31 days of hire do not have to complete a health care questionnaire. Long-term care is the care you need when you require assistance with day-to-day functions like dressing, eating, and getting into and out of bed due to medical problems caused by illness or accident. The cost of this insurance is dependent upon one's age and level of coverage. Check with the benefits office for specific costs.

Optional Long-Term Disability

Long-term disability income insurance helps to protect your income when, due to a covered illness or injury, you are disabled. It has been designed to cover a disability sustained on or off the job. The plan provides up to 60 percent of your basic monthly earnings after 180 days of disability. The cost varies depending upon age and level of coverage.

Personal Accident Insurance

Personal accident insurance is available for the employee, spouse, and dependent children and helps protect against losses due to accidents. A full benefit is paid for accidental loss of life; loss of use of both upper and lower limbs; loss of both hands, feet, or eyes; loss of speech; or loss of hearing in both ears. Partial benefits are paid in the event of loss of any one hand, foot, eye, both legs, or both arms. The firm pays all costs.

Transportation Reimbursement Account

You may contribute to a parking reimbursement account and/or a transportation account, which covers mass transit or vanpooling. These are two separate accounts. Contributions are pre-tax, deducted from your paycheck. You can contribute up to $185 per month for the parking account and $100 per month for the transportation account.

Optional Pre-Paid Legal Plan

A pre-paid legal plan which, for a monthly payroll deduction of $19.20, provides legal services such as traffic court representation, first offense DUI court representation, will preparation, credit/warranty disputes, financial contract or lease review, uncontested divorce, uncontested adoption, and purchasing or selling a primary residence.

Tuition Assistance

Educational assistance is available for full-time employees with at least one year of service. Our firm will pay for a maximum of 15 credit hours for the year—six credit hours in the fall, six credit hours in the spring, and three credit hours in the summer. Courses must be work- or degree-related and taken at a fully accredited college or university.

80 EXERCISE
Executive Perks

I. OBJECTIVES

A. To familiarize you with the wide variety of perks often given to top executives.

B. To familiarize you with the arguments for and against various executive perks.

II. OUT-OF-CLASS PREPARATION TIME: none

III. IN-CLASS TIME SUGGESTED: 30–40 minutes

IV. PROCEDURES

At the start of class, your instructor will divide the class into groups of three to five. Your group is to assume that you are all members of the compensation committee for a large firm. Your committee is composed of independent members of the firm's board of directors. It is responsible for establishing annual and long-term performance goals for the firm's executives, for evaluating the performance of these officers, for setting the compensation of these officers, and for making recommendations to the board with respect to new compensation plans. The firm's current CEO has announced her retirement, so a new CEO will be chosen soon. Given the controversy regarding executive perks that arose after the 2009 federal bailout of the U.S. banking system, your committee has been asked by the board of directors to review the current CEO perks to determine if they should also be offered to the new CEO. You are to assume that the current CEO has a base salary of $863,000 and earned an additional $1 million from bonuses. Below is a list of the CEO's current perks. Your task is to evaluate each of the following in terms of whether it should be provided. So, for each item, circle "Y" or "N." Then, write below each item the reason behind your decision.

A. Physical Exams — Y or N

Reason: ______________________________

Estimated Cost: $4,000–$8,000 per year

B. Personal Financial Counseling — Y or N

Reason: ______________________________

Estimated Cost: $5,000–$10,000 per year

C. Company Car — Y or N

Reason: ______________________________

Estimated Cost: $12,000 per year

D. Memberships in Country/Exercise Club(s) — Y or N

Reason: ______________________________

Estimated Cost: $10,000 per year

E. First-class Air Travel for Overseas Travel — Y or N

Reason: ______________________________

Estimated Cost: $40,000–$60,000 per year

F. Chartered Plane for U.S. Travel — Y or N

Reason: ______________________________

Estimated Cost: $80,000–$100,000 per year

G. Personal Liability Insurance Protection Against Law Suits Y or N
Reason: ____________________
Estimated Cost: $6,500 per year

H. Chauffeur Service to Meetings/Airport/Home Y or N
Reason: ____________________
Estimated Cost: $18,000–$20,000 per year

I. Reserved Garage Parking Y or N
Reason: ____________________
Estimated Cost: $5,000 per year

J. Clothing Allowance Y or N
Reason: ____________________
Estimated Cost: $6,000 per year

K. Stock Options (allows executive to buy company stock in future years at favorable prices) Y or N
Reason: ____________________
Estimated Cost: Up to $1,250,000 per year

L. Golden Parachute/Severance Pay (given if the executive's employment is terminated before end of contract) Y or N
Reason: ____________________
Estimated Cost: $900,000 one-time payment

M. Guaranteed Pension Y or N
Reason: ____________________
Estimated Cost: $600,000 per year for life

N. Bonuses Y or N
Reason: ____________________
Estimated Cost: Up to $1,250,000 per year

81 INCIDENT

Retiree Health and Pension Benefits

Frank Sears was a blue-collar worker for a large chemical company in the Northeast for his entire career and retired in 2003 at age 60. Sears felt quite secure about his situation at the time of retirement. The union had negotiated very generous health insurance and pension benefits for its retirees. His home mortgage had been paid off in 1992, so his only household expenses were property taxes, repairs, and routine maintenance.

While their health and pension benefits have failed to keep up with inflation since 2003, Sears and his wife have adapted by eating out less often and postponing some needed home repairs. Since their pension benefits were not indexed to inflation, they had reconciled themselves to learning to live on less or to one or both of them going back to work. In conversations with other retirees from the same companies, they learned that others were also considering going back to work to augment their income. The only problem they faced was that unemployment in their area is currently 12.2 percent. Job opportunities at wage rates much above minimum wage are few and far between.

But their retiree health insurance premiums, purchased through Sears's former company, were a particular concern. Their premiums had increased 21 percent and 26 percent, respectively, for each of the past two years. Mrs. Sears called a number of other health insurance companies to determine how much it would cost to purchase insurance on their own directly from another insurer. To her amazement, she learned that direct purchase would cost them less.

After checking with two other retired couples who were insured with the original company, she learned they had switched a year ago when they found out that the original company had viewed retiree health insurance as a profit center and had charged accordingly. She promptly switched to a new insurer and felt their problem had been solved.

Yesterday, she received a letter from an executive of a company she had never heard of indicating that the new company had purchased the original company. The letter went on to say that, effective immediately, no more health or pension benefits would be paid to them or any other retiree. She was no longer concerned about the health insurance benefits, since these were paid directly out-of-pocket anyway. However, their ability to pay for the health insurance was dependent upon continued lifetime pension benefits as the union contract stipulated at the time of Sears's retirement.

QUESTIONS

1. Do companies have either a moral or legal obligation to honor all terms and conditions associated with an employee's retirement that were in effect at the time of that retirement? Why or why not?
2. Does the purchase of the original company by another company, or changing economic circumstances, obviate the employer's obligation concerning retiree benefits? Why or why not?
3. Could Mr. and Mrs. Sears expect to receive any retirement benefits as a result of ERISA?

82 INCIDENT

The Educational Leave Problem

Rollermakers Corporation is a midwestern manufacturer of rollers used by most industrial firms to move products and packages from one location to another. For example, the U.S. Postal Service uses rollers to slide packages from one area of the post office to another, thereby minimizing the lifting of heavy parcels. Coal companies use rollers underneath conveyor belts to move coal from the mine to empty coal train cars. Rollers are usually made to customer specifications rather than mass produced. Typically, customers determine the type of rollers needed with the help of design engineers or Rollermakers's sales staff.

Rollermakers's staff consists of a production crew, inside sales force, outside sales force, and administration. Administration and the inside sales force work together to process quotes, orders, and invoices in the most efficient manner possible. The inside sales force is hired using a placement firm, and employees are trained internally. Administrative staff are usually hired from the same recruiting agency, with some exceptions. Purchasing managers and accounting positions are salaried and are filled through advertising and recruiters. In the recent past, the company has faced threats of racial discrimination lawsuits from former inside sales employees, and lawyers have contacted the firm on behalf of those who are issuing these threats. No lawsuits have been filed, but management has become more careful in all human resource matters.

The present purchasing manager was hired from another competitor a little over a year ago. At that time, the manager was also attending an evening MBA program at a local university and, as part of his compensation package, would be allowed tuition reimbursement and time off to attend classes with the understanding that the classes would not cause a major disruption to the daily work schedule. For the past year, this has worked well because classes do not start until 5:45 P.M.

With the new fall semester starting, two inside sales employees informed the inside sales manager of their intentions to return to college on a part-time basis. Jan Thornton, an African-American female, wanted to return to college to finish a degree in Accounting. She is a junior now and hopes to finish within the next two years. She is scheduled to take two Accounting classes, one on Tuesday and Thursday from 11:00 until 12:20, and the other on Monday, Wednesday, and Friday from 2:00 until 2:50. These are the only times the required classes are offered. The college is located about five minutes from work. Thornton has made it known that she will be leaving the company upon graduation. She has been with the company for 18 months and is well-liked and competent. She is one of the more efficient and accurate of the inside sales staff.

The second employee, Josephine Green, is a white female, starting community college after achieving a GED. She would like to take classes that meet from 2:00 until 2:50 and from 3:00 until 3:50 on Monday, Wednesday, and Friday. The community college is located within 20 minutes of work. She also plans to earn a degree or certificate in accounting and has stated that she wishes to stay with the company "for as long as they will have me." She wants to earn more money and was told if she obtained her degree she would be eligible to be promoted to an appropriate position. The current bookkeeper is planning on retiring in three years, and Green has her eye on this job. Green is also well-liked by most, but not all, of the inside sales force. Her error rate on specifications and pricing of specialty work is higher than most others.

Green submitted her class schedule to the inside sales manager as a request and had not registered or paid for classes. Thornton had registered and paid for her classes. The schedules chosen by the employees drastically conflicted with the regular business day. Nonetheless, both employees asked that their schedules be worked around and accommodated. They contended that the precedent set by the purchasing manager should apply to them. Rollermakers Corporation does not currently have any formal policy regarding educational leave. However, both employees were told when they were first hired that they were expected to be at work during business hours.

QUESTIONS

1. Should Rollermakers Corporation allow the two inside salespeople to miss work in order to attend classes? Should it pay for their tuition? Why?
2. Should the firm continue to allow the purchasing manager to attend the evening MBA program and to pay his tuition?
3. Should there be a formal policy regarding educational leave or should it remain informal? If the firm decides to formalize its policy, what provisions should it contain?

83 INCIDENT

The Lost Vacation Days

Ships, Inc. is a large shipbuilding company located in one of the eastern states. One September afternoon, the firm made the decision to shut down operations due to an approaching hurricane. This was based on the forecasted arrival of tropical storm force winds to the local area as early as noon on Wednesday. They made that decision at approximately 2:00 P.M. on a Tuesday afternoon, and some employees were told Tuesday by supervisors that the shutdown would occur beginning with the next morning's shift and that they were not to report to work. They were also told that the time they lost would be excused with pay.

By Tuesday evening, it was very clear that the hurricane would not hit the area until Thursday at the earliest. Nonetheless, the shipyard decided to maintain the decision to shut down on Wednesday. The emergency hotline message confirmed this information, but also said that missed time for salaried personnel would be charged against each employee's vacation bank.

By Wednesday evening, the emergency hotline message was updated to state that the shutdown would be continued through the first shift on Thursday, with normal operations commencing on the second shift. The hurricane subsequently hit the area Thursday night (during the second shift), leaving many roads littered with branches and debris.

On Friday morning, when all personnel reported for work again (many of them without electricity at home), they were hit with the fact that they had just lost two days of vacation—two days "gone with the wind." Hourly personnel had the option of charging the two days off to their vacation bank or taking time off without pay, but salaried personnel did not have a choice—they were required to charge the leave to their accrued vacation bank. This action was in line with the company's policy for complete shutdowns despite what some personnel were told prior to this shutdown.

Within a few days, many salaried employees became very upset with the way the company handled the situation and with the fact that they just lost two vacation days for no good reason. Why did the firm close down operations so soon instead of waiting for the storm to hit? Why didn't it close down operations on Thursday, the day the storm actually did arrive? Some employees had already scheduled vacation for the Thanksgiving and the Christmas holidays and now realized that they had insufficient vacation days left in their vacation bank. Those who had already paid for their airline and cruise tickets were particularly upset. Others were offended by the fact that they would now need to work uncompensated overtime to make up for the work missed, an action expected of all salaried employees.

The company's vacation policy states that salaried employees accrue vacation time based on length of service. Employees with less than five years' seniority receive one day per month, those with five to ten years' seniority earn one and one-half days per month, and those with more than ten years earn two days per month. Employees have the right to carry over unused vacation time to the next year. The policy also states that if the shipyard is shut down for any reason, the time lost by salaried employees will be charged to each person's vacation bank. Furthermore, the policy states that in the event of a partial shutdown, salaried employees who report to work and are then sent home will be paid for any time missed and will not be required to charge lost time to their vacation banks.

QUESTIONS

1. What, if anything, should Ships, Inc. do with regard to salaried personnel who have vacations planned later this year and now do not have enough vacation time?
2. What, if anything, should the firm do regarding the lost vacation time for all of the other employees, both salaried and hourly?
3. Should the firm change its current policy that requires salaried employees to charge their vacation bank whenever a shutdown occurs?

84 INCIDENT

The Medical Leave Problem (FMLA)

Maura Currier has been working for ComputerTech for four years as a lead supervisor. During the past two years, Currier's mother has needed frequent medical attention for her diabetes. Being the only child, Currier has helped her mother, Jane Currier, as often as her work schedule would allow. Unfortunately, during the past two years, her mother's condition has worsened.

With the passage of the Family and Medical Leave Act (FMLA), Currier asked the firm for, and was granted, an unpaid leave to care for her mother in accordance with company policy (see the policy in Exhibit 4.9). The agreement stated that Currier could miss work every Friday for 60 weeks rather than take off 12 straight weeks. At the end of 60 weeks, Currier returned to work full time and immediately began missing work to care for her mother until all of her allotted vacation and sick leave days were exhausted. She then asked that her Friday

EXHIBIT 4.9 *Family Medical Leave Policy*

Employees who have worked for at least one year and worked 1,250 hours during the 12-month period preceding the commencement of the leave year are eligible to take up to 12 weeks of unpaid job-protected leave during any 12-month period for one or more of the following reasons:

1. Because of the birth of a son or daughter of the employee and to care for such son or daughter;
2. Because of the placement of a son or daughter with the employee for adoption or foster care;
3. To care for the spouse, son, daughter, or parent of the employee, if such spouse, son, daughter, or parent has a serious health condition; or
4. Because of a serious health condition that makes the employee unable to perform the functions of the position of such employee.
5. For qualifying exigencies arising out of the fact that the employee's spouse, son, daughter, or parent is on active duty or call to active duty status as a member of the National Guard or Reserves in support of a contingency operation.

We will also grant an eligible employee who is a spouse, daughter, parent, or next of kin of a current member of the Armed Forces, including a member of the National Guard or Reserves, with a serious injury or illness, up to a total of 26 weeks of unpaid leave during a single 12-month period to care for the service member.

If two spouses are employed by us, they are limited in the amount of family leave they may take for the birth and care of a newborn child, placement of a child for adoption or foster care, or to care for a parent who has a serious health condition, to a combined total of 12 weeks (or 26 weeks if leave to care for a covered service member with a serious injury or illness is also used). Leave for birth and care, or placement for adoption or foster care, must conclude within 12 months of the birth or placement.

Under some circumstances, employees may take FMLA leave intermittently—taking leave in separate blocks of time for a single qualifying reason—or on a reduced leave schedule-reducing the employee's usual weekly or daily work schedule. When leave is needed for planned medical treatment, the employee must make a reasonable effort to schedule treatment so as not to unduly disrupt our operation. If FMLA leave is for birth or care, or placement for adoption or foster care, use of intermittent leave is subject to our approval.

Employees who wish to take advantage of this policy must fill out a Leave Request Form at least 30 days prior to the date they wish the leave to commence, or as soon as possible in cases where the reason for the leave (such as sudden illness) was unforeseeable. You will be entitled to return to your same job or an equivalent position as the one you held before, and all normal benefits will be restored. Eligible employees will also be entitled to maintain group healthcare coverage during the period of leave to the same extent as if they had continued to work during the leave period.

leave be extended indefinitely, because her mother's condition remained serious and she required ongoing assistance.

The firm's human resource director was uncertain what her response should be in this situation. ComputerTech needed Currier to be at work regularly because of the increasingly heavy workload, the fact that her job duties were critical, and because other supervisors and employees preferred not to have to cover for her. On the other hand, Currier was an excellent supervisor and had worked four years for ComputerTech. In addition, everyone was concerned about the welfare of both Currier and her mother and wanted to be supportive of them.

QUESTIONS

1. What are the advantages and disadvantages of extending Maura Currier's leave?
2. If you were the human resource director, would you grant her request? Explain your answer.

85 CASE

Disaster Preparedness

Winston Hotels is a national hotel chain based in Orlando, Florida. The company employs 2,100 staff members in the United States, of which 118 are employed in the home office, 256 are employed in hotels in the Orlando area, and 1,726 are employed in hotels outside of Orlando. In 2004, Hurricane Charley blew through Central Florida and was followed by two other hurricanes within a 30-day period. During each of the three hurricanes, the two Orlando hotels were damaged by falling tree limbs and the accumulation of rainwater in some rooms.

The company required employees to work around the clock in these hotels even though the home office and the Orlando hotels lost power for one to three days during each hurricane. In addition, many telephone lines in Central Florida were down for various periods of time during these hurricanes. Some workers refused to work around the clock since they or family members had suffered major or minor damage to their homes and were attempting to arrange repairs or rebuilding. All of these employees were dismissed. One employee gained notoriety by appealing his dismissal based on his citizen's right to protect his home and property. He and his lawyer stated that this right superseded his employment contract.

In addition, some employees filed a lawsuit against the company because they were promised a higher pay scale for working continuously during the hurricanes. However, after the hurricanes, management decided either not to pay the employees for all of their extra hours or not to pay them overtime rates. Still other employees filed lawsuits because the company failed to provide adequate sleeping accommodations or food for those employees who remained on site.

George Baker is director of human resources for Winston Hotels. He has been told by lawyers representing the company that the lawsuits would be easier to defend if the company had a disaster preparedness plan in place to deal with extraordinary events such as hurricanes, floods, earthquakes, volcanoes, SARS, bird flu, bioterrorism, and other terrorism events. Baker knows that while the probability of any one of these occurring is very low, the company will function more smoothly during such events, recover more quickly, and be less vulnerable to lawsuits if it follows a clearly communicated disaster plan.

Up to this point, the company has had no disaster plan and managers "played it by ear" when the hurricanes struck. The only policy that existed was a general policy that each employee had to either report to work during his or her scheduled work hours or give adequate notice so a replacement could be scheduled. No possibility for extraordinary circumstances was provided in the policies.

Many of the lawsuits are still under appeal by the company and have not yet been resolved. Baker is very aware that the company is vulnerable to lawsuits and large financial losses as a result of not having a disaster plan. Yesterday he read in *The Wall Street Journal* that his company is not alone; 75 percent of all employers do not have a disaster plan. The article went on to say that the disaster plan needs to include policies and procedures for addressing employee absenteeism, operating with a reduced workforce, communicating with employees and customers, addressing payroll and employee benefits policies, addressing supply shortages, providing back-up electricity, maintaining information technology, maintaining security, assuring occupational health and safety, and minimizing litigation. In groups of two to four students, answer the questions below.

QUESTIONS

1. What policies and procedures do you suggest George Baker propose to his company to address each of the areas identified above in *The Wall Street Journal* (i.e., employee absenteeism, etc.)?
2. Given the central Florida location of Winston Hotels, what types of disaster threats are most likely to occur and why? Which disasters are most likely in your current location?
3. What are the components of today's corporate disaster plans with which you are familiar? Access company Web sites to determine the components of existing plans. Are these plans adequate to address the challenges of various kinds of disasters? If not, what additional policies or procedures would you suggest?

86 EXERCISE

Safety and Health Programs

I. OBJECTIVES

A. To familiarize you with contemporary health and safety policies and procedures.

B. To give you an understanding of the possible gaps that may develop between health and safety policies and procedures and actual practices on the job.

II. OUT-OF-CLASS PREPARATION TIME: 3 hours

III. IN-CLASS TIME SUGGESTED: 45 minutes

IV. PROCEDURES

A. You or your group of three or four students (at the option of your instructor) select(s) one organization and obtain(s) its policies concerning health and safety. Examples might include workplace injuries, AIDS, employee assistance programs, and smoking. The information is often contained in the Employee Handbook.

B. You or your group then interview(s) one person in the organization who is knowledgeable about these policies.

C. You or your group then write(s) a brief report that answers the following questions:

1. What safety and health policies/procedures currently exist? Are any changes in these policies contemplated for the near future? If so, why?
2. What safety and health problems were the policies above designed to eliminate or minimize?
3. To what extent do employees abide by these policies? How do employees feel about these policies? Why?
4. Are these policies enforced and who is responsible for enforcement? If the policies are not enforced, why not?
5. What impact does the Occupational Safety and Health Act (OSHA) (together with the agency) have on the organization?
6. What future changes does the organization anticipate in the areas of health and safety?

D. At the option of the instructor, you or your group report(s) the results of your study either to the class as a whole or to a small group.

E. The reports are then turned in to the instructor.

87 INCIDENT

The Safety Problem

Belcher Manufacturing Company employs 300 workers at its main plant in the upper Midwest. One of its major product lines is compressors for air conditioners. All compressors are tested when they come off the assembly line. Two years ago William Carlson was 28 years old, a high school graduate, and had been employed in the compressor division for five years. His job was to test each compressor using a standard procedure. Each inspector goes through an extensive training program where proper procedures for testing compressors are explained and demonstrated. In addition, inspectors are required to follow the detailed procedures for testing each unit specified in the company manual. No deviations from those procedures are permitted by company policy.

Two years ago Carlson was testing a compressor when it exploded and he was killed on the spot. The Belcher Manufacturing Company expressed sympathy to the family but also indicated that the company had provided proper training, proper clothing, proper warnings, and proper procedures. It reiterated its commitment to employee safety and implied that the cause of the explosion was probably due to improper employee testing procedures, which were neither known nor approved by the company.

Carlson's family hired an attorney on a contingency basis to pursue a lawsuit against the Belcher Manufacturing Company. Recently, the case was heard in federal district court. During court testimony it was revealed that most of the inspectors, including Carlson, had developed various "shortcuts" to reduce the time required to test each compressor. Some continued to use the shortcuts even after the accident. The plaintiff's lawyer argued that it was not clear that Carlson had violated procedures, but if he did, the company had an obligation to know about the deviations and take steps to bring inspectors back to the proper testing procedures. In addition, he argued the company was responsible for providing training, periodically reinforcing proper procedures, and monitoring practices to assure conformity to proper procedures. The jury then retired to consider a verdict and, if the company was found guilty of safety violations, to assess appropriate penalties.

Belcher Manufacturing then brought in an attorney from corporate headquarters to defend the company. Thomas King had a law degree from Northwestern University School of Law and had been practicing law for 27 years, and 12 of those years he had been counselor for Belcher Manufacturing with an excellent track record of defending the company in areas of safety and health. King had focused his law practice in the area of health and safety and was always up-to-date with information regarding data and trends in this field. For example, he knew the following:

- There are approximately 4.3 million injuries per year among private sector firms.
- Each year the cost of occupational injuries and illness total more than $165 billion.
- In any year, approximately 80 million working days are lost because of on-the-job injuries.
- In the most recent year, 6,480 employees died from work accidents.

King knew that Congress passed the Occupational Safety and Health Act (OSHA) in 1970 to ensure the safety and health of American workers by setting and enforcing standards;

providing training, outreach and education; establishing partnerships; and encouraging continual improvements in workplace safety and health. The most recent fatality numbers were only about one-third of the number of worker deaths reported in the late 1960s. Consequently, most observers believed the Act has been effective in reducing workplace injuries.

King was also aware that a supervisor at another company's construction site was charged with criminal negligence because he had failed to take "reasonable steps to prevent bodily harm" that caused a worker's death on his watch. Five years ago the supervisor pleaded guilty to eight counts of failing to ensure compliance under OSHA and received a $50,000 fine. Subsequently, the same company was charged with criminal negligence for causing another death related to failure to correctly package cement blocks on pallets. The company subsequently pleaded guilty and paid another fine of $110,000 dollars. King knew he needed to prove to the jury that Belcher Manufacturing had done everything they could to develop safety policies, communicate these policies to all employees, and train new and current employees periodically regarding safety procedures.

QUESTIONS

1. In this particular case, was the Belcher Manufacturing Company guilty or innocent of safety violations that resulted in the death of William Carlson?
2. Irrespective of the jury's decision in this case, what should the company do now to avoid a similar incident in the future?

PART

5

Enhancing Employee Relations: Discipline, Motivation, and Labor Relations

88 CASE

The Drug Testing Problem at Standard Chemical

Standard Chemical Company's Camden Division processes volatile toxic chemicals that are sold for commercial use. The division consists of 500 employees, and approximately half are in the bargaining unit of the Machinists and Aerospace Workers Union at the Division. Safety is a critical issue at the plant because of the potential for environmental hazards resulting from accidents.

Vicky Jacobson, the human resource manager, had attended a seminar on drug abuse in the workforce and was concerned that some of the job-related accidents in the Camden Division might be due to drug use. As a result of Jacobson's concerns and the concerns of management at the other plants, the company decided to implement a Drug and Alcohol Program.

Notification was sent to the president of the local union. When Jacobson met with union representatives at the plant, she found little opposition to the policy. However, there was concern about how the policy would be enforced. Bob James, union representative, was concerned that the policy would be used by supervisors in a "witch hunt" to get rid of people they did not like. Jacobson assured him that there would be checks and balances so that the program would be administered even-handedly. She further assured the union that the emphasis would be on rehabilitation, not termination.

NOTIFICATION OF THE PROGRAM

The program was presented to employees during a series of group meetings. Jacobson read a prepared statement at each meeting to be certain that the policy was presented uniformly to all employees:

> *Standard Chemical is implementing a company-wide Alcohol and Drug Abuse Program effective January 1. We do not believe we have a serious problem with drug or alcohol abuse at Standard. However, we are committed to maintaining high standards of job performance and to protecting the safety of our employees, our community, and our environment. Therefore, we have implemented a policy that will significantly reduce the possibility that our employees or our environment might be harmed through alcohol or drug use of any individual employed at Standard Chemical. Please familiarize yourself with the policy as described to you in the brochure.*
>
> *(Brochures were distributed to each employee at the group meetings. See Exhibit 5.1 for a description of the brochure's contents.)*

SUSPENSION UNDER THE PROGRAM

During the time in which the policy has been in effect, Jacobson has, in practice, enforced the policy by suspending employees when there was reasonable suspicion of drug use. Suspended employees were then given three options regarding drug testing:

1. Refusing to undergo drug testing which resulted in immediate termination.

EXHIBIT 5.1 *Excerpt from the Brochure Given to Employees during the Group Meetings*

Standard Chemical Alcohol and Drug Abuse Policy

1. Use or abuse of any substance that may have an adverse effect on job performance or safety is a violation of Company policy.
2. Reporting to work or working while under the influence of alcohol or unauthorized drugs is a violation of Company policy.
3. Unauthorized drugs are any drugs that cannot be obtained legally or have been illegally obtained. Prescription drugs obtained without a prescription, or over-the-counter drugs used other than as instructed, are considered to be unauthorized drugs.
4. Drug testing is required as a condition of employment when there is reasonable suspicion of drug or alcohol use.
5. Reasonable suspicion is a basis for drug testing when, in the opinion of management, a job-related accident may have been caused by human error that may be drug or alcohol-related.
6. Employees who test positive may, if circumstances warrant, be permitted to continue employment provided they agree to undergo periodic drug/alcohol screening and participate in the Company-approved Employee Assistance Program (EAP).

2. Taking the drug test. If the drug test was negative, back pay was awarded for the time on suspension. If the drug test was positive, the employee was given the opportunity to participate in the Employee Assistance Program (EAP).
3. Enrolling directly in the EAP's drug and alcohol program in lieu of submitting to a drug test.

On March 7, Jacobson was in her office when John Martin, the company's security guard, asked to speak to her. "Ms. Jacobson, I thought I better report this to you. The forklift driver on the last shift must have been out of it when he parked that machine. The blade was driven through the crack between the concrete floor and the outer steel wall. The next shift driver is out there and he's having a heck of a time getting it out." The guard also told Jacobson that other employees had commented that "It was probably that 'pothead' Peter Carpenter."

When Jacobson and the guard walked over to the forklift, she noticed that the lower portion of the steel wall had buckled. During that day, she talked to several employees who had information about the accident. She discovered that Peter Carpenter was the driver of the forklift and that he had been seen driving the lift too fast around the corner at the end of his shift. Carpenter had worked for Standard Chemical for five-and-a-half years.

Jacobson met with Carpenter, his supervisors, and union representatives and questioned him about the forklift accident. According to Jacobson, the following conversations took place.

"Look, Ms. Jacobson, I admit that I parked that forklift there, but I had no idea I had parked so close to the wall."

Jacobson responded, "Mr. Carpenter, I have worked in this plant for 23 years and have seen my share of accidents. The blade of the forklift was wedged in the crack between the wall and the floor with enough force to buckle the steel wall. In my opinion, this accident is evidence enough for reasonable suspicion of drug or alcohol abuse."

After talking to Carpenter's supervisors and conferring with the plant manager, Jacobson met again with Carpenter and told him, "Mr. Carpenter, you are suspended effective immediately, based on reasonable suspicion of drug or alcohol use on the job. Company policy requires that you submit to a drug test or be terminated, effective immediately. If your

Contributed by Dr. Susan Corriher

drug test is negative, you will be paid for the time of your suspension. If it is positive, then you must enroll in the Employee Assistance Program and demonstrate a sincere commitment to the treatment program. You do have the option of enrolling directly into the EAP's alcohol and drug program. If you choose that option, you can forego the drug test at this time."

"Ms. Jacobson, I'd like to go ahead and get some help. I'll go on and get started with the EAP," replied Carpenter.

In Jacobson's presence, he then signed the company's EAP consent form which included the following statement:

> *If I fail to meet my obligation to the EAP program, I will be subject to disciplinary action, including termination of employment.*

After Carpenter signed the form, Jacobson telephoned the EAP (conducted by the local Alcoholism Council). Carpenter was given an appointment the next evening, March 8. Carpenter kept this scheduled appointment. During that first meeting with the counselor, he signed a Release of Information form authorizing the EAP to release information about his participation in the program, including keeping appointments, following EAP suggestions, and reporting to the designated lab for drug testing. He refused to give the EAP counselor permission to release the results of his drug tests to Standard Chemical.

REPORT FROM THE COUNSELOR

Robert Johnson, the EAP counselor, telephoned Jacobson to confirm that Carpenter had kept his appointment and explained that he had not given permission for the EAP to disclose results of the drug testing. Johnson also recommended that Carpenter be allowed to return to work while attending counseling sessions on an outpatient basis.

On March 13, Jacobson sent Carpenter a letter stating that his discharge was "held in abeyance" while he received counseling sessions. The letter further stated that Carpenter must attend counseling sessions and follow the guidelines of the program and submit to urine testing if instructed to do so by his EAP counselor. The letter also included the following statement:

> *Any incident in the future, which indicates failure to comply with the EAP program, will result in disciplinary action up to and including termination of employment.*

Carpenter attended EAP sessions regularly for the next eight weeks. Reports to Jacobson from his supervisors during that time period were extremely positive. His job performance was excellent and he had no safety violations.

On May 9, Johnson, the EAP counselor, called Sarah Green, the plant nurse, to discuss several EAP-related matters. They specifically discussed Carpenter's case because of Johnson's concerns about him. He noted that while Carpenter had attended every session and his supervisors reported that he had been an exemplary employee, his lab tests showed ascending levels of cannabinoids (marijuana metabolites). Johnson intimated that he was not sure that the EAP counseling sessions would be successful.

Green called Jacobson and reported that Carpenter's lab reports were positive. Jacobson telephoned Johnson and confirmed what had been said to the plant nurse. She also telephoned the company's medical department and was told that cannabinoids normally stay in a person's system for 35–45 days.

Later that same day, Jacobson met with Carpenter and the union representatives and confronted him with the information she had received about his drug tests. Carpenter argued with Jacobson and said that he did not understand why she was questioning him. He told her that he had attended every counseling session and felt like the sessions were helping him. Carpenter told her that his performance and his safety record had been great since he started the program. Carpenter further told her that he knew that his supervisors had reported his excellent work record to her. He also told her that he had stopped smoking marijuana. Jacobson then asked him to submit to a urine sample test. She told him that if he refused he would be terminated in compliance with company policy. Carpenter agreed to take the drug tests.*

On May 17, the lab reported that the results of both drug tests were positive. Later that same day, Jacobson met with Carpenter and informed him that he was fired. Carpenter immediately filed a grievance.

On May 26, the union recommended that Carpenter take another drug test. Standard Chemical agreed to take into consideration the results. Later that same day, Carpenter took the drug test.*

On May 30, Standard Chemical received the lab report that was negative for cannabinoids. On June 21 and July 12, Carpenter's drug tests were again negative for cannabinoids. Ten months later, Carpenter took another drug test that was also negative.

QUESTIONS

1. Was Peter Carpenter's suspension justified?
2. Was his termination justified?
3. Evaluate the adequacy of the Standard Chemical Company's drug and alcohol abuse policy. Are there any components that need improvement?
4. Were Carpenter's privacy rights protected?

*The company uses two tests: the enzyme-multiplied immunoassay technique (EMIT) and gas chromatography/mass spectrometry.

89 CASE

Violence at Work

Eastern State University is a state school with about 15,000 students. Half of the student population are commuters, and the rest live in university dormitories, apartments, or fraternity/sorority houses. The university does not have high admissions standards, believing that students should be given a chance to prove themselves academically. About half of the freshman class needs to take either remedial English or math. The business school at the university often attracts students who could not succeed academically in other fields such as engineering or chemistry.

Because the university wants to improve its graduation rate, faculty in the business school are encouraged to work with students so that they do not fail and drop out. Nonetheless, grading standards are high, and it not unusual for 30–40 percent of the students to get a "D" or "F" in Introductory Economics or Accounting classes. Students who get low grades are rarely asked to leave the university. Rather, they are allowed to take the class again and substitute the new grade for the original one. Nonetheless, many students drop out, realizing they will never graduate.

In recent years, the university has experienced a serious increase in student misbehavior, ranging from swearing at faculty members to not leaving class when asked. Some of the faculty blame this on the university's admission and retention policies. Several times each semester, a faculty member has needed to ask a security officer to come to class and escort out one or more students. Fortunately, no student has ever physically harmed a faculty member.

One of the professors at the university, Roy Morris, has taught Marketing and Public Relations courses for over ten years. He is known for being a hard but fair grader, and his student evaluations are always high. He expects a lot from the class and is a stickler for meeting assigned deadlines. Morris rarely gives make-up exams and expects all papers to be turned in on time with no exceptions. He includes his expectations in his syllabus and repeats them orally throughout the semester.

Usually, Professor Morris is a happy, upbeat individual, but one December day he appeared very upset when he walked into the faculty lunchroom. Everyone there saw the expression on his face and knew that something serious had occurred. Morris sat down in a chair and exclaimed, "You will not believe what the chief of security and the dean of student affairs have just told me!"

Professor Morris further explained that after his Principles of Marketing class had ended earlier that morning, he had gone back to his office and was confronted by a student, Paul Lewis. Lewis was an older student who had served in the U.S. Marines prior to returning to school. He was majoring in Marketing, and most of the faculty knew him because he was so outspoken. He was at best a "C" student and liked to argue with other students during class discussion. Lewis was six feet, five inches tall and had an intimidating physical appearance.

Lewis told Professor Morris that he was unable to turn in a term paper due that day because he had been sick recently. He said he knew that Professor Morris had stated repeatedly when the paper was due and that no late papers would be accepted, but he wanted an exception in his case. The paper accounted for 10 percent of the course grade, and Lewis said he did not want to receive an "F" on it. Professor Morris said that he was sorry, but

Lewis had had 13 weeks to complete the paper and that, in fairness to all of the other students, he could not grant an exception.

Lewis argued vehemently that the policy was completely unfair, that he could not help it if he got sick, and demanded that an exception be made. Again, Professor Morris told him he was sorry, but if he made an exception for him, he would have to do it for all of the other students in the class. At this point, Lewis exploded and said in a loud voice, "This issue isn't over until I say it's over. You will regret your decision!!!" Shaking his fist at Professor Morris, Lewis walked out of the office and slammed the door behind him.

Professor Morris stated that he was dumbfounded by Lewis's actions. He was not sure what to do, so he called the campus chief of security. The chief told him there was nothing he could do about Lewis now, but that if further problems arose, and it got more serious, to call back and a guard would come to his office or classroom. Unhappy with this response, Professor Morris called the dean of student affairs, explained what had happened, and asked the dean to suspend Lewis from the university. He told the dean that he did not take Lewis's threat lightly and that he also feared for his safety. The dean's response was that he could remove Lewis from Professor Morris's class but not from his other classes. He would give Lewis an "I" in the class and allow him to take it again next semester without charging him tuition. The dean told Professor Morris that if any further problems occurred with Lewis, he should call security.

After Professor Morris finished talking, the faculty members in attendance looked at each other in amazement. "What kind of solution is that?" they asked each other. Several of those present also had Lewis in their classes, and as he was not performing well, they were worried about their own safety. What might Lewis do to them, particularly if they did not grant him an exception or gave him a failing grade? The faculty members agreed that they wanted Lewis permanently removed from the university. One professor reminded the others that violence on campus was increasing all over the country and pointed out that over 30 students and teachers were killed at Virginia Tech in 2007 by one disgruntled student. She added that calling security would not have prevented this massacre. She would not want to see Lewis in her Business Policy class the next semester. Another professor agreed by saying that calling security would definitely be "too little too late" and stated that he would henceforth lock his classroom door once class began, spend less time in his office, and keep his office door shut when he was there. He also said he would keep a watchful eye out for Lewis and suggested that the others do the same.

QUESTIONS

1. What action do you believe Eastern State University should have taken with regard to Paul Lewis? Do you agree with the dean's solution to the problem? Why or why not?
2. If you were Professor Morris, what preventive action would you take to insure your safety and prevent Lewis from harming you?
3. What steps should the university take to insure the safety of faculty?

90 CASE

Surfing the Internet on Company Time

Helen Barnett was shocked by what she was seeing on the computer screen at the desk of James Erskine. On the screen was a picture depicting a sexual act! The picture appeared on a porn Web site that Erskine had evidently visited. Helen supervises 15 customer service representatives for National Insurance, a company specializing in home insurance. The job of a customer service representative is to assist clients with claims, insurance quotes, and other queries. Each customer service representative works in a cubicle furnished with a computer, a desk, and a phone headset. Only Barnett has a personal office. National Insurance prides itself in its efforts to make greater use of electronic technology in servicing its clients. Quotes for insurance and even samples of policies are often sent to clients via the computer. Most of the information representatives need to answer customer queries is available at their fingertips.

Erskine had been employed with National Insurance for the last six months. His 90-day performance review had been satisfactory. Lorraine Smalls, a co-worker who sat in a cubicle close to Erskine, had inadvertently discovered the pornographic picture. When her computer malfunctioned, Smalls had gone to Erskine's cubicle to quickly retrieve some data to respond to a customer's query. It was not unusual for representatives to use another staff member's computer. Erskine was out to lunch and his computer screen was in standby mode. When Smalls hit the enter key, the picture appeared and its graphic nature disturbed her greatly. She immediately called Barnett over to the workstation. When Barnett checked Erskine's browser, it seemed that he had visited the Web site more than a dozen times that morning. She felt that she needed to confront him about using company time in such an unproductive manner.

When Erskine returned from lunch, Barnett told him about her discovery. He was irate with her. Erskine told her that he had visited the site on his break time, not on company time. Furthermore, he felt that it was an invasion of his privacy that both a co-worker and Barnett had gained access to his computer. Barnett told Erskine she had no recourse but to report his behavior to the human resource manager. After he left Barnett's office, Erskine himself went to the human resource manager, Dale Gibbons. Erskine believed that the supervisor's actions violated his constitutional rights to privacy. Gibbons told him, "Even though the company does not have a written policy prohibiting visiting Web sites, all employees are expected to use their computers for work-related purposes. Unnecessary surfing ties up our ISDN line capacity and could impact service delivery. In addition, you exposed two of your fellow employees to pornography." He went on to say, "National Insurance operates on a trust basis in all its relationships with employees."

Two days later, Erskine was suspended for using the company's computer system for nonproductive, personal purposes. When he received his suspension notification, Erskine told Gibbons that he would sue National Insurance for violating his right to privacy. He also told Gibbons that he knew of many other employees who surfed the Internet and used the company's e-mail for personal purposes.

QUESTIONS

1. Did Helen Barnett's actions invade James Erskine's right to privacy?
2. Was National Insurance justified in suspending Erskine?
3. What should be the key elements of an employee computer and Web use policy?

91 Exercise

Developing an Employee Dress Code

I. Objectives

A. To improve your skills in developing a new dress code.

B. To familiarize you with the reasons why firms develop dress codes.

C. To familiarize you with the content of different dress code policies.

II. Out-of-Class Preparation Time: 1–3 hours

III. In-Class Time Suggested: 30–45 minutes

IV. Procedures

At the end of the class prior to the beginning of this exercise, your instructor will divide the class into small groups of two or three. Each group will meet outside of class and write up a dress code policy for one specific job at a firm. The instructor will assign each group a job from the list provided below or from his or her own list. The exercise begins by having each group state the job they were assigned and presenting their dress code policy to the class. This will be followed by a critique of the policy by class members and the instructor. The exercise ends when the last group finishes its presentation.

In writing a policy, keep in mind that firms typically develop dress policies for one or more of three major reasons:

1. To provide employees with a safe and healthy workplace as required under the Occupational Safety and Health Act (OSHA). For example, those working on construction sites may need to wear hard hats, ear protection, eye protection, and/or hard tip shoes.
2. To meet health ordinances and laws. For example, employees who handle food may be required to wear hair nets and plastic gloves to reduce the spread of germs and disease.
3. To enhance a legitimate business interest. For example, some firms state in their policies that they do not allow employees to wear any clothing that others might find highly offensive such as shirt with a swastika, a Confederate battle flag, a nude person, or a religious slur such as "God is Dead."

More commonly, many firms state in their dress policy the type of clothing they want employees to wear in order to create a favorable impression or specific image of the firm. For example, a firm that sells imported clothing from Scotland may legitimately ask employees to wear kilts while waiting on customers. Likewise, Walt Disney theme parks can legitimately ask employees to wear costumes that portray Mickey Mouse and Donald Duck.

It is important to note that dress policies should not be based on the personal whims of management. Firms have the burden of proof to show that their dress code enhances the firm's success. Keep in mind also that the policy must not be discriminatory and violate federal or state discrimination laws.

In writing a dress code policy, the following items need to be addressed:

1. What clothing is the employee required to wear and/or not wear on your assigned job? Hats? Shirts/blouses? Pants? Footwear? Safety or health attire? Company uniform? Name tag? Other?

2. Are there any requirements for your assigned job regarding hair style, length, or color? Are mustaches and beards permitted?
3. Does the dress code for your job need to include provisions that address items such as lipstick, false eyelashes, perfume, after-shave lotions, and false fingernails, and/or polish?
4. Should the dress code for your assigned job address the wearing of jewelry such as bracelets, rings, necklaces, ear/nose jewelry?
5. Should the policy for your assigned job address personal hygiene issues such as using deodorant, wearing clean clothes, or taking baths/showers?
6. Should the dress code for your job be the same for men and women? If not, how should they differ?
7. What disciplinary or other action will be taken if someone violates the policy?

Listed below are possible jobs for which your group could write a dress policy:

1. A horseback trip leader at a guest dude ranch.
2. A chain saw operator working for a logging firm.
3. A cook at a large expensive restaurant.
4. A salesclerk working at a retail store that sells clothing, apparel, and shoes that appeal to pop culture customers.
5. A barber or hair stylist.
6. A student at your college.
7. A bank vice president who makes loans to large corporations.
8. A life guard at a country club swimming pool.
9. A personal trainer working at a fitness center.
10. A nurse working at a hospital emergency room.
11. An exterminator who sprays chemicals around homes.
12. A pharmaceutical sales representative calling on doctors.
13. A TV weather announcer.
14. A realtor who shows houses to clients.
15. A hostess at a popular chain restaurant.
16. A professor at your college.

92 INCIDENT

Facebook Posting: I Hate My Stupid Boss

Shanti Williams, HR manager at a large retailer received a Facebook friend invitation from Marisa Hernandez, a senior clerk in the company's finance department. She and Hernandez had attended the same high school several years ago and had only recently discovered they were employed at the same company. During high school, they had been in several classes together, and Williams readily remembered Hernandez. She had met Hernandez again at one of the retailer's training programs she had launched about three weeks ago. When Williams saw the Facebook request, she quickly accepted it.

A few months later, she saw a Facebook posting from Hernandez to her friends that read: "I hate my stupid boss. My new boss is a total jerk and makes each day a big pain in the xxx. He treats us finance clerks like we are his slaves. I can't wait to leave this job because I would rather eat beans than spend another day working for a moron! Help!"

That evening after reading the posting, Williams did not sleep very well. She wondered what action she should take as HR manager against Hernandez, if any, about what she had read in the Facebook posting.

QUESTIONS

1. What issues does this Facebook incident raise about social media and the workplace: (a) from the perspective of an employee, (2) from the perspective of management/managers, and (3) from a legal perspective?
2. Should Shanti Williams have accepted the friend invitation? Why or why not?
3. If you were in Williams's position, what would you do now? Why?

93 INCIDENT

Can He Wear an Earring at Work?

Peter Wood was hired as a personal services representative at South Town Bank, a small bank serving South Town for over 30 years. The bank had a reputation for being one of the more conservative places of employment in town. Because it offered good wages and benefits, the bank had no problems finding employees.

Personal service representatives sat at desks in the wood panel lobby of the bank to assist bank customers with account queries and other problems. All bank personnel were required to dress according to company rules. Men were expected to wear dress shirts and ties, while women were required to wear dresses or skirts. Recently the bank instituted "Casual Friday" on the last Friday of each month. On that Friday, employees could wear business casual clothes. Men could wear golf shirts or other shirts with collars. Women could wear slacks with appropriate blouses and/or sweaters. No jeans, shorts, halter tops, or t-shirts were allowed. Employees with tattoos were required to wear clothes that would cover tattoos.

When Wood reported for his first day at South Town Bank, he came dressed appropriately in a shirt and tie. He also had a discreet, but noticeable gold loop earring in his left earlobe. When the branch manager saw the earring, he told Wood to remove the earring since it was not consistent with the bank's employee dress policy. Wood became upset and pointed out that no one had told him during the employment interview that he could not wear an earring to work. The branch manager pointed out that if Wood had worn the earring during the job interview, he probably would not have been hired. He further stated that, because of the earring, Wood did not present the professional image the bank desired for its personal service representatives. Wood pointed out that female personal service representatives were allowed to wear earrings at work. The branch manager said it was customary in society for women to wear earrings but not men. He again asked Wood to remove the earring. When he refused, Wood was fired.

Wood felt that he had been discriminated against and vowed that he would take legal action against. The following statement regarding earrings appeared in the employee handbook: "Visible jewelry must be small and tasteful as determined by management. Jewelry must not interfere with job performance."

QUESTIONS

1. Is Peter Wood a victim of discrimination?
2. Evaluate the branch manager's comment that Wood would not have been hired had he worn the earring during the employment interview.
3. Evaluate South Town Bank's dress policy. Is it clear? Is it appropriate? Is it legal?

94 INCIDENT
Spiked Milk

A reputable northeastern construction company employs six experienced construction supervisors for its various construction jobs. These supervisors have the overall responsibility of hiring and firing and seeing that the construction proceeds as close to time and cost schedules as possible. They also have the responsibility of overall quality control of the construction.

Larry Werst, age 55, has been a supervisor for this company for many years. He is never absent and has established a reputation for getting the job done right and close to schedule. He has supervised the construction of several prominent buildings and is now supervising the construction of a college fraternity house. Werst's approach to handling his employees is firm and sometimes harsh. He does not allow any back talk, and everyone who works for him usually earns his or her pay or is not on the job for very long.

The owner and manager of the company had become concerned about Werst because rumors were circulating that he was an alcoholic and that he drank on the job. The owner knew that Werst drank a lot and had a stormy home life, but he did not know whether he was drinking on the job.

One day, when the manager was talking with Werst, he smelled alcohol on his breath. This had happened on several occasions when office and storeroom employees noticed the odor when they talked to him. Also, the storeroom clerk noticed that almost every day Werst would come into the store, buy two Cokes, and then leave in his company truck, presumably to go back to his job site.

The manager decided to talk to Werst about this situation. When he confronted Werst with the rumors, his alcoholic breath, and the purchasing of two Cokes at a time, Werst denied that he was drinking on the job. He replied that the rumors were just that and that the two Cokes were for himself and his carpenter supervisor. The manager told him that he would have to let him go if he were caught drinking on the job. He reminded Werst that the firm's progressive discipline system included a rule that states, "No employee is permitted to go on duty or remain on duty if he or she possesses, is under the influence of, or is consuming an alcoholic beverage. Violation of this policy will result in dismissal."

About a year later, when the construction season was again in full swing, stories began circulating about Werst's drinking. His fellow employees now pondered over the quart of milk he drank every day. They wondered if he spiked the milk and/or used it to cover his alcoholic breath. Sometimes his speech seemed slurred, but Werst was gravel-voiced and had sloppy speech habits anyway. The workers were amused by the stories he would tell about things that had happened to him. They were just stories, of course, but lately they were becoming pathetically farfetched and made no sense at all.

The manager soon heard about some of the new rumors about Werst, and he wondered what he should do about the situation again. Werst still had never actually been caught drinking on the job. His construction project was proceeding satisfactorily, but it was a little behind schedule due to the inability to hire good carpenters and laborers at the beginning of the construction season. And worker turnover was perhaps somewhat higher on this project than the average turnover.

QUESTIONS

1. What course of action should the owner-manager follow? Why?
2. To what extent should the owner-manager go to try to catch Larry Werst drinking on the job?
3. What action, if any, should the owner-manager take if Werst confesses to being an alcoholic?
4. Does the owner-manager presently have sufficient proof that Werst is working under the influence of alcohol?
5. Critique the construction company's alcoholism rule.

Contributed by Arno F. Knapper, School of Business, The University of Kansas

95 INCIDENT

Caught in the Act: Immoral Behavior at Work

It was about 1:30 in the morning when Mike Morrison, night supervisor at HITEC Corporation, a West Coast manufacturer of computer software, finally returned to his office to finish up a report. As he began writing, he heard a strange noise coming from the quality control lab down the hall. He knew that no one was assigned to work in the lab at that time, so he walked down to investigate. After knocking, he opened the door and was stunned to see two of his lead employees. Jim Harris, a lead maintenance supervisor, had his back turned to the door and was pulling up his pants. Mary Bridge, a lead production line supervisor, was next to an inspection bench and was likewise pulling up her pants. Morrison quickly shut the door and returned to his office, aghast at what he had just witnessed. Given the embarrassing nature of the situation, he decided to take no action.

Two weeks later, Teya Simpson, the human resource director, was talking to another lead supervisor when she heard about the incident. Apparently, everyone in the plant knew the story, except top management, because both Harris and Bridge had spread the word that they were "caught in the act" by Morrison.

Simpson immediately called Wayne Purdy, plant manager, to see what action, if any, should be taken. Both recognized that the firm had no work rule that specifically covered sexual relationships on the job and that the offense had occurred two weeks ago. On the other hand, both believed that the employees' behavior was highly unprofessional and noted that both managers had left their work areas unattended. Furthermore, they were concerned about the effect that this incident might have on future employee behavior if no disciplinary action was forthcoming.

QUESTIONS

1. What action should HITEC Corporation take, if any, with regard to Jim Arnold and Mary Bridge? Justify your answer.
2. What action should the firm take, if any, with respect to Mike Morrison? Why?

96 INCIDENT

Motivating and Maintaining Morale during Downsizing

The Rutledge Company is an organization involved in the retail industry, operating more than 100 retail stores. The company's headquarters is going through what is termed "modernization." A new information system, which will completely alter the way the firm does business, is being implemented. In addition, the new system will affect the staffing required by the company. The company began implementing the new software last year, and it is projected that at least another year is required before the rollout will be complete. All personnel within the corporate office, including the large clerical staff, attended a four-day, comprehensive computer training program and were told to immediately incorporate the new software into daily use.

The completion of the rollout will primarily affect the clerical staff. It is the company's objective to eliminate the majority of these individuals. The technology of the new software will enable all management-level personnel to perform their jobs efficiently without the need for clerical support. The Rutledge Company has informed its large clerical staff that most, but not all, of their jobs will disappear once the rollout is complete. The prospect of future unemployment, along with the uncertainty regarding when their jobs will be terminated, has greatly affected the staff morale. Complacency, lack of initiative, and complaints all have accompanied the loss of morale.

The firm has another problem: some of the clerical staff are long-term employees who are accustomed to how the company operated ten years ago. These employees have not adapted to the new software or to the other new programs that have been implemented. Thus, these employees do not provide the full clerical support needed by management. Rather, they perform only those aspects of their jobs that existed prior to the introduction of the new software plus other menial jobs sufficient to keep them busy.

Individual managers must determine how to motivate all of the clerical support staff for the remaining time that they will be employed and must also determine how to motivate some employees to use the new software. It must also be determined which clerical help should be retained once modernization is complete. The firm would like to retain all of its clerical staff until that time.

QUESTIONS

1. What actions should be taken in order to increase the morale and motivation level of the clerical staff at the Rutledge Company?
2. What actions can be taken to motivate those employees who are not using the new technology required of their job?
3. What criteria should be used to determine which clerical employees should be retained?
4. Should the firm attempt to solve its motivational problems by conducting further training?

97 INCIDENT

Motivating Employees during a Buyout

Radio, Inc. is a holding company for over 20 radio stations located throughout the West Coast. At its headquarters, the company employs approximately 65 media professionals. The firm has been in the news lately with speculations of a buyout, and both Wall Street analysts and news broadcasts indicate that the company is for sale. These statements have been circulating for a month now, and insiders know that they are not unfounded. Radio, Inc. is viewed as a "cash cow" and has been coveted by many outsiders for years because of its large listening audience.

Earlier this week, Radio, Inc. was visited by the president of a large firm. As he toured the facility, everyone recognized him and rumors reached a feverish pace. Accountants were asked to prepare current financial statements which added fuel to the rumors. Officially, this has all been "hush-hush," but staff members at headquarters had worked many overtime hours to provide the needed financial information. Employee morale is at an all-time low and most employees are fearful about their jobs and their future.

Meanwhile, the performance improvement and awards committee is finalizing plans for the second-quarter meeting. This committee was created several years ago to promote continuous improvement, reward individuals for performance excellence, and plan an off-site quarterly meeting. The first-quarter meeting was a huge success. Awards were presented with great fanfare and specific accomplishments of every recipient were cited. Slides of employees at work and play, gathered over the previous six months, were shown. The meeting boosted employee morale and provided incentives to improve performance with hopes of gaining recognition at the next quarterly meeting. The committee has created numerous awards that employees cherish. These include:

- People's Choice Award—given to the employee who has an infectiously positive influence on the company and on co-workers. This person is nominated by peers, voted on by management, and ultimately selected by the committee.
- Fiscal Responsibility Award—given to an employee who implements a program that saves the company the most money. The recipient is nominated by department heads or middle/senior management and is ultimately selected by the committee.
- Winning Attitude Award—given to the employee who performs both routine and special job tasks with a cheerful, can-do attitude.
- Extra Effort Award—given to an employee who gives extra effort, goes the extra mile, and contributes more than 100 percent to accomplish his or her job.
- Technical Achievement Award—given to the employee who invents and implements a new program or process that uses technology and results in improvements for internal/external customers.
- Out-of-the-Box Award—given to the employee who thinks of innovative, new ways of accomplishing his/her job, or contributes fresh ideas that focus on continuous improvement, or coordinates department efforts that enhance the change process.

Since March, the committee has prepared for the second-quarter event. They have scheduled the Shark Room at a local marine science aquarium for the afternoon, put together a great slide show, ordered sandwiches from a well-known catering firm, solicited senior and middle management for award nominations, and purchased gifts for the award recipients.

The quarterly awards meeting is scheduled to be held on Friday. However, on the preceding Wednesday, the president of Radio, Inc. receives an attractive buyout offer that she knows the firm's board of directors will accept. The details of the sale are expected to be finalized and announced on the same day as the awards banquet. The announcement cannot be postponed due to the risk of having confidential information leak out to the public. The president is now faced with the issue of whether the awards meeting should be held.

QUESTIONS

1. Should the awards banquet be held as scheduled or should it be canceled or postponed?
2. Assuming that Radio, Inc. is bought, what can the firm do to retain desirable employees and to enhance employee motivation and morale?

Labor Relations

98 Case

Union Organizing at SGA Industries

Introduction

President White sat in his office at SGA Industries thinking about the union election taking place at the plant auditorium. He felt that the company had waged a successful campaign to persuade workers that their best interests would be served only if the company remained union-free. As he awaited the election results, his mind began to wander back to the events leading up to today's election.

Background

SGA Industries is known as the world's largest producer of women's hosiery and employs approximately 6,500 people at ten plants in five communities in Georgia and South Carolina. The company's headquarters is located in Anderson, Georgia. The company's sales subsidiary, SGA Inc., has 12 offices in major market areas throughout the United States and sells its products directly to distributors around the world. The company's strategy of strong identification with the customer has made SGA one of the most recognized names in the entire hosiery industry.

SGA was founded in 1907 by Sam Gerome Anderson. Anderson built the company, and the surrounding community was named after him in 1910. Ever since, the fortunes of Anderson residents have been interwoven with those of SGA. Over the years the company supported the community, donating land and money for churches, schools, and hospitals, and providing jobs for nearly a third of the town's residents. As the years passed, further expansion and product diversification occurred, and the company gained a reputation as an industry leader in the design, production, and marketing of women's and men's hosiery and undergarments.

After the death of the last Anderson family member, SGA was managed by four chief executive officers in less than a dozen years. Then, the company was purchased for $550 million by Jack Phillips who is a well-known Atlanta entrepreneur and business leader. Soon after the purchase, Phillips appointed Ted White as president of SGA.

Labor-Management Relations

Over the years, SGA enjoyed a reputation as a steady job provider in an unstable industry. The company provided for its workers and treated them like family members. Many believe that the company's generosity to both its employees and the town of Anderson helped to defeat an earlier union organizing drive by the Textile Workers of America, by a vote of 3,937 to 1,782. At the time of the vote, the chairman called it "an expression of confidence by employees." The SGA vote was viewed as a severe blow to union organizing efforts in the South.

Contributed by Dr. Gerald Calvasina, Southern Utah University

When Phillips purchased SGA, he announced that his major goals would be to improve the community and to improve the quality of life for SGA employees and their families. Phillips invested over $100 million to reach these goals. The total included funds for pay increases; new job benefits; capital improvements, including the use of robots on the production line; community improvements; and other contributions. These improvements were also accompanied by a shift in management philosophy. The theme of the new philosophy was self-sufficiency, and it signaled an end to the benevolent paternalism that had so long characterized employee relations at SGA. Greater emphasis was henceforth placed on employee performance and productivity.

During the mid-1980s, the entire hosiery industry experienced major problems. Growing foreign competition and imports had a negative impact on domestic hosiery manufacturers. Many manufacturers attempted to reverse the impact by intensive capital investments in new technology, by the reorganization and downsizing of plants, and by instituting programs to improve employee productivity and efficiency. SGA was not spared from this competition. Its international sales fell dramatically from $26 million to $10 million. Faced with increasing imports and weak consumer sales, the company was forced to lay off 1,500 employees, reduce pay scales, and rescind many of the perks that the workers had enjoyed under the Anderson family. Many of these changes drew worker protests and created a good deal of tension between workers and management.

Wages in the industry had been rising steadily but were still lower than wages in the manufacturing sector in general. On a regional basis, the differential was still quite wide, with a study showing that wages ranged from $10.56 per hour in South Carolina to $14.90 in Michigan. In addition, as technology advanced, more skilled operatives were required, thus increasing the cost of turnover to companies. Employers in the industry also were becoming increasingly more dependent on women and minorities for employees. At SGA, 40 percent of the employees were women and 35 percent of the total workforce were minorities. Minorities and women made up less than 2 percent of the management staff.

The Election Campaign

Despite its earlier defeat, the Amalgamated Clothing and Textile Workers Union (ACTWU) was back in Anderson, armed and ready for an organizing effort that would divert the attention of SGA management for several long, tense months.

While many employers learn of union organizing efforts by their employees only after the National Labor Relations Board informs them, the ACTWU's efforts to organize SGA employees were clearly out in the open a full nine months before the election. With a union office in downtown Anderson and a healthy budget, the ACTWU, led by Chris Balog, engaged in one of the most sophisticated union organizing efforts ever seen in the area. Using computerized direct mailing to stay in touch with workers, as well as extensive radio and television advertising, the union effort at SGA attracted wide attention. Many observers felt that the outcome of ACTWU's drive would have significant implications for the ability of labor unions to make inroads into traditionally nonunion regions of the country.

Union's Campaign

The campaign issues developed and communicated to workers were, for the most part, predictable. Job security was brought to the front early and was easily introduced to the campaign in the wake of over 1,500 layoffs and selective plant closings by SGA management. In addition, in an attempt to become more competitive in the face of increasing foreign competition, increased workloads and reduced wage rates were key issues raised by the union. The union repeatedly accused Phillips of engaging in unfair labor practices by threatening to sell or close the company if the union were to win bargaining rights for SGA workers. To a certain extent, the union did expand on the traditional wage, hour, and working condition issues typically raised in organizing efforts. As the campaign progressed, Phillips became a focal point of union rhetoric, and the union attempted to portray Phillips as a greedy and ruthless city slicker from Atlanta who was not interested in the long-term survival of SGA and its employees.

Management's Campaign

While Phillips became a focal point of union criticism as the campaign wore on, his role in management's response to the organizing efforts was critical throughout the months preceding the election. With President White leading the anti-union campaign, backed by a sophisticated strategy developed by an Atlanta law firm specializing in anti-union campaigns, SGA was able to quickly respond to every issue raised by the union.

The SGA strategy to defeat the union organizing effort included extensive meetings with community, business, and religious leaders in an attempt to influence workers' views about the union. Viewing anti-union films was required for workers on company time. Letters sent to workers' homes by President White and Phillips emphasized the need for team spirit, not only to keep the union out, but to overcome the threat created by hosiery imports. President White put it this way:

"We intend to do everything that is proper and legal in this campaign to defeat the union. This is essential if we are to remain competitive in the hosiery business. Every day, we are facing more foreign competition. Not only do our workers understand this, but I think the public does also. We have been able to communicate with our workers in the past, and we don't need a third party voice. We all must work together as a team. The only way SGA can beat the encroaching foreign competition is to streamline and consolidate our operations."

White and Phillips made repeated visits to plants to shake hands and listen to workers' concerns. The weekly employee newsletter was filled with anti-union letters written by workers and community members. Late in the campaign, a letter was sent to SGA workers from Jack Phillips explaining why they should vote against the union (see Exhibit 5.2). In response to the union claim that Phillips was attempting to sell the company, Phillips told the workers that "SGA is not for sale, but if I determine that the company cannot operate competitively, I can and I will cease to operate SGA. This is entirely up to me and nobody can stop me—including this union."

Employees' Views

The employees were divided over the union organizing campaign. Several employees formed an Anti-Union Committee, which organized an SGA Loyalty Day. At one rally sponsored by the Anti-Union Committee, "No Union" badges, "Be Wise—Don't Unionize" t-shirts, and "Vote No" hats were worn by several hundred employees. A statement by Terry Floyd, a shift leader, summed up the view expressed by some employees:

"We, as employees of SGA, do not feel that it is in the best interest of our company and its employees to be represented by ACTWU. Many generations of the same families have worked at this plant; part of our strength is family heritage. I'm afraid a union will destroy that strength. We feel that a union is not needed and that we can work with management as a team."

EXHIBIT 5.2 *Letter to SGA Employees*

To All SGA Employees:

It is only fair for you to know SGA's policy on unions. Our policy is quite simple. We are absolutely opposed to a union at any of our plants. We intend to use every legal and proper means to stay nonunion.

As you know, the hosiery industry has been under great pressure and competition from foreign firms. Sales in the industry have dwindled over the past few years, and we are in a poor profit position. Our government has done little to protect your jobs and stop the imports from eroding our sales. Only you and I can save this company and your jobs.

Our whole industry has been forced to modernize our production process to make it more efficient. In fact, you know that many firms have merged together to strengthen their market position. Our company, too, will have to explore the possible advantages of pooling resources and products. In the long run, such strategy can only benefit employees and management alike. I know bringing in the ACTWU at this time will only drive up our operating expenses and jeopardize our chances of making such arrangements. Only management has the right to decide how to operate this company. If we find we cannot operate this company profitably, we may be forced to consider other options.

We are convinced that unions have the tendency to create an adversarial relationship between employees and management. Cooperation and teamwork cannot exist in such a hostile environment. It is only through cooperation and teamwork that we will get through the crisis.

No SGA employee is ever going to need a union to keep his/her job. We know that ACTWU cannot help this company or you and will probably cause us to lose even more of our market and threaten your job security. I urge you—do not vote for the union. Let's all pull together and remember the goodwill of the Anderson family and how it has stood behind you all of these years.

Sincerely,

Jack Phillips

Jack Phillips
Chief Executive Officer

Others workers expressed support for the union. One worker stated, "We need a union for protection. At least it would give us a voice. Supervisors can be too arbitrary." Others pointed to pay increases and bonuses for top management in the wake of wage cuts and layoffs for plant workers. Many older employees, who remembered the generosity of the Anderson family, also expressed bitterness toward SGA and worried about their pensions.

QUESTIONS

1. What was the impetus for the Amalgamated Clothing and Textile Workers Union (ACTWU) organizing effort at SGA Industries?
2. Discuss SGA's strategy in managing the representation campaign.
3. Discuss any potential unfair labor practice charges SGA management might face as a result of their campaign strategy.

99 CASE

The Give Back: A Case of Union Busting

Three years ago, Local 974 of the United Tireworkers of America made significant contract concessions to the North American Tire plant in Bailey, Georgia. The union concessions were made for the company's economic survival and for the plant to remain open. Now, as the U.S. economy was struggling to recover from what some had called the worst recession since the Great Depression, North American Tire and its union was back at the bargaining table. While the U.S. economy had shown some signs of recovery, the union was not looking to give back again but to recover some of what was given up in previous negotiations. The union's position was that its previous concessions had facilitated North American Tire's survival and that it had already done its part to ensure the company's viability. However, the company had other goals for negotiations.

The company's initial proposals did not satisfy the union's negotiating team, a strike resulted, and both sides indicated their resolve was strong. While picket lines and demonstrations at the plant were rather uneventful, a war of words was fought in the media. On the one hand, full-page ads appeared in the local papers condemning the company for going back on their word to make up for the givebacks of the past. On the other hand, the company claimed it needed to maintain its competitive position in an industry undergoing a shakeout of underperforming competitors. North American Tire's parent company, Swiss Financial, of Alpsland, Switzerland, reported that operating profit rose 20 percent to $68 million on sales of $1.1 billion in the most recent quarter. North American's other nonunion plants were operating at capacity, and the company recently announced the purchase of Mexico's largest tire maker.

Negotiations broke down when the union rejected what management called its best offer. The company stated that the contract proposal was well above average for the Bailey, Georgia area. However, the union countered that it was well below industry standards. In addition, the union filed unfair labor practice charges with the National Labor Relations Board (NLRB). The union alleged that the strike was caused by unfair labor practices including the company's refusal to bargain over medical insurance or to bring its decision makers to the bargaining table.

Supervisors and clerical employees kept the North American Tire plant in Bailey operating at less than 30 percent of capacity, and plans were made by management to hire strike replacements. Striking employees were invited to return to work, but only a small percentage returned. The company began to advertise, interview, and hire strike replacements. Although the labor market was tight and Bailey's unemployment rate was less than 3 percent, there was no shortage of applicants. The company increased production at the Bailey plant, and production was also stepped up at its nonunion plants. While the union cried foul, the company continued to increase production. A federal mediator was appointed to get both sides back to the bargaining table to resume negotiations.

QUESTIONS

1. What are the pros and cons of North American Tire's strategy of hiring replacement workers? How ethical is the behavior of management?
2. Assuming that the firm's goal is to break Local 974 of United Tireworkers of America, what are the advantages and disadvantages of this strategy?
3. What standard should the firm use in setting wage rates (industry or geographic)?

Contributed by Gerald E. Calvasina, Southern Utah University and Joyce M. Beggs, University of North Carolina at Charlotte

100 EXERCISE

Applying the NLRA

HOW DO YOU RESPOND?

I. OBJECTIVES

A. To help you understand the application of the National Labor Relations Act (NLRA).

B. To help you understand the court's interpretation of the NLRA.

C. To help you understand the meaning of the terms "decertification election," "union salting," "strike replacements," "Excelsior List," and the rights of supervisors under the NLRA.

II. OUT-OF-CLASS PREPARATION TIME: 60 minutes

III. IN-CLASS TIME SUGGESTED: 45 minutes

IV. PROCEDURES

A. Read the exercise, review the National Labor Relations Act, and complete any additional reading assigned by the instructor.

B. The class should be divided into groups of four.

C. Each group should read each of the case incidents that follow and develop responses to each situation.

1. You are finishing up some paperwork at the end of a hard day. As the human resources manager, you have been involved in the company's negotiations with the union regarding the truck drivers' new contract with your firm. The negotiations have not been going well and all signs indicate that a strike will be called in a matter of days. As you are preparing to leave your office, three long-time truck drivers ask to have a word with you in private. They inform you that they are not happy with their union and that a number of the other drivers feel the same way. They ask you to help them get rid of the union.
2. You have been interviewing an applicant for a production line opening. The applicant seems to have all of the necessary KSAs to do the job. You feel certain that he will be one of the three candidates you recall for a second interview with the production manager. As you are about to close the interview, the applicant informs you that if he is hired, he intends to encourage his co-workers to form a union.
3. The negotiations between your company and the union representing the 110 production workers in your firm have reached a dead end. Union members have already voted to go on strike. At a meeting of the key managers involved in running the company, the production manager suggests utilizing the remaining clerical, accounting, and managerial staff as replacements to keep the plant running. She also suggests contacting a temporary employment agency to help fill any remaining critical positions while the union members are on strike. As the human resources manager, how would you respond to this suggestion?
4. You are the human resources manager of a 150-employee retail establishment. The mix of employees in the store is 50 full-time sales associates, 50 part-time sales

associates, 20 full-time shipping and receiving employees, and 30 supervisory/managerial employees. You receive a call from the regional office of the National Labor Relations Board (NLRB) informing you that a petition for a representation election has been filed by your sales associates. Three weeks later, the NLRB informs you that an election has been ordered. The NLRB representative calls again and asks you to send him a copy of your current payroll complete with names and addresses of the employees in the potential bargaining unit. This list, you are told, will be turned over to the local union seeking to organize your employees.

5. You are the store manager for a regional supermarket chain. Your store is nonunion. When a local union attempts to organize your employees, you receive orders to terminate those employees of your store who have signed union authorization cards. Your regional manager also orders you to prepare termination slips for each of the fired employees detailing false reasons for their termination.

Contributed by Dr. Gerald Calvasina, Southern Utah University

101 EXERCISE

Labor Arbitration

I. OBJECTIVES

A. To familiarize you with the arbitration process.

B. To give you practice in presenting a case before others.

C. To examine issues relating to contract administration.

II. OUT-OF-CLASS PREPARATION TIME: 40–50 minutes

III. PROCEDURES

Either at the beginning of or before class, each student should read the exercise. To start the exercise, the instructor will divide the class into the following three groups:

A. Union representatives (approximately five individuals)

B. Company representatives (approximately five individuals)

C. Arbitrators (all remaining participants, divided into groups of three to five members)

The union representatives should meet together and carefully examine "The Union Position" and prepare to argue and defend this position. The company representatives should do the same with reference to "The Company Position." Meanwhile, the arbitrators should read both positions and discuss among themselves the arguments for and against each position.

After both the union and company representatives have prepared their position statements, each should present their case to the arbitrators. Each group will be allowed five minutes for their presentation, and then an additional five minutes to counter the other group's position.

After all presentations are complete, each group of arbitrators will be given ten minutes to discuss the case and reach a decision. These decisions should be presented, along with the reasoning behind them, to all participants. Finally, the instructor may (optionally) present the arbitrator's actual decision in this case.

THE ISSUE

Was the grievant discharged for just cause? The company claimed the employee's negligence of duty resulted in the discharge, and the union claimed poor performance was the issue. If the union is right, what should be the remedy?

PERTINENT PROVISIONS OF THE UNION AGREEMENT

Article I. Purpose of the Agreement

1.3 The management of the company and the direction of the working force, including the right to plan, direct, and control operations, the right to hire, suspend, transfer, or discharge for just and sufficient cause, to relieve employees from duties because of lack of work or for other legitimate business reasons, and the right to introduce new or improved methods or facilities of production, is vested exclusively in the company; provided, however, that such rights shall not be exercised for the purpose of discriminating against any employee, and such rights shall not conflict with the provisions of this agreement.

Contributed by Dr. Gerald Calvasina, Southern Utah University

Article 33. Discipline and Discharge

33.1 In cases of poor job performance, the following procedure dealing with discipline will be accomplished with written notification to the union:

a. Formal written warning in the first instance with copy to the employee.

b. In subsequent instances, formal written warning and/or suspension without pay for a period not to exceed five working days.

c. In the event three or more instances occur, one of which results in a suspension, within any two-year period, discharge for just cause will be accomplished.

33.1.1 For purposes of this article, job performance shall include consideration of the following factors:

a. Attendance record, including absenteeism, tardiness, and proven abuse of sick leave.

b. Adherence to industrial safety rules.

c. Adherence to company house rules.

d. Ability to perform assigned tasks satisfactorily.

33.2 In cases of personal misconduct, the disciplinary action taken, including discharge, will be consistent with the gravity of the offense.

BACKGROUND

The grievant was employed as a service technician for the ABC Petroleum/Gas Company from August 2003 to April 2009. On January 26, 2009, grievant was dispatched to a customer who reported a strong odor of gas. Grievant's service report showed that he spent 26 minutes on the call, that no leaks were found, and that no repairs were made. The grievant did not take a pressure/manometer test.

Later that same day, in response to a second call, another technician was sent to the customer's home. The second technician checked the gas tank and gauge readings, added some gas, used the track, and did the pressure/manometer test. He tested the lines and isolated the source of the gas odor at a leak in the heater connector after the shutoff valve on the heater. The leak was located less than two feet from the pilot light on the water heater, which was lit. The technician replaced the heater connector and put the old one in the back of his truck. Subsequently, the grievant's immediate supervisor talked with the second technician and examined the damaged heater connector.

On January 28, 2009, the supervisor met with the grievant and informed him that he was being suspended, pending an investigation. The reason for the suspension was "Negligent in responding to report of gas odor on January 26, failure to perform leak investigation according to company procedures, leaving party with hazardous condition." By letter on April 16, 2009, grievant was notified that he was being terminated based on the company's findings indicating that "the incident was of such serious nature that we would be remiss in continuing your employment as a technician."

THE COMPANY'S POSITION

The company contends that the grievant failed to follow normal procedures necessary to determine whether there was a gas leak, and that leaving the customer in a hazardous condition constituted just cause for discharge. The grievant's failure to find or repair the gas leak was not poor performance but negligence of duty. The company defined poor performance as involving a lack of skills or intelligence and that the grievant's behavior was not caused by a lack of skills or innate inability. The company specifically refers to Article 1.3 that permits the company to discharge an employee for "just cause" and that, under Article 1.3, no prior warnings are required. The company also noted in its presentation that the employee was previously suspended for five days in 2004, and that he has been reprimanded on numerous occasions for various infractions.

The Union's Position

The union contends that the grievant should have been disciplined under Section 33.1 for poor job performance. The union contends that grievant performed three of the four tests usually performed and that, at worst, used poor judgment in not pressure testing the system. Further, the union contends that the company failed to give grievant adequate notice of the rule or the consequences of his action. The grievant did not have knowledge that he could be discharged for negligence in performance of his duties. Further, the union claimed that the company did not conduct a proper investigation and relied solely on the report of the second technician sent to the customer's home. The company made no attempt to visit the job site to determine firsthand if grievant had followed company rules.

102 Skill Builder

Employee Communications during Union Campaigns

I. **Objectives**

A. To give you practice in preparing an effective company communication during a union campaign.

B. To help you understand the practical application of the National Labor Relations Act.

II. **Time Required to Complete:** 1 hour

III. **Instructions**

Your company, Fruit Canners, Inc., has recently become aware that the United Food and Commercial Workers Union is attempting to convince employees in your plant to sign authorization cards. Management is somewhat surprised by the campaign because employee relations have generally been good. Prepare a one-page letter to be sent to all plant employees stating the company's position on the union drive and the company's desire to remain nonunion. Be certain that the content of your letter does not violate the provisions of the National Labor Relations Act.

Contributed by Dr. Gerald Calvasina, Southern Utah University

PART 6

International HR and Term Project

International HR Issues

103 CASE

Selecting a Manager for a Nigerian Facility

Victoria Oilfield Equipment is a supplier of drilling equipment for oil and gas exploration. It is headquartered near Houston, Texas. The company has seven offices and warehousing facilities near potential markets for its equipment. Only 30 percent of Victoria's profits come from selling equipment; the rest comes from leasing the equipment. Within the company's leasing operations, half the profit comes from supplying operators for the equipment. Victoria has over 25 years of experience in Texas and Louisiana, and 10 years of experience in several Latin American countries. Most of its customers are large multinational oil companies. However, approximately 20 percent of its contracts are with small, independent exploration companies.

Victoria has just completed construction of a new facility near Port Harcourt, Nigeria—its first venture into Africa. Nigeria is the most populous country in Africa and has one of the fastest growing economies in the world and is the 12th largest oil producer. During the past few years, several armed militant gangs have disrupted life and commerce in the city. These gangs claim to fight for the interest of the indigenous people and ask for a share of Nigeria's oil wealth. However, they are mostly known for random and targeted killings, arson, bombings, and kidnappings of both foreign workers and indigenous people.

The machinery, trucks, and equipment to operate this facility are to arrive within the next three months. You are the assistant human resource officer for Victoria Oilfield Equipment and have been instructed to review the records of the three leading candidates for manager of this new facility. You must recommend one of the three to your boss, the human resources director.

Before you examine the records, you make a list of personnel and political factors that you believe should be taken into consideration:

1. The general criteria for this position are education, experience, job knowledge, desire, and stability.
2. The Nigerian facility will be in the start-up phase.
3. Victoria wants to develop some of its current managers in international operations.
4. Few Nigerians have experience in the technical aspects of drilling for oil, yet Victoria has built its reputation on the expertise of its managers and customer acceptance of its managers as knowledgeable professionals.
5. Although some of Victoria's managers have had experience in Latin America, none have had experience in Africa.
6. Political power within the Nigerian government shifts periodically, and many of those with whom Victoria negotiated its move into Nigeria are no longer in the government.
7. The supply of trained oil-drilling equipment operators in Nigeria is much less than the demand.

The three candidates are:

Henry Smith: Age 34, United States citizen, graduate of Texas A & M, served three years in the Army and then joined Victoria Oilfield Equipment. In his ten years with Victoria, his record has been outstanding, and it is often said that he will be president of Victoria someday. He has never been outside of the United States.

Juan Lopez: Age 46, Venezuelan citizen, has been with Victoria for 21 years and worked his way up in several offices in Latin America. He spent two years in company headquarters planning operations in Latin America and is well respected throughout the company. He currently manages Victoria's facility in Ecuador.

Matthew Ohwueme: Age 52, Nigerian citizen, educated in England, member of the Ibo ethnic group. He is the owner/manager of the largest Honda dealership in Lagos but has had no experience with oilfield equipment.

QUESTIONS

1. Would it be best for Victoria Oilfield Equipment to select a manager who is a local (citizen of Nigeria), a home-country national (citizen of the United States), or a third-country national (citizen of some country other than Nigeria or the United States)? Why?
2. Which of the factors to be considered would favor the selection of Henry Smith? Juan Lopez? Matthew Ohwueme?
3. Which candidate would you recommend? Why?

Contributed by Sam C. Holliday, formerly with the University of Southern California

104 CASE

Outsourcing Jobs to India

Argus Publishers Inc. is a New York City–based publisher specializing in college textbooks in the Social Sciences and Business. One of their best-selling texts is *Cases and Exercises in Marketing Management*, now in its seventh edition. This book is the fourth best-selling text in the field of marketing. Two of the authors are based in the southeastern United States (Professors John Sexton and Bruce Nystrom), and the third author is currently teaching at a British university (Professor Donna James).

Six months ago, the authors agreed to prepare an eighth edition to their text and deleted some cases and exercises while adding some new ones based on reviewer comments. The reviewers were faculty members who had used the seventh edition of the book. Their comments reflected what they liked and disliked as well as case or exercise topics they would find useful in the eighth edition of the text.

For the first seven editions over the previous 23 years, the authors had worked with various editors in the United States to whom the publisher had outsourced the editorial work. After finishing the revision for the new edition, the authors sent the manuscript to the publisher and waited for the edited manuscript, which they would proofread. It was agreed that each author would receive edited manuscript only for his or her chapters. In addition, the edited manuscript always came with detailed instructions from the editor indicating what they needed from each author and by what date.

This time, however, all three authors received hundreds of pages of manuscript from an editor, a Mr. Reddy, who was based in India, with no instructions at all. Each author received all parts of the revised text including those written by his/her co-authors. They also noted that some of the sentences and paragraphs were in red type within these manuscripts, but no explanation for the red type was provided. The three authors then called each other and tried to figure out what Reddy, the editor, wanted from them since no instructions were provided with the manuscript. Reddy was then replaced by two new editors at various points who also e-mailed large quantities of edited manuscript without instructions. In each case, the new editor indicated that the previous editor had left the company or was on vacation. Continuity of the editorial staff seemed to be nonexistent.

The three authors then e-mailed the managing editor, Sarah Shelly, that they had no clue what was going on with their revision, what the editors wanted from them, and what they should do with the hundreds of manuscript pages each had been sent. Shelly told them they had been sent the edited Parts I and II of the text and that five other Parts would be sent later to them. However, she was unclear as to what the Indian editors were asking of the authors. She further noted that a corporate decision had been made to outsource all editorial work to India for cost control reasons.

Further e-mail communications between the authors and the editors continued to be muddled. The authors could never get the editors to clearly communicate what they wanted from them and by what date. So each author downloaded the electronic manuscript files that had been sent to them, opened only those that they had authored, and proceeded to make their own edits and comments. This was frustrating since the authors had specifically indicated to everyone on the editorial team which author was responsible for which materials.

All three authors commented to the managing editor that they wished they could go back to the previous system where the text had been edited by U.S. citizens.

QUESTIONS

1. What are the advantages and disadvantages of publishers and other employers outsourcing editorial work or other activities to Third World countries?
2. What changes, if any, would you suggest for the publisher to better serve their authors during the editorial process? Why?

105 CASE

Fred Bailey: An Innocent Abroad

Fred Bailey gazed out the window of his 24th floor office at the tranquil beauty of the Imperial Palace and its gardens amidst the hustle and bustle of downtown Tokyo. Only six months ago, Bailey had arrived with his wife and two children for this three-year assignment as the director of Kline & Associates' Tokyo office. Kline & Associates is a large, multinational consulting firm with offices in 19 countries worldwide. Bailey was now trying to decide if he should pack up and tell the home office that he was returning home, or whether he should somehow try to convince his wife (and himself) that they should stay and finish the assignment. Given how excited Bailey thought they all were about the assignment originally, it was a mystery as to how things had gotten to this point. As he watched the swans glide across the water in the moat that surrounds the Imperial Palace, Bailey reflected upon the past seven months.

Seven months ago, the managing partner of the main office in Boston, Dave Steiner, asked Bailey to lunch to discuss business. To Bailey's surprise, the "business" was not the major project that he and his team had just finished, but was instead a very big promotion and career move. Bailey was offered the position of managing director of the firm's relatively new Tokyo office which had a staff of 40, including seven Americans. Most of the Americans in the Tokyo office were either associate consultants or research analysts. As managing director, Bailey would be in charge of the entire office and would report to a senior partner who was in charge of the Asian region. It was implied to Bailey that if this assignment went as well as his past ones, it would be the last step before becoming a partner in the company.

When Bailey told Jenny, his wife, about the unbelievable opportunity, he was shocked at her less-than-enthusiastic response. She thought that it would be difficult for their children to live and go to school in a foreign country for three years, especially when Christine, the oldest, would be starting middle school next year. Besides, now that the children were in school, she was considering going back to work—at least part-time. Jenny Bailey had a degree in fashion merchandising from a well-known private university and had previously worked as an assistant buyer for a large women's clothing store.

Her husband explained that the career opportunity was just too good to pass and that the company's overseas package was generous enough to allow for a relatively luxurious lifestyle. The company would pay all the expenses to move whatever belongings the Baileys wanted to take with them. The company had a beautiful and spacious house located in an expensive district of Tokyo that would be provided to them rent-free, and the company would rent their house in Boston during their absence. Also, the company would provide a car and driver, education expenses for the children to attend private schools, and a cost-of-living adjustment and overseas compensation that would nearly triple Bailey's gross annual salary. After two days of consideration and discussion, Bailey told the managing partner, Dave Steiner, that he would accept the assignment.

The previous managing director was a partner in the company, but had only been in the new Tokyo office for less than a year when he was transferred to head a long-established office in England. Because the transfer to England was presently taking place, the Baileys were given about three weeks to prepare for the move. Between getting things at the office transferred to Bob Newcome, who was being promoted to Bailey's position, and the logistical hassles of getting furniture and other belongings ready to be moved, the Baileys did not have much time to find out much about Japan and its culture.

When the Baileys arrived in Japan, they were greeted at the airport by one of the young Japanese associate consultants and the senior American expatriate. They were all tired from the long flight, and the two-hour limousine ride back to Tokyo was a quiet one. After a few days of becoming familiar with the new environs, Bailey spent his first day at the office.

Bailey's first order of business was to have a general meeting with all the employees of associate consultant rank and higher. Although he was not aware of this at first, the Japanese staff always sat apart from the American staff. After Bailey introduced both himself and his general ideas about the potential and future direction of the Tokyo office, he asked a few individuals for ideas about how their responsibilities would likely fit into his overall plan. From the American staff, Bailey received a mixture of opinions with specific reasons about why certain ideas might or might not fit well. From the Japanese staff, he only received vague answers and no outright opinions. When Bailey asked for more specific information, he was surprised to find that some of the Japanese staff made a sucking sound as they breathed and said that it was "difficult to say." Bailey sensed the meeting was not entirely fulfilling his objectives, so he thanked everyone for attending and said he looked forward to everyone working together to make the Tokyo office the fastest growing office in the company.

After they had been in Japan about a month, Fred's wife complained to him about the difficulty she had finding some everyday products like maple syrup, peanut butter, and quality cuts of beef. She said that when she could find these items at one of the specialty stores they cost three to four times what they would cost in the United States. She also complained that the washer and dryer were too small and that she had to spend extra money by sending clothes out to be dry-cleaned. Additionally, unless she went to the American Club in downtown Tokyo, she was never able to enjoy the company of English-speaking adults. After all, her husband was at the office 10 to 16 hours a day and their children were at school most of the day. Unfortunately, at the time of this discussion with his wife, Bailey was preoccupied with a big upcoming meeting between his company and a significant prospective client—a well-respected Japanese multinational company.

The next day, Bailey, along with the lead American consultant for the potential contract, Ralph Webster, and one of the Japanese associate consultants, Kenichi Kurokawa, who spoke perfect English, met with a team from the Japanese company. The Japanese team consisted of four members—the VP of administration, the director of international personnel, and two staff specialists. After shaking hands and a few awkward bows, Bailey said that he knew the Japanese team was busy and he did not want to waste their time, so he would get right to the point. Bailey then asked Webster to lay out their company's proposal for the project to include project costs. After the presentation, Bailey asked the Japanese clients for their reaction to the proposal. The Japanese did not respond immediately and so Bailey quickly launched into his summary version of the proposal, thinking that the translation might have been insufficient. But, again, the Japanese team had only the vaguest of responses to his direct questions.

His recollection of the frustration of that initial business meeting was enough to shake Bailey back to the reality of the situation. The reality was that, in the five months since that first meeting, little progress had been made and the contract between the companies had yet to be signed. "I can never seem to get a direct response from a Japanese person," he thought to himself. This feeling of frustration led him to remember a related incident that happened about a month after his first meeting with the Japanese client.

Bailey reasoned that little progress had been made because he and his group did not know enough about the client to package the proposal in a way that was appealing to them. Consequently, he called in the senior American associated with the proposal, Ralph Webster, and asked him to develop a research report on the client so the proposal could be reevaluated and tailored to better meet their needs. Jointly, they decided that one of the more promising Japanese research associates, Tashiro Watanabe, would be the best employee to take the lead on this report. To impress upon Watanabe the importance of this task and the great potential they saw in him, Bailey and Webster decided to have the young Japanese associate meet with them. During the meeting, they presented the nature and importance of the task. At that point, Bailey said to Watanabe, "You can see that this is an important assignment and that we are placing a lot of confidence in you by giving you this assignment. We need the report this time next week so that we can revise and re-present our proposal. Can you handle this?" After a somewhat pregnant pause, Watanabe responded hesitantly, "I'm not sure what to say." Bailey smiled, got up from his chair, and walked over to the young Japanese associate, extended his hand, and said, "Hey, there's nothing to say. We're just giving you the opportunity you deserve."

The day before the report was due, Bailey asked Webster how the research report was coming along. Webster said that since he had heard nothing from Watanabe, he assumed that everything was under control, but that he would double-check with him. Webster later met one of the American research associates, John Maynard, in the office hallway. He knew that Maynard was hired for the Tokyo office because of his Japanese language ability and that, unlike any of the other Americans, he often went out after work with some of the Japanese research associates, including Watanabe.

Webster asked Maynard if he knew how Watanabe was progressing on the report. Maynard then recounted that, last night at the office, Watanabe had asked if Americans sometimes fired employees for being late with reports. He had sensed that this was more than a hypothetical question and asked Watanabe why he wanted to know. Watanabe did not respond immediately and, since it was 8:30 in the evening, Maynard suggested they go out for a drink. At first Watanabe resisted, but then Maynard assured him that they could have a quick drink at a nearby bar and come right back to the office. At the bar, Maynard got Watanabe to express his concerns.

Watanabe explained the nature of the research report that he had been requested to produce. He went on to say that even though he had already worked many hours to complete the report, he found the task to be impossible; he had doubted from the beginning whether he could complete the report in a week.

At this point, Webster asked Maynard, "Why the hell didn't he say something in the first place?" Webster did not wait to hear whether Maynard had an answer to his question and headed to Watanabe's office. The incident then escalated as Webster lashed out at Watanabe and then went to Bailey explaining that the report would not be ready and that Watanabe did not think it could have been from the start. "Then why didn't he say something to us during the meeting?" Bailey demanded. No one had any clear answers, and the entire incident left everyone involved more suspect and uncomfortable with each other.

There were other incidents, big and small, that had made the last two months in Tokyo especially frustrating, but Bailey was too tired to remember them all. It seemed as if there was too much of a language and cultural gap between the Americans and the Japanese to overcome. Bailey felt that he could not communicate with his Japanese colleagues and that he could not figure out what they were thinking. This drove him crazy and made him feel as if he was not a success in his new position.

Then, on top of all the work-related problems, his wife had laid a bombshell on him last evening. She wanted to go home, and yesterday was not soon enough. Even though the children seemed to be enjoying their stay in Tokyo, his wife was tired of being stared at, of not understanding anybody or being understood, of not being able to find what she wanted at the store, of not being able to drive and read the road signs, of not having anything to watch on TV, and of not being involved in anything. Because of her feelings of isolation, she wanted to return to the United States and to their previous life. She reasoned that they owed nothing to the company because the company had led them to believe this was just another assignment, like the two enjoyable years they had spent in San Francisco, and it was anything but that!

Bailey looked out the window of his office once more, wishing that somehow all the problems could be solved or that time could be turned back. Down below, the traffic was backed up in the always crowded Tokyo streets. Though the traffic lights changed, the cars and trucks did not seem to be moving. Fortunately, in the ground below the streets, one of the world's most advanced, efficient, and clean subway systems moved hundreds of thousands of people to their destinations about the city.

QUESTIONS

1. What factors (individual, work, and organizational) contributed to Fred and Jenny Baileys' lack of adjustment to Japan?
2. What mistakes did Bailey make at work because of his lack of understanding of the Japanese culture?
3. What criteria would be important in selecting employees for overseas assignments?
4. What special training and development programs might have been beneficial to Fred Bailey and his family prior to his assignment in Tokyo?
5. Imagine that you are Dave Steiner and you receive a telephone call from Bailey in which he talks about his difficulties adjusting to life in Tokyo. How would you respond? What should be done now?

Contributed by J. Stewart Black, Insead

106 CASE

A Clash of Cultures in the Workplace: German Managers in South Africa

Dr. Christa Kriek was preparing for a lecture on cultural intelligence to her International Human Resource Management elective class when her cell phone rang. It was a call from a former student, Johan Coetzee, a quality manager in the Logistics Division of German Auto Manufacturer, Inc. (GAM). GAM had recently resumed business in South Africa after having left in response to the international boycotts against firms doing business in a country that practiced apartheid.* Its plants in the country assembled luxury cars for the domestic market and neighboring countries in southern Africa. Coetzee asked her if she would be able to assist the Division with morale and motivation problems among their associates by giving a motivational talk to staff. Coetzee said he was calling because his boss, Walter Koch (Division Head) had complained about low staff morale and motivation, especially among associates. Dr. Kriek asked if she could meet with Coetzee to hear more about the problem. At their meeting a week later, he provided her with additional details about the structure of the Division and its current personnel problems.

THE SITUATION AT LOGISTICS DIVISION

The Logistics Division was responsible for the supply of parts, subassemblies, and other items to the production line. This Division employed 425 people including a management staff of eight. The management team was culturally diverse and consisted of four German nationals, one of whom was Walter Koch, a British expatriate who had been in South Africa for two years, a black South African, and two white South Africans. In the GAM human resource management system, all shop floor employees were referred to as associates, and this is a practice they followed in their South African operations. The shop floor staff consisted primarily of black South Africans with different ethnicities, but were largely Sotho-speaking as they came from the surrounding townships located about 20 to 25 miles from the Division. Many of them relied on the taxis that operated daily from the townships to business areas for transport to and from the plant as few, if any of them, owned cars. Management staff, however, were provided with company cars as part of their compensation package.

When the Logistics Division started operations six months ago, Koch, an engineer by training, had been appointed Division Head. He had never worked in South Africa before but had been successful in previous company assignments throughout Europe. GAM's human resource approach to expatriate assignments was to rotate managers every three years at different international sites. Maureen Kaiser, vice president of Global Human Resources, explains,

> "Our approach to international assignments complements our international business strategy. We believe our brand is known in the automobile market for its uncompromising quality and precision. Therefore, we want uniform standards across the globe, no matter where we operate. Thus, we assign our managers to three-year rotations so that they learn how to install our values and goals in any context."

*Apartheid was based on a system of legislated racial categorization and separation dividing the population into different racial groups. This separation governed every sphere of life, from education to employment, and resulted in legislating discriminatory practices by minority whites toward the black majority.

GAM believed this approach was the best way for their managers to develop the skills and knowledge to be effective in international assignments. In line with this philosophy, managers assigned to an international site were expected to draw upon their previous experiences to perform well. No country training was done prior to the assignments other than a review of management's strategy for operations in the country. Koch confessed to his fellow managers that he knew little about South Africa prior to arriving, but had believed that the company's well-defined strategy and performance culture would ensure success during his assignment.

When Koch arrived at the Logistics Division, he promptly put a strategic plan in place that was aligned to the company's goal to make sure all world-wide operations were "world class" no matter in which country they did business. Within the company, this goal was referred to as "Keeping the Rhythm." In line with the plan, performance metrics were set within a performance management system that covered all employees from management to associates.

Coetzee described the culture as both task-oriented and performance-driven. People were rewarded based on how well they performed in respect to the set targets. Each month, Koch held a communications session with employees to inform them about progress toward performance goals. These sessions were held in a large auditorium with the management team sitting behind a table at the front of the room and employees seated theatre-style in the spacious auditorium. Typically, Koch would make a 15-minute PowerPoint presentation with graphs and brief everyone on operations and progress toward goals. Generally, none of the other managers or team leaders made presentations. Once Koch finished his presentation, he would ask if there were any questions. In the five months he had been conducting these communications sessions, no one had asked a single question. Koch had told Coetzee on more than one occasion that he really believed all staff, including associates, really understood what needed to be achieved at the Division.

Yet, all was not going well. There was high absenteeism among shop floor employees as well as a problem with lateness in some of the departments. The team leaders who had been appointed by the management team complained of uncooperative workers and discipline problems. Additionally, in recent months they had experienced incidents of theft from the stores. All of these problems began to be reflected in the Division's performance on key metrics, and recently there had been an increase in complaints from the Production Division about delays in receiving parts. Koch was quite concerned because he had aspirations for one day becoming part of the top management team at GAM. He had two very successful international assignments under his belt and wanted this one to be just as successful.

Koch called a meeting of his management team to discuss what was transpiring at the Division. During the meeting, the South African managers were mostly quiet. Typical of his leadership style, Koch seemed to have the problem all figured out. He believed the problem was a lack of motivation among the workers. In his previous assignments in Belgium and the United Kingdom, workers had always responded well to tasks and set goals. He thought a "motivational" talk from a local expert might help to motivate the staff. He had then asked Coetzee for his assistance in finding a good speaker on motivation.

Dr. Kriek's Intervention

Dr. Kriek, an experienced human resources consultant, convinced Koch and the rest of the management team that she needed to do a survey of staff to really find out more about "the motivational problems." Koch agreed as long as Dr. Kriek ensured them that she would get to the "bottom" of the problem. She decided to survey a random sample of 50 percent of the staff as well as conduct 30-minute interviews with management. The original idea of surveying the shop floor associates was not feasible because of the insufficient literacy of most of them. Instead, Dr, Kriek held focus group discussions with the associates about the climate and culture of the Division.

The results of the interviews and focus group discussions revealed a huge gap between the perceptions and feelings of associates and management. Exhibit 6.1 contains what Dr. Kriek heard from each side. The majority of associates said they do not understand the behavior of the Germans. One associate expressed a view that most had agreed with during the focus group sessions: "They act strangely, including Mr. Koch. They have no manners. They come into the shop floor in the morning but they do not greet us. They just wave at us with their hands. What is this kind of behavior? We work for them every day." Another associate stated, "I do not think they really care about us. They rush everything, including the monthly meetings held in the big auditorium. We have been working here for almost seven months, and they do not know our names. But we know their names."

Another issue raised by the associates was about how the team leaders had been appointed. John Dube, who appeared to be a spokesperson for the associates in his focus group session said, "Team leaders were appointed by the Germans without consulting us. They are not our natural leaders, and we do not really trust them." When Dr. Kriek asked the associates what they expected from management, they readily offered a number of suggestions. Exhibit 6.2 contains a copy of what she wrote on a flip chart during the sessions.

The interviews with the management team presented a very different view of the problems. There was also a difference in the views of the local South African managers and the German nationals. Koch and the other German managers expressed the view that the workers were lazy and not willing to work hard. They felt the monthly forums were an excellent form of communication and did not understand why the associates never asked questions. Koch had stated during his interview that

> I feel like I have really done everything by the book in bringing staff up to speed on 'Keeping the Rhythm.' I also believe in keeping an eye on the shop floor, and I make it a regular task to walk through the departments each morning.

EXHIBIT 6.1 *Perceptions of Associates and Management Collected from Interviews and Focus Groups*

Perceptions of Associates	Perceptions of German Managers	Perceptions of South African Managers
■ German managers are cold and do not communicate with us ■ German managers do not greet us properly ■ Feeling of not belonging ■ Not recognized ■ Not important ■ Lower class ■ Hate being called an associate ■ Us versus Them ■ We feel invisible ■ Early and late shifts cause serious transport problems	■ We are good communicators ■ This is a business and work comes first ■ Associates are here to work and meet goals ■ Being on time is very important ■ We care about associates ■ We have a good bonus system based on performance ■ Performance management system works well ■ The division will be successful if associates work harder and are more motivated	■ German managers are arrogant ■ They do not listen to us ■ The focus is on reaching goals ■ German managers don't understand the South African culture or how to motivate associates

EXHIBIT 6.2 *Focus Group Notes*

- ✔ We want the Germans to treat us with respect by calling us by our real names.
- ✔ They must greet us properly and show courtesy by asking how we are feeling.
- ✔ In our culture, it is important that people are respectfully acknowledged.
- ✔ Do not just give us facts and figures at the monthly communication forums, there should be more dialogue.
- ✔ Let us have input in selecting the team leaders because we know who our leaders are in the community and who people will respect and respond to.
- ✔ Don't divide us by giving individuals bonuses instead of a group bonus.
- ✔ We are willing to work hard but do not feel we are really part of the company.
- ✔ Stop calling us associates and use our names instead.

He went on further to state:

> The workplace is about delivery and performance. It is not about making people feel good. Our company has been successful because of the precision and quality of our automobiles. That only happens when there is strict adherence to world-class standards.

When Dr. Kriek asked the German managers what they expected of staff, their list was rather straightforward. They expected everyone to work hard, be on time, and meet the performance goals set for the Division.

The South African managers had a different view about the situation than their German colleagues. They felt the Germans were arrogant and did not solicit their knowledge of local realities. Pieter Smit, warehouse manager, put it this way:

> They tell us what to do and do not ask for our opinions. There is a very formal, impersonal style of interaction which we South Africans are just not used to. We don't think the Germans really understood the culture among the shop floor employees.

After compiling these results, Dr. Kriek decided to share what she had heard from the associates and the non-German managers with Koch. Koch was shocked and could not understand how they could hold such views. Koch told her:

> Of course, we care about all the staff, especially the associates. I have made every effort to communicate the goals and the challenges of supply parts and subassemblies in a just-in-time production process. I thought everyone was clear that we are to produce and that the expectations of employees are high. Why haven't they ever told me these things at the forums we hold monthly?

Dr. Kriek's Proposed Solution

Based on what she had heard during her sessions with staff and management, Dr. Kriek decided a motivational talk was not going to adequately address these issues. Instead, she proposed a two-day cultural awareness and sensitivity workshop for the management team to address what she saw as primarily a clash of cultures—German versus South African. Exhibit 6.3 contains Dr. Kriek's proposal for the workshops and the topics that she planned to present and discuss. When she shared the proposal with Koch, he was doubtful that it would address the real problem with the Division. He told Dr. Kriek:

> I really don't understand this culture business. We have been successful wherever we have operated by applying our world-class standards and ways of doing business. But, you are the expert so I am willing to give the workshops a chance but things have to improve soon or our Division is in trouble.

EXHIBIT 6.3 *Cultural Awareness and Sensitivity Workshop*

Objectives of the Workshop

The objective of this workshop is to provide participants with an opportunity to:

- Understand how national cultures differ
- Understand how cultural differences impact organizations
- Develop leadership skills for managing cultural diversity
- Develop their cultural intelligence

Proposed Content

1. What is culture?
2. How cultures of countries differ in terms of:
   - Power Distance
   - Uncertainty avoidance
   - Individualism/Collectivism
   - Universalistic versus Particularistic
   - Masculinity versus Femininity
   - Long-term versus Short-term Orientation
   - Monochronic versus Polychronic Time
3. How culture shapes and influences approaches to management
4. Cross-Cultural Communication Skills
   - Communicating in Low-context Cultures
   - Communicating in High-context Cultures
5. Becoming a Culturally Intelligent Manager
   - Developing Self-Awareness of One's Own Culture
   - Social Awareness of Other Cultures
   - Adapting Behavior in Cross-Cultural Situations

QUESTIONS

1. Why are the views of the German managers and associates so different? What are the underlying cultural values that may be causing the differences?
2. Do you agree with the GAM's view that the best preparation for an international assignment is "learning on the job" instead of formal training programs?
3. What are the human resource problems associated with a multinational company adopting a global human resource management strategy rather than a local strategy for operations outside its home base?
4. Evaluate Dr. Kriek's approach and actions. Do you agree with the approach she took? Why or why not?
5. Evaluate her proposal for the cultural awareness and sensitivity workshop for management. What are its strengths and weaknesses? What effect do you think it will have on the managers?

Case was prepared by Professor Yvonne du Plessis, Department of Human Resource Management, University of Pretoria (South Africa)

Term Project

107 TERM PROJECT

Human Resource System or Subsystem Evaluation

I. **OBJECTIVE** To help a student group of two to four students critically analyze a human resource management system or subsystem, identify problems, and recommend constructive improvements.

II. **OUT-OF-CLASS PREPARATION TIME:** 30–40 hours per group (10–15 hours per individual student) for a total human resource system evaluation and 20–25 hours (5–10 hours per student) for a subsystem evaluation.

III. **IN-CLASS TIME SUGGESTED:** None, unless an oral report is required by the instructor. In that case, each group will make a 15–20 minute presentation to the class.

IV. **PROCEDURES**

Option 1: Students will self-select or be assigned into groups of two to four students, identify a real organization, and receive permission from either the CEO or the human resources director to study the organization's human resource system. Once permission is received, the group should arrange to interview as many of the following as possible: the human resources director, other human resources department employees, and employees performing different functions at different levels in the organization. As an option to completing the entire Human Resource System Evaluation outlined here, the instructor could assign only specific sections to a given student group. In that case, all groups would complete Sections I and VII and then be assigned Section II, III, IV, V, or VI.

Option 2: Same as above except student groups select an organization and study information available on its Web site in order to answer questions and analyze that organization's human resources system or subsystem.

V. **GENERAL PURPOSE**

The study will focus upon the selected organization's human resources and employee relations objectives, structures, policies, practices, and selected administrative problems or challenges. It will give you the opportunity to learn firsthand about the management of human resource systems in actual organizations. It will also provide you with the opportunity to develop field research methodologies and evaluation skills that should prove beneficial in future academic and professional assignments. Finally, for the organization cooperating with each of the student projects, the results of these studies may prove helpful in future efforts to improve the efficiency and effectiveness of their human resource systems.

The final reports of both the in-person and the Web site evaluations may be turned in to the organization at the discretion of the instructor. The final product of this study will be a comprehensive written report to be submitted on the date determined by the instructor. Each student should assume the stance of an outside consultant who has been called in to evaluate the human resource system or subsystem of the particular organization. At a minimum, the paper should reflect the items contained in the Evaluation Guide as a whole in Sections I and VII, as well as one other part of the Evaluation Guide that follows.

EVALUATION GUIDE

I. *The Organization and Its Mission* (This section to be completed with both options.)

A. When and why was this organization established?

1. Under what statutory or legal authority was it created?
2. What are the principal needs and objectives that the organization is designed to fulfill?

B. What budgetary constraints confront the organization?

1. What are the sources of revenue for this company?
   a. for capital expenditures?
   b. for operating expenditures?
2. What changes have occurred in the organization's budget in recent years?
   a. Have there been any noticeable increases or decreases in revenues?
   b. Have there been any new sources of funding?
   c. Have any old sources of funding been reduced or eliminated?
   d. How have these trends affected management of the organization?

C. What is the total employment complement of the organization?

1. How are these employees distributed throughout the organization?
   a. by department or operational function?
   b. by skill, e.g., managerial, professional, technical, clerical, skilled craftsperson, semi-skilled operatives, unskilled laborers, etc.?
2. What have been some of the noticeable employment trends in recent years?
3. Does the organization operate overseas? If so, do you employ Americans or foreign nationals overseas?

D. What are the major strategic threats and opportunities confronting this organization?

1. Does the organization have a strategic management plan including goals, objectives, and timetables?
2. What strategies have you been pursuing and with what degree of success in order to address these challenges?

II. *The Human Resource Function, Diversity, and Legal Issues*

A. Does this organization have a formal and identifiable human resource function or department?

1. When was this department or function formally established and why?
2. How is the human resource function or department organized to carry out the objectives of the organization?
3. How many individuals are directly associated with the human resource function or department?

4. What are the academic and employment backgrounds of those involved in the function or department?

B. To what degree is human resource management centralized of decentralized?

C. To what degree has the human resource function used information technology to manage information?

D. How have shifting workforce demographics impacted the human resource function?

E. What is the perceived importance of the human resource function or department relative to other functional operations of the organization?

F. Does the human resource function provide support in foreign countries? What problems or challenges does this present?

G. To what degree has the human resource function been involved in any organizational restructuring (i.e., mergers, outsourcing to other companies or countries, etc.)?

H. To what degree and how does the organization support a goal of diversity in the workplace?

I. To what degree is the human resource function achieving diversity goals for professional and managerial positions?

J. What legal challenges (if any) is the human resource function currently addressing?

K. What recommendations do you have (if any) for reorganizing the human resource function? Why?

III. *Meeting Human Resource Requirements: Job Analysis, Planning, Recruitment, and Selection*

A. To what degree is human resources management integrated into the strategic management of the organization? How?

B. Who is responsible for human resource planning and forecasting for the organization?

1. What methods are used to determine staffing needs?
2. Does the organization focus primarily upon short-term or long-term human resource needs, or both?
3. Are job analyses and job descriptions made for each position in the organization? To what degree are they updated periodically?
4. Is any human resource planning done?
    - How is it being done?
    - If not, why not?
    - Has the lack of human resource planning had any negative impact? Explain.
5. Does the organization provide career planning and career counseling for employees? Why or why not? If yes, how is this done and how effective is it?

C. Once staffing needs are established, what procedures are utilized for filling job vacancies?

1. Who is responsible for staffing the organization—the human resource department or the respective functional departments?
2. What methods are used to recruit new employees?

3. What methods and criteria are used for evaluating and selecting job applicants? Have these methods been validated? How?
4. Have you used employee recruitment through social network sites and through the Internet? How effective are these?
5. To what extent are new employee recruitment, evaluation, and selection procedures aided or restricted by
    a. established policies or practices of the organization?
    b. provisions contained in employment laws?
    c. factors associated with local labor markets?
6. To what degree does the organization seek to fill existing job vacancies from among present employees or by recruiting new employees, and why?
7. What selection processes and criteria do you use to select employees?
8. How have these criteria been validated?
9. What options do you provide for flexible employee work schedules?
10. To what degree does the staffing reflect the skills, knowledge, and abilities necessary to successfully implement the strategic goals of the organization?
11. What does the organization do to enhance the work and family interface?

D. To what degree has the organization outsourced or downsized positions?

E. What specific problems have been encountered in the employment staffing process?

1. To what can these be attributed?
2. What are the major alternatives for resolving these problems?
3. Which solutions are most feasible, and why?

IV. *Developing Effectiveness in Human Resources: Training, Career Development, and Performance Appraisal*

A. Has the organization supported programs for employee training and development? Why or why not?

1. What kinds of programs have been established? Have they been oriented toward
    a. job skills?
    b. supervisory and leadership skills?
    c. basic educational skills?
    d. knowledge, skills, and abilities necessary for strategic goal attainment?
    e. orientation of new employees?
2. How do these programs relate to the organization's strategic and operational objectives?
3. Does the organization maintain its own training staff or are outside organizations used for training purposes?
4. What proportions of employees have participated in training (in both general and specific job categories) and development programs supported by the organization?

5. Are training and development offered in-house, outside the organization, or both?

6. How has the effectiveness of employee training and development been evaluated?

B. To what extent have the organization's programs of employee training and development been used in making decisions related to promotions and transfers within the organization?

C. What processes and programs, if any, do you offer for employee career development?

D. What options, if any, do you provide for flexible employee work schedules?

E. What problems, if any, have been encountered in the administration of employee training and development programs within the organization? What suggestions for improvement can you make? Why?

F. What methods are used for evaluating employees for the purpose of determining their effectiveness and any merited salary increases?

a. What methods of appraising employee performance are currently being used?

b. Do employee performance appraisal systems actually reflect job performance? Why or why not?

c. How adequate or inadequate are the performance appraisal methods currently being used? Why?

d. Do they reflect the knowledge, skills, and abilities needed to successfully implement the particular organization's strategic goals?

e. What factors other than job performance influence employee performance appraisal outcomes? Explain.

V. *Implementing Compensation Systems and Security*

A. How are wage and salary levels and annual improvements determined?

1. Does the organization conduct periodic internal and external wage surveys?

2. Are salary levels adequate to enable the organization to attract and maintain an effective work force? Why or why not?

3. Do differentials in salary grades appropriately reflect differentials in skills and responsibilities?

4. How do salary levels compare with those of other comparable organizations for the same or similar occupational and experience groupings?

5. Does the current reward system adequately reward employees with the requisite knowledge, skills, and abilities necessary to implement the strategic plan?

6. What trends have taken place in salary levels over the past few years?

7. To what degree is merit pay and incentive compensation used and in what areas? How effective are they in achieving high levels of employee performance?

8. Do you provide bonuses for executives? If so, how are these bonuses determined? Do they reflect individual and/or organizational performance?

B. How adequate are non-wage fringe benefits?

1. How are they determined?

2. How do they compare with those of other organizations?

3. How have they changed in recent years and how will they change in the future?
4. Do you provide domestic partner benefits? If so, please describe.
5. Do you provide for family and medical leave? If so, please describe.

C. Does the organization provide employee health insurance coverage? If so, how have their benefits changed over time and how are they likely to change in the future as a result of healthcare reform?

D. Has the organization introduced any special programs or activities to improve health and safety conditions on the job (i.e., violence in the workplace)?

E. Has the organization developed, periodically reviewed, and implemented a disaster preparedness plan? If so, please describe.

F. What efforts, if any, are utilized to maintain employee morale and job satisfaction?

G. Does the organization provide for flexible work options such as telecommuting or job sharing? Please provide details.

H. What retirement pension benefits are currently offered and how are they expected to change in the future?

I. What improvements in compensation, employee motivation, and health and safety should be made? Why?

VI. *Enhancing Employee Relations: Employee Discipline and Labor Relations*

A. What methods and procedures are available for resolving employee complaints and grievances?

1. Have there been large numbers of such grievances? Why?
2. Has the volume of grievances been growing or declining? Why?
3. What are the problems eliciting the majority of employee grievances?

B. Have there been many employee discipline problems?

1. Are there clearly spelled-out formal procedures within the organization for handling discipline cases? What are they?
2. How often are employees disciplined or discharged?
    a. What are the major causes of such problems?
    b. How have these been dealt with by the organization?
    c. Do you have any serious problems with employee violence or use of controlled substances in the workplace? How have these been addressed?

C. To what extent have employee tardiness, absenteeism, and turnover been problems?

1. Have these problems been studied to determine their most likely causes? What are they?
2. What steps have been taken to resolve these problems, if they exist? What steps should have been taken? Why?

D. What employee restrictions (if any) does the organization impose on employee free speech, surfing the Internet, and unhealthy behavior (smoking or drug use) on or off the job?

E. Have any of the employees sought to join labor organizations for the purpose of engaging in collective bargaining over wages, hours, and working conditions? Explain.
   1. Why have, or have not, such organizing activities taken place?
   2. What is the official position of the organization toward acceptance or rejection of unionism for its employees?
   3. If a labor union exists in this organization, what effect has the union had upon
      a. overall decision-making within the organization?
      b. the efficiency and productivity of the organization?
      c. the administration of the human resources function?
      d. the relations between the managers of the organization and its non-managerial personnel?
      e. the interpersonal relationships among non-supervisory employees?

F. What has been the relationship between management and union leaders (e.g., cooperative, neutral, cold, hostile)?
   1. Have there been any noticeable changes in the nature of this relationship in the recent past? Why or why not?
   2. Have there been any work stoppages among employees in order to pressure management into agreeing to union demands?
      a. What were the issue(s)?
      b. Why did the dispute occur?
      c. How was it resolved?
      d. What has been its subsequent impact upon
         i. the operation of the company?
         ii. employee performance?
         iii. the work environment?
         iv. the decision-making process involved in personnel matters?

G. What suggestions would you make for minimizing employee grievances and improving the labor relations climate (if applicable)? Why?

VII. *Summary and Evaluation* (This section is to be completed with both options.)

A. How effectively is the human resource function of this organization contributing to the fulfillment of its mission, objectives, and strategic plan?

B. What are some of the problems of human resources management that have been adequately solved or are now in the process of being solved by the organization?

C. What are some of the major human resource problems that remain to be confronted and solved?

D. What would appear to be among the most desirable solutions to these problems? Provide specific detail and justifications for your recommendations.